Anti-Ugly

I recommend ....

....

for the 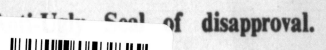 Anti-Ugly Seal of disapproval.

...estmoreland Terrace, London, S.W.1.

Anti-Ugly

Anti-Ugly

Excursions in
English Architecture and Design

Gavin Stamp

First published in Great Britain
2013 by Aurum Press Ltd
74-77 White Lion Street
London N1 9PF
www.aurumpress.co.uk

Front endpaper: An 'Anti-Ugly' recommendation card issued by
the New Architecture Group in 1962.
Rear endpaper: The frontispiece to Pugin's Apology for the
Revival of Christian Architecture, 1843.

A catalogue record for this book is
available from the British Library.

ISBN 978 1 78131 123 3

1 3 5 7 9 10 8 6 4 2

2013 2015 2017 2016 2014

Typeset in Dante MT by SX Composing DTP, Rayleigh Essex

Printed by CPI Group (UK) Ltd, Croydon, CR0 4YY

Contents

Foreword	vii
A Vision of England	1
Anti-Ugly	6
The Curse of Palladio	12
Palladian Games	18
Surreal Recall	23
Guinness isn't Good for You	28
Keeping an Open Mind	34
Robert Byron	39
Cartoon History	44
Betjemanic	49
Hawksmoor Redivivus	55
Shakespeare in Stone	60
The Destroyer	65
Slightly Subhuman?	69
God's Architect	74
Midland Grand Hotel	79
The Second Greatest Briton?	84
The Spirit of Ernest George	89
Forgotten Prophet	94
Spence's Charm	99
Knight's Tale	104
Dreaming Towers	109

Englishmen's Castles   114
Flogging Off the Silver   119
Nature Versus Culture   124
Gothic Revival   129
Inspired Patronage   135
Sell the Rubens   141
A Tomb for a King   146
The Empty Plinth   151
A Canova for Today   157
Too Many Memorials   162
The War Goes On   168
Tragic Triumph   173
Steam Ahead   178
Long Journey's End   183
Battlebridge   188
Tent for a Prince   192
An Artist's Villa   197
Villa Frankenstein   202
Post-Haste to Closure   207
In Carceri   212
Taking the Plunge   218
Aerial Travellers   223
Streamlined   227
Bring Back the Railings   233
Out With the Old   238
Looking After Liverpool   244
Dreamland   249
Lost Lululaund   254
List of Illustrations   259

Foreword

Architecture is the only art you cannot escape. We can go through life oblivious to music, of painting, of sculpture, but buildings have a profound effect on the way we live, work and feel. Yet it is difficult to find places to write about them seriously. Newspapers grudgingly acknowledge architecture but are more interested in what a building costs than in who was responsible for the way it looks, and why. And as architects decline to criticise each other and shelter behind jargon and professional exclusivity, the architectural journals do not engage with the wider public. Architectural criticism is less well established than art or literary criticism, and critics enamoured of the new often have no interest in or knowledge of the old. As for architectural history, it can be an esoteric and dull business. All of which makes *Apollo magazine*, in which I have written about architecture both new and old for almost a decade, an admirable and precious publication.

As a freelance architectural historian, I once wrote for newspapers and weekly journals for my bread and butter. 'One doesn't keep journalism, does one?' Sir John Summerson once remarked. It is true that most journalism is ephemeral and much of it hastily and thoughtlessly composed, although that cannot be said of the journalism produced by this great architectural historian and writer. One of his earliest articles – in the *Scotsman* in 1930 imagining the Edinburgh of the future (mercifully unrealised) as 'a glittering spectacle of steel, glass and concrete' – is often still quoted. Summerson's career, indeed, suggests that journalism can be good training for producing readable architectural history and criticism.

It depends in part on the publication. Articles dashed off overnight for a newspaper's deadline are different from pieces written for a regular column or commissioned by a specialised journal. In the case of *Apollo*, the 'International Art Magazine', there is more time for reflection as it appears only monthly. And we authors know that *Apollo*'s readers are serious and informed. I therefore like to think that my regular column on architecture in the magazine encourages me to ponder, research and write as best I can. The results are, I hope, worth keeping.

The articles reprinted here are almost half of those I wrote for *Apollo* between 2004 and 2013. A criterion for selecting them was that they should be about England (very occasionally about Britain) or Englishmen. My thoughts on architecture and art abroad – in Berlin, St Petersburg, Budapest, Malta, Istanbul, New Delhi, Bombay and elsewhere – must remain, for the moment, in back numbers of the magazine. Rereading my articles to make this selection made me realise that many are, to a degree, autobiographical but I hope this may be forgiven. I have been writing about buildings for over forty years and it is natural that in my pieces for *Apollo* I draw upon personal enthusiasms and experiences.

The articles here reflect my love of churches, both ancient and modern, and many of the articles were the result of my continuing interest in and enthusiasm for Victorian architecture, acquired at an early age (I am proud to record that I joined the Victorian Society when still, just, at school because of the threat to St Pancras Station). Out of this came my long-standing interest in the work of the Scott dynasty: in the great Sir Gilbert, in his brilliant tragic son, George Gilbert Scott junior, in his son, the great Sir Giles, and in *his* son Richard, an underrated talent and a dear friend. I have also never lost my enthusiasm for the monumental, sublime architecture of Nicholas Hawksmoor, to whose London churches I think I was first pointed, again as a schoolboy, by *Nairn's London*, an inspiring book by that great eponymous architectural journalist: Ian Nairn. From that followed my admiration for the work of the greatest of English architects, Sir Edwin Lutyens.

Some articles are the result of other long-standing enthusiasms: for railways – still the most civilised and enjoyable form of transport – and railway stations; for war memorials and in the melancholy, sublime architecture of the memorials and cemeteries of the Great War which grew out of my passion for Lutyens. It is sad, perhaps, that war memorials remain a topical subject as so many – too many, mostly of deplorable quality – have been erected in Britain in the last couple of decades: a phenomenon which may well engage and puzzle future historians. They deserve comment as they are, by their nature, public monuments and public art and sculpture require more attention than they usually receive. In this context I have written about the work of Alexander Stoddart, the modern Classical sculptor who I regard as an artist of rare skill and of genius. For this I make no apology, for although he is a Scot his work is to be seen in London and elsewhere in England.

Re-reading what I have contributed to *Apollo*, I am surprised that there is so little about Scotland where I lived and worked for over a decade. There is nothing, for instance, about another architect-hero, Alexander 'Greek' Thomson of Glasgow, but I conclude that when I came back home to England in 2003 I had banged on long enough about Scottish matters and was, as it were, written out on the subject. In consequence, much of what I have written for the magazine concerns English architecture and English concerns: hence the subtitle of this book, *Excursions in English Architecture and Design*. After all, I cannot help being English myself, and am decidedly not a 'Brit'.

My first article in *Apollo*, in May 2004, was an opportunity to rehearse the scandal of the mutilation and desecration of one of the great Mediaeval buildings of Europe, King's College Chapel, perpetrated when I was an undergraduate in Cambridge and still not rectified. On the whole, however, architecture has greatly improved over the intervening decades, becoming more varied, better made and sometimes more influenced by tradition. I cannot, however, join in the current glass-worship which operates at the expense of other more important architectural qualities. It has been extraordinary to see how Modernism, once shoddy but altruistic, has morphed into the vulgar style of arrogant capitalism. Nevertheless, over the same period, the fight for conservation (of the ordinary as well as of the best, in all styles and of any date) and for a less destructive approach to urban development would seem to have been won – as symbolised by the resurrection of once-doomed St Pancras (never could I have imagined when I first saw the despised and neglected Victorian Gothic hotel that, over forty years later, I would stay overnight in the magnificently restored building prior to its triumphant reopening) – although, at the time of writing, what with the ruthless economies being imposed by an ideologically-driven government on English Heritage as well as on local authorities, the future for many historic buildings looks bleak and more big battles may come.

I was able to bang on about King's Chapel and much else thanks to Michael Hall, who worked wonders for *Apollo* after he took over the editorship that year. I am most grateful to him, and to his successor, Oscar Humphries, for allowing me to republish so many of the articles I contributed. And I must thank Graham Coster at Aurum Press, whose idea it was to gather my articles together as a book. I am flattered that he saw something in them worth republishing and intrigued that he detected in them the theme of Englishness.

What are printed here are my original texts, that is, without benefit of the intervention of the sub-editors. This may well mean the loss of improvements they introduced but it does involve the restitution of necessary cuts that I regretted, guilty as I am of often writing too much for my two-page spread. The articles have not otherwise been altered or amended. This, inevitably, does lead to occasional repetitions in a collected volume, which I hope the reader may forgive. If anything has occurred since the original publication of consequence to my arguments, or has been rendered redundant or incorrect by events, this has been recorded as an afterthought. But by their nature as journalism these articles are period pieces, and I hope none the worse for that.

Forest Hill
May 2013

A Vision of England

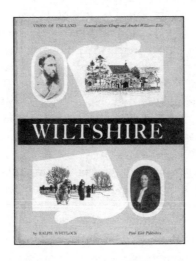

There is nothing like destruction – or the threat of destruction – to make people value things. The threat of aerial bombardment and the loss of so much historic and beautiful architecture during the Second World War resulted in the passing of the legislation designed to protect those that were left: the Town & Country Planning Act of 1946 which first introduced the statutory 'listing' of buildings. It also stimulated the writing and publication of a wide range of guide and travel books about the architectural riches and landscape of Britain. The decade which saw the intense flourishing of a native Neo-Romantic Art – often concentrating on buildings and landscape (as with the work of Eric Ravilious, John Piper, Edward Bawden and many others) – also saw the launching of several series of guides intended to extol and to catalogue the towns, villages and buildings of England (and Wales and Scotland).

The 1940s and early 1950s can now be seen as one of the golden ages of British publishing, particularly for illustrated books. There were the *King Penguins* and so much else from the firm established by Allen Lane. There were the many Batsford books which continued that firm's pre-war coverage of Britain's buildings, places, landscapes and customs. And then there were the guide books. There were *The County Books*, launched by Robert Hale in 1948, which were not intended as 'a mere recital of facts' but rather to 'give a true and lively picture of each county and people set against the background which has made it what it is'. In a similar vein, but more interesting and more concerned with buildings both distinguished and quaint, were the *Shell Guides*. These had been begun before the war, in 1934, by John Betjeman, soon afterwards helped by John Piper. With each county volume written by an interesting author, with their imaginative use of typography, photography, old prints and photomontage, together with a witty quirkiness that reflected Betjeman's involvement, the early volumes are highly sought after by those of us suffering that form of mental illness that results in the compulsive buying and collecting of books.

The *Shell Guides* faltered after the war, however, before they were resumed. So Betjeman and Piper, no doubt mindful of the old red-bound *Murray's Handbooks*, persuaded John Murray to fill the breach and start publishing similar county architectural guides. *Berkshire* and *Buckinghamshire* appeared in the late 1940s (and *Lancashire* a few years later) before the project came to a halt and the *Shell Guides* resumed under Betjeman's editorship. Because of the tiresomely over-emphasised antipathy between John Betjeman and Nikolaus Pevsner, these are sometimes seen as a rival to the latter's *Buildings of England* volumes published by Penguin. In truth, Pevsner was trying to do something rather different. Beginning with *Cornwall*, published in 1951, these books were intended to give 'full particulars of the architectural features of all ecclesiastical, public and domestic buildings of interest in each town and village of the county concerned'. And the extraordinary thing is that – unlike the *Shell Guides* – this wonderful, essential series was sustained until every English county was eventually covered and continues today with the *Buildings of Wales, Scotland and Ireland.*

Much has been written about the *Shell Guides* and the *Buildings of England.* But in the considerable literature on all these guides and the bibliographical achievements of Betjeman and Pevsner, another interesting contemporary series of architectural guides has been unaccountably ignored: this is the *Vision of England* series published by Paul Elek between 1946 and 1950. This is odd as the general editors were well known: Clough and Amabel Williams-Ellis, who had earlier written *The Pleasures of Architecture.* Clough Williams-Ellis was, of course, the engaging Welsh country-house architect whose 1928 book, *England and the Octopus,* had railed against the despoliation of the countryside and towns by advertisements, bungalows and that most destructive agent, the motor car (the sense that England was under threat well predates the intervention of the Luftwaffe).

The *Vision of England* books were clearly inspired by the pre-war *Shell Guides* and, like the *Murray's Architectural Guides,* were intended to fill the void left by their (temporary) cessation. As with the *Shell Guides,* each was written by a different author and the books were illustrated by well-chosen photographs. They did not, however, contain an alphabetical gazetteer of places listing buildings of interest. 'Well-known authors here give their own impressions of – and their personal associations with – particular parts of England in a series of books which are intimate and discursive in style rather than formally descriptive.' But what makes these books so covetable is that each was illustrated by a different artist. Line drawings, or, occasionally, wood engravings, of buildings, village scenes and architectural details relieve the text and most also contain colour plates. The results vary in style, and quality. Some of the artists may now seem obscure – I know nothing of Malvina Cheek, Sven Berlin or Dorrit Deck – but their work usually has considerable charm. But some of the artists are now well-known: Michael Rothenstein, Humphrey Spender, Kenneth Rowntree and – above all – Barbara Jones.

Barbara Jones illustrated two of the books with her decorative and evocative drawings: Aubrey de Sélincourt's *Dorset* and G.S. Fraser's *Vision of Scotland*. The series was not in fact confined to England and there was also a *Vision of Wales* volume on *South Wales and Monmouthshire* by Tom Richards. Nor were all the volumes devoted to particular counties. Oddly enough, the first to appear was the guide which explored *The Black Country*, that seldom-visited industrial landscape (actually full of interest) between Birmingham and Wolverhampton. Individual volumes followed on *The Cotswolds*, *The Chilterns*, *The Isle of Wight* and *The Scilly Isles*. And then it all came to an end. Further titles were promised – on Devon, Lancashire, Cambridgeshire and the East and North Ridings of Yorkshire – but they never appeared (what is it about Yorkshire? The *Shell Guides* never covered that huge county either, although the indefatigable Pevsner managed it).

No doubt the reason was financial. There are stories that royalty cheques from the publisher sometimes failed to materialise, but his heart was in the right place. Paul Elek was one of those many émigrés from Continental Europe who did so much to enrich and stimulate the cultural life of staid, provincial Britain in the mid-20th century. Hungarian-Jewish, he was the son of a Budapest printer who first came to London in 1929 as a student and settled here nine years later with his wife Elizabeth. He first set up as a printer during the war and then managed to establish a publishing company in Hatton Garden. Over the following three decades he published over a thousand books. Many of these were on the visual arts, and illustrated. There were monographs on artists and the *Cities of Art* series. A highly cultured man, and a collector, he cared about the appearance of his books and wished to emulate the production of Faber & Faber. In the late 1940s, in addition to the *Vision of England* books, he published two books by Clough Williams-Ellis on the work and possessions of the National Trust entitled *On Trust for the Nation*. The first of these, illustrated by Barbara Jones, began with a dedication by the author: 'to all the beauty of my country, natural and other, in gratitude and grief. The grief is for all the destruction of lovely buildings and for the spoiling by war of beautiful places almost throughout the world.'

One of the last books published by Paul Elek before his death in 1976 was *The Rape of Britain* by Colin Amery and Dan Cruickshank. This depressing little volume catalogued the contemporary despoliation of city after city in Britain by the combined efforts of local authorities, commercial developers, town planners and architects. It makes a poignant contrast with the *Vision of England* series which – like so many of the handsome books of that now-distant era – celebrated the beautiful buildings and landscape of Britain which, after six years of war, then seemed so precious.

April 2008

[I should also have mentioned that Clough Williams-Ellis was the creator of the picturesque fantasy village of Portmeirion in North Wales.]

Anti-Ugly

George Ferguson, the current President of the Royal Institute of British Architects, has proposed a national 'X-list' of buildings worthy of demolition. 'Vile buildings are an affront to our senses,' he insists; 'What I seek is public intolerance of the worst and demand for the best. This is about repairing damaged places.' The suggestion may be well intentioned, if clearly intended to generate publicity; it is also naïve, for taste changes and today's eyesore can become tomorrow's masterpiece. After all, if such a list had been drawn up fifty years ago it would have contained many 'hideous Victorian' buildings an earlier generation had been taught to despise – major monuments like St Pancras Station which we now, rightly, cherish. Is Mr Ferguson really so sure of his judgement that he is prepared to promote the destruction of buildings designed by members of the Institute over which he presides?

Of course we all can think of buildings that the environment would be better without and I agree that, for example, the horrible St James's Centre in Edinburgh did much damage and deserves replacement. But even the most unlikely buildings have their defenders. The Tricorn Centre at Portsmouth, an assertive example of raw concrete Brutalism designed by Rodney Gordon of the Owen Luder Partnership, was once regarded as the epitome of bad 1960s design, yet its recent demolition provoked protest – not least from Jonathan Meades. Similarly, Gateshead City Council (which has just built the offensively obtrusive Sage Centre) cannot wait to see the back of the 1960s concrete shopping precinct and multi-storey car park which looms over the south bank of the Tyne, yet this extraordinary structure, designed by the same architect, has achieved cult status – partly because it starred in the Michael Caine film, *Get Carter*. Is it on the President's X-list, I wonder?

Mr Ferguson counters such objections by saying that he is only concerned with mediocre buildings which damage their surroundings, and on their sins we can surely all agree. But can we? Such arguments are equally subjective. What about Embassy Court in Brighton, a building whose horizontal emphasis and overweening bulk wrecks the stuccoed urbanity of the Hove seafront? Its removal would please the Regency Society of Brighton and Hove, but would dismay the Twentieth Century Society as it is a pioneering 1930s Modern Movement masterpiece by Wells Coates which is now – very properly – listed. And I might myself propose the new Lloyds of London for the X-list as an ill-mannered and crude exercise in Neo-Meccano high tech which wrecks its surroundings, but the President of the RIBA is unlikely to agree as it is, of course, a masterpiece by Lord Rogers of Riverside.

We already have a list, and one that is positive rather than negative. This is the statutory list of buildings of architectural and/or historical importance, and inclusion on that is the result of careful thought and expert opinion rather than knee-jerk prejudice. It is this official list that determines whether, after debate, a building survives or not if it comes up for demolition, and that is surely the way it should be. A *prescriptive* list of buildings meriting destruction, however, is simply philistine. It is, after all, difficult to imagine the President of the Royal Society of Literature proposing a list of books suitable for burning. The X-list is also offensive because of its crude populism, and it comes as no surprise to learn that there is to be an associated television series on Channel 4 in which viewers will nominate contenders for demolition and which will end – to quote the RIBA press release – with 'a spectacular celebratory demolition of one of the nation's nastiest eyesores'. As far as I am concerned, that is the equivalent of a public hanging, and no more edifying.

The real point is that there is no need for an X-list. When bad buildings come to the end of their useful (and sometimes largely useless) lives and the statutory listing system detects no merit in them, they can be demolished and replaced by something better. It is getting something better that is the problem. And it is here that an earlier, wittier and considerably more stylish form of Mr Ferguson's X-list might have something to teach us.

In December, 1958, a new group called Anti-Ugly Action demonstrated outside two new buildings they found offensive: Caltex House in the Old Brompton Road and Agriculture House (the monumental Neo-Georgian headquarters of the Farmers' Union, since demolished) in Knightsbridge. Soon afterwards, to coincide with the foundation stone-laying ceremony at the new Barclays Bank headquarters in Lombard Street (a very posthumous work by Sir Herbert Baker, who had died in 1946), the group placed a black coffin on the pavement outside bearing the legend: *Here lyeth British Architecture.* Subsequent targets included the Air Ministry in Whitehall, the new Guildford public library and the new dining hall of Emmanuel College, Cambridge (a building so dreary it is surprising that anyone got worked up about it, although Pevsner thought 'it may one day be loved'). Perhaps these tactics were ultimately successful as at least two of these post-war buildings have since been replaced (although in the case of Barclays Bank by something much worse).

So who were the Anti-Uglies, otherwise known as the New Architecture Group? Significantly, the founders were not architects but students at the Stained Glass Department of the Royal College of Art who also attended lectures on architecture and became aware of the low quality of so much new building. Later they were joined by architecture students at the RCA and eventually there were representatives from three other London architectural schools – the Bartlett, the Regent Street Polytechnic and the Architectural Association – on the executive committee. Interestingly, the secretary was that antithesis of ugliness who has become a Sixties feminist cult figure, Pauline Boty, who told the *Daily Express* that 'I think the Air Ministry building is a real stinker, with the Farmers' Union H.Q., the Bank of England [that's the huge curved block along New Change by Victor Heal], and the Financial Times as runners-up.'

Cards were printed for members of the public to recommend buildings 'for the Anti-Ugly Seal of disapproval' and although some were sniffy about demonstrations by long-haired, duffle-coated students, others welcomed debate about architectural quality. 'I think it is a healthy sign these things are happening,' wrote John Betjeman in the *Daily Telegraph*. 'Art is coming into its own again after the worship of science and economics. What is more important, the art of architecture is at last coming in for the public notice it deserves.' But it is clear from the list of targets that the Anti-Uglies were not so much concerned with ugliness as with architectural conservatism. Almost all were examples of modern traditional buildings designed by architects who were either disinclined or too old to embrace the new orthodoxies of modernism. The fact that the marchers down Knightsbridge cheered as they passed Bowater House

– the block that straddles the entrance to Hyde Park which I, for one, would be happy to see go – confirms that their agenda was really ideological.

Another prominent victim was the new Central Library at Kensington, a well-made, carefully detailed red-brick essay in monumental Classicism. Over two hundred Anti-Ugly activists were led by a blinkered figure in 17th century dress in a bathchair, symbolising the architect, and a town crier, who read out extracts with a megaphone from the real architect's apologia for his design. 'The library should be a building of good manners...' 'It's an outrage,' roared the demonstrators; 'It is in modern English renaissance style in keeping with the Royal borough...' 'It's an outrage!' The architect was, in fact, E. Vincent Harris, the *doyen* of town hall builders who had been awarded the RIBA Royal Gold Medal in 1951 and whose work now commands respect (and is mostly listed). Harris was 82 years old when his Kensington Library was attacked, and he commented that the demonstrators were 'quite irresponsible. As a matter of fact, these students have had no training at all. Just because they have passed a few exams, they think they are fully fledged architects.' He surely had a point.

Such traditionalists may well have had the last laugh. One of Pauline Boty's runners-up, Bracken House, was designed for the *Financial Times* in pink brick and stone by Sir Albert Richardson, who posed as 'The Last of the Georgians' in the 1950s but who had been a progressive designer anxious to develop the Classical tradition. Bracken House did not deserve the abuse of the Anti-Uglies as it was an elegant and sophisticated response to a difficult brief which drew upon the work of Cockerell and Schinkel. Its modernist critics could surely never have imagined that, when threatened with demolition in 1987, this building would become the first Post-War building in England to be listed after the Twentieth Century Society campaigned in its favour. A further irony is that, in consequence, the printing works in the centre of Richardson's modern

Neo-Classical sandwich was subsequently replaced by a clever and harmonious new structure by Sir Michael Hopkins who, three decades earlier, along with his wife Patty, had been an active Anti-Ugly. Did they once protest against Sir Albert's masterpiece, I wonder?

All of which might suggest that the history of taste – of changing perceptions of vileness and ugliness – is rather less straightforward than the President of the RIBA would have us believe.

January 2005

[Bowater House did go, but to be replaced by something much worse: One Hyde Park, the overweening block of luxury flats for the stinking rich designed by Rogers Stirk Harbour & Partners*. Victor Heal's civilized building in New Change next to St Paul's Cathedral has been torn down to make way for a pretentious glass lump by the French architect Jean Nouvel (the Johnny Halliday of architecture). Rodney Gordon's car-park in Gateshead has also since disappeared. For more on Anti-Ugly Action, see my article in* Blueprint *for January 2007, and a forthcoming article in* Architectural History, *the Journal of the Society of Architectural Historians of G.B. I made one mistake: Anti-Ugly Action was not the same as the New Architecture Group – the latter attempted to revive Anti-Ugly protests in 1962.*

Interest rightly continues to grow in the work of Pauline Boty, with an exhibition, Pauline Boty: Pop Artist and Woman, *held at Wolverhampton Art Gallery in 2013 and her role in Anti-Ugly action acklowedged in the accompanying book by Sue Tate.*

I am also happy to record that George Ferguson, ex-PRIBA, became the first elected Mayor of Bristol in 2012.]

The Curse of Palladio

Raymond Erith – some of whose exquisite drawings are currently on display in the centenary exhibition at Sir John Soane's Museum – has long been the most celebrated of those so-called traditionalist architects who carried on building after the Second World War despite the active opposition of the ascendant Modern Movement. Many of his projects remained on the drawing board and most of his work consisted of building or altering country houses, but after he reconstructed the interiors of nos. 10, 11 and 12 Downing Street for the Macmillan government interesting jobs came his way, notably the library at Lady Margaret Hall, Oxford. This last, at least externally, is like a large, austere Soanian warehouse, and Soane, indeed, was a hero or mentor for the young Erith. Like others of his generation who intelligently recognised an affinity between the abstraction of Soane and the aesthetic of Modernism, Erith considered him 'a very rare

bird, and unique among the great architects, in being a progressive Classicist'.

There seem to me to be two things that matter about Erith.
One is that he saw the continuing value of traditional styles
and methods of construction, so that his buildings were beauti-
fully made. The other is that he was a good designer. This last
consideration is too often forgotten in the tiresomely polarised
debate about Modernism and Classicism which continues to
rage. It is a debate in which blinkers tend to be worn on both
sides – something encouraged by the Prince of Wales tendency,
which naively regards anything with a flat roof as clearly
bad and any building with columns as indisputably good.
Modernists, of course, adopt precisely the reverse position.
What this reveals is merely conventional opinion. It is instructive to note that, when the first Modern Movement houses
were built by Maxwell Fry and Connell, Ward & Lucas in
Hampstead in the 1930s, there was ferocious local opposition
to these alien intruders spoiling the precious local character. Yet thirty years on, when Erith designed that charming
essay in Georgian vernacular, *Jack Straw's Castle*, the denizens
of Hampstead opposed it because it was traditional and not
'modern'.

Intelligent modern architects such as Denys Lasdun and
Philip Powell held Erith in high regard, but perhaps this was
partly because he was no threat and had a rather specialised
practice. Indeed, Erith has become a sort of hero or prophet for
those who are committed to Classical architecture. This may
reflect English snobbery, that is, the undue reverence given to
the architecture of country houses, for in truth, despite his early
admiration for Soane and his belief in a progressive Classicism,
Erith's work has less to teach about the adaptability of tradition
to modern conditions that that of certain other twentieth-century
Classicists. There was Lutyens, of course, who expanded
and enriched the language of Classicism with astonishing
originality until his death in 1944. More to the point, there was

Sir Albert Richardson who, although he parodied himself as a reactionary Georgian squire, designed Bracken House for the Financial Times in the 1950s – a modern commercial building (since cleverly altered by Michael Hopkins) that showed how the Neo-Classicism of Schinkel and Cockerell could still be appropriate and practical in the City of London.

Above all, perhaps, there was Erith's contemporary Donald McMorran and his younger partner George Whitby, who, inspired by the legacy of Lutyens and that great town-hall builder Vincent Harris, rose to the challenge of modern administrative and technical requirements. Their Classicism was truly progressive and they designed municipal buildings at Exeter and Bury St Edmunds and university colleges at Nottingham that were both traditional and modern, abstracted but civilised structures that met their users' needs and were intelligently detailed. Most impressive, perhaps, are two buildings in the City: their police station in Wood Street, which has a stone-faced residential block that is a miniature skyscraper, and the extension to the Edwardian Baroque Old Bailey, where the simplicity of treatment and the abstraction of monumental forms create a grandeur worthy of Vanbrugh. Yet McMorran and Whitby were largely ignored by the architectural press and are little known today.

The tragedy of modern British architecture is that the sane, progressive alternative to doctrinaire Modernism was undermined by the comparatively early deaths of these men: McMorran in 1965, Whitby and Erith both in 1973. Although this was the very time when the arrogant assumptions of the Modernist establishment were beginning to be questioned, these departures left the field empty, with only Erith's younger pupil and partner, Quinlan Terry, to hold aloft the torch of Classicism – something he was, I fear, quite unfitted to sustain. Yet Terry went on to build up a hugely successful country-house practice, largely for the new money of the Thatcher years. There are two unfortunate things about this earnest and rigid traditionalist. The first is that he has grasped the dead hand of that perennial curse of English architecture: Palladianism. Erith, at least when young, was much more broad-minded, holding to 'the tradition of all western architecture: Greek, Roman, Gothic, Renaissance, and all the rest, including the tradition of the great modern engineers. It is the tradition from which architecture ought never to have deviated'. His early designs, inspired by the Regency, were drily witty. Later, however – perhaps under Terry's influence – his work drew more on Palladio, and became more pedantic and boring.

The second unfortunate aspect to Terry's being fêted as the leader of a new generation of continuing Classicists in Britain is that he is, I am sorry to say, a mediocre architect. He goes in for a sort of photocopy-Palladian, with Classical details stuck on to dull boxes. Although undoubtedly well made, his architecture is stiff, pedantic and uninspiring. Particularly revealing is the Howard Building at Downing College, Cambridge, a vaguely Palladian design which turns its back on the Greek Revival style of the original campus. Ineptitude is demonstrated by the complete failure to integrate – or interpenetrate – a lower Doric order with a double-height Corinthian, as Cockerell, or, for that matter, Palladio knew how to do, while it is simply excruciating to see down-pipes slicing through plinths. And then there are the eight false windows, four of them in symmetrical pairs and so, as balancing elements, redundant. Far from aspiring to a progressive Classicism, this is crude, drawing-board architecture that undermines efforts to take a modern Classicism seriously, yet Quinlan Terry has been consistently praised by the Country Life/Prince of Wales Institute lobby.

Of course, the other side is equally partisan and blinkered. Poundbury, the new development outside Dorchester promoted by the Duchy of Cornwall, i.e., the Prince of Wales, is undoubtedly twee in aspects of its traditionalism. It has, however, been carefully planned by Leon Krier to realise progressive and socially humane ideas about traffic, social diversity and community, yet few critics seem to have a good word for the experiment. Similarly, the new Queen's Gallery at Buckingham Palace has largely been ignored by architectural critics, despite its clear success, simply because its designer, John Simpson, uses the language of the Greeks as refined by Schinkel. Now Simpson may not be a great architect, but in the handling of space – something that Modernists constantly bang on about – he displays genius. At Buckingham Palace he has brilliantly threaded new rooms and staircases through an existing building while the quality of his detail and his mastery of technology and construction commands respect. The Queen's Gallery deserves to be taken very seriously indeed.

Even so, the sad truth is that, despite much hype, the new Classicism that has flourished to a degree since the 1980s has been rather a disappointment. Even if Terry is taken out of the equation, no designer has emerged who has made the immensely rich language of Classicism glow and 'become as plastic clay', as Lutyens put it. There is Robert Adam who, with considerable intelligence, has argued that Classicism must adapt and embrace new technologies, but his designs are too often clunkingly gauche and slightly vulgar. There is Demetri Porphyrios, who can be elegant and austere when he keeps to a Greek Revival style, but whose attempt at Tudor Gothic at Magdalen College, Oxford, is so painful as to make the whole enterprise seem contrived and posturing. More promising is the work of Craig Hamilton, who has had the benefit of an old-fashioned training in South Africa and who seeks to play with the Classical orders informed by a broad-minded knowledge of history. With his work, I cannot help feeling that the further he moves from Palladio, and the simpler it becomes, the more convincing it is – but I fear that is not what his clients want.

The late Sir Nikolaus Pevsner has received much stick, particularly from David Watkin in *Morality and Architecture*, because of his disapproval of traditional architects who declined to follow the orthodoxy of Modernism after the 1920s.

Yet I am increasingly being forced to admit – especially when contemplating all this unremarkable and self-conscious New Classicism – that perhaps he was right all along in that, yes, there really is a *Zeitgeist*. Of course architects should have the freedom to reject the spirit of the age and learn from the past, but I suspect that true originality and artistic success is only possible when a designer is working with that spirit. Any alternative seems to be doomed to be pedantically striving and unsophisticated. Even Erith's buildings became less interesting as the climate became more alien. Even so, it would help if critics on both sides used their eyes rather than just following party lines.

November 2004

[Craig Hamilton has since emerged as a major talent, and almost the only new Classical architect able and sophisticated enough to go way beyond Palladio and embrace the lessons offered by 19th and 20th century Classicists such as Lutyens, Holden, Plečnik and Piacentini.]

Palladian Games

'In architecture Palladio is the game!!' wrote Edwin Lutyens in a much-quoted letter to Herbert Baker written in 1903. The English architect, having made his name with romantic vernacular houses, was then discovering the possibilities of the Classical language and revelling in the geometrical and formal discipline it could impose. As he would soon demonstrate in New Delhi and elsewhere, Lutyens would handle that language with astonishing originality – playing games and bending the rules. But in fact Palladio was not a major influence on Lutyens, and in Italy (which he only visited for the first time in 1909) he was much more impressed by the Mannerism of Sanmichele in Verona.

Sanmichele, however, was scarcely as well known as Palladio and certainly never gave his name to a style. Born five hundred years ago – on 30 November – in Padua, Andrea Palladio became one of the most revered and influential architects in history. Thanks to his *Quattro Libri* on Architecture, the Classical language was understood beyond Italy through Palladio's drawings and Palladianism would become a dominant, not to say ineradicable, taste in the English-speaking world in particular. Whether that legacy did justice to Palladio's own creations, and whether, indeed, his influence can be seen as benign or pernicious, are interesting questions and ones that may be provoked by the major quincentenary exhibition which is currently on show in Vicenza, where he built so much. This exhibition will then travel to Britain, where it will open at the Royal Academy at the end of January next year, before moving on to the United States.

The anniversary itself is, however, being celebrated this month in London by an imaginative exhibition at the Plus One Gallery called 'Celebrating Palladio'. Organised by the architectural artist and perspectivist Carl Laubin, this consists of personal responses to the Italian architect's work and his legacy by modern artists and architects. Laubin himself is contributing two of his magnificent *capriccios*, one of which – 'Cinquecentenario' – does for Palladio what he has already done for Hawksmoor, Cockerell and Ledoux; that is, gather together all of the master's churches, palaces and villas in an ideal landscape. Other artists represented include Ben Johnson and Alexander Creswell, who depict buildings by Palladio and his contemporaries in their very different but characteristic styles. And then there are the architects. These, of course, belong to the traditionalist party in the tiresomely polarised situation which now exists: architects who produce modern Classical designs which are ritually derided by the modernist establishment. So John Simpson shows a design for a rumbustious market hall which he proposed in his unexecuted scheme for redeveloping Paternoster Square next to St Paul's Cathedral, and Julian Bicknell shows his executed design for a modern Palladian country house in Cheshire.

This, Henbury Hall, appears in pride of place in Laubin's

other *tour-de-force*, 'Palladius Britannicus', which depicts many of the Palladian bridges, garden pavilions, country houses and other buildings raised in Britain since the 17th century by Inigo Jones, Lord Burlington, Colen Campbell and more recent devotees. As for Henbury Hall, built in the 1980s, a house originally inspired by a painting by the late Felix Kelly, the uninitiated might well mistake it for Campbell's Mereworth Castle in Kent of the 1720s, which was itself little more than a realisation of Palladio's published design for the celebrated Villa Rotunda. Now there is absolutely nothing wrong with designing Classical buildings today. The trouble is that so many of the projects are pedantic, literal recreations of Palladian precedents, with an emphasis on correct detail, rather than attempts at an imaginative, creative reinterpretation of the Classical language in response to modern conditions – such as early 20th century architects like Lutyens or McMorran & Whitby strove for.

An earlier quincentenary exhibition, of so-called 'New Palladians', held at The Prince's Foundation in London, confirmed this sad state of affairs. Although it purported to demonstrate 'the continuity of a Timeless, Robust and Sustainable Culture of Building and Design into the 21st century' in the hands of the 'World's Leading Practitioners', the display was dominated by derivative designs for Classical country houses, each with a grand portico. Unfortunately, there seems to be no shortage of rich men, on both sides of the Atlantic, who want to build nothing more than a Neo-Palladian house – always with a big portico – to show off their wealth. It is a craven taste which has sustained the lucrative career of that most pedantic and unimaginative of modern Classical architects, Quinlan Terry. The problem, perhaps, is the very nature of Palladianism, for not only did the superior foreign manner become snobbish by association but , in the hands of that prissy, intolerant aesthete, the Earl of Burlington, who could only understand architecture by reference to Palladio's books, it became a mere formula for producing grand houses. What, surely, is regrettable is that this taste for elegant boxes with porticoes brought to an end the glorious native phase of the English Baroque, of the original and truly monumental interpretations of Classical precedent achieved by Wren, Hawksmoor and Vanbrugh.

Not all Classical architects have been in awe of Palladio, however. Notwithstanding the Classical revival of the early 20th century, Lutyens's contemporary, that combative architect and historian Reginald Blomfield, dared to criticise the 'fetish-worship' and the 'Palladian superstition of the eighteenth century' in an essay he published in 1905. Palladio, Blomfield argued, was as a reactionary figure in his time, for, 'with the touch of pedantry that suited the times and invested his writings with a fallacious air of scholarship, he was the very man to summarise and classify, and to save future generations of architects the labour of thinking for themselves'. As for Palladianism, the 'weaker men' who succeeded Wren, he argued, 'had to fall back on rule and text-book, and Palladio recovered his ascendancy in England because his method adapted itself to the taste of the English virtuoso of the eighteenth century'.

Now, in truth, Blomfield – not the greatest of Classical architects (though his Menin Gate at Ypres is a fine thing) – was both ignorant about and unfair to Palladio's own work. There was much more to Palladio than the Palladians singled out for admiration. They were principally interested in those glorious and undeniably elegant essays in geometry which are his country villas in the Veneto, but he also designed town houses and, of course, churches of great spatial complexity and sculptural richness, while some late works, like the Palazzo Valmarana and the tantalising Loggia del Capitaniato in Vicenza are subtle, inventive Mannerist compositions with much to teach any modern architect who truly wants to explore the possibilities of Classicism. But the blinkered Palladians ignored these problematic buildings, although some more intelligent architects admired them; as David Watkin writes in the catalogue to the *Celebrating Palladio* exhibition, 'different ages find in Palladio what they want to find: for Inigo Jones and Burlington it was purity, for Cockerell richness'.

It is not Palladio's fault, but the sad fact is that Palladianism has had – and continues to have – a stultifying effect on British architecture. In his book on the architect, Bruce Boucher observed that 'most of the buildings dubbed "Palladian" have only the vaguest connection with Palladio's own work; columns and symmetry alone were never a passport to immortality'. In conclusion, therefore, it is worth continuing with the quote from that famous Lutyens letter about the 'big game', the 'high game' of Classicism: 'It is so big – few appreciate it now, and it requires training to value and realise it. The way Wren handled it was marvellous. Shaw has the gift. To the average man it is dry bones, but under the hand of a Wren it glows and the stiff materials become as plastic clay.' That was certainly true as well of Andrea Palladio – whose 500th birthday is well worth celebrating – but not, alas, of most of his many English-speaking disciples.

November 2008

Surreal Recall

'I try to create fantastic things, magical things, things like in a dream...,' wrote Salvador Dali in 1940. 'We can make the fantastic real, and then it is more real than that which actually exists.' Although architectural ideas and fantasies can have an existence on paper, it is both the glory and the drawback of architecture that it has to be real, to exist in three dimensions as a masonry construction that actually stands up. A Surrealist architecture might therefore seem a contradiction in terms, even though it may sometimes be possible to build dreams. But buildings can have a surreal, oneiric effect – even unintentionally: John Summerson famously writing in 1945 how it was possible to visit Milner Square in Islington many times 'and still not be absolutely certain that you have seen it anywhere but in an unhappy dream'.

There certainly was a Surrealist architecture and, even more important, a Surrealist interior, in which extraordinary effects were created by curtains, upholstery, murals, weird furniture and objects and unexpected juxtapositions. There was, for instance, the Parisian apartment designed by Le Corbusier for Carlos de Beistegui whose roof garden had a Rococo chimney-piece set into the parapet wall above which was a mirror open to the sky. Furthermore, as Alan Powers has argued, there were several Modern Movement interiors which were not so much Functionalist as anti-functionalist and even Surrealist in intention. The Italian Fascist buildings with their repetitive arcades or colonnades inspired by the paintings of de Chirico might also be cited. And above all, there were the interiors created at Monkton House and elsewhere in the 1930s by that greatest, most intriguing and most creative of Surrealist patrons, Edward James, who, for Dali, was 'the most surrealist of us all'.

Some of these works figure in the current major exhibition of *Surreal Things* at the Victoria & Albert Museum. As far as I am concerned, this is the best – and certainly the most enjoyable – of the big themed exhibitions mounted at the museum in recent years, perhaps because the subject lends itself to humour and glamour. Objects which once contributed to Surrealist interiors, like the plaster palms, console tables and other furniture by Emilio Terry and Alberto Giacometti, are on show. And there is, rightly and inevitably, a whole section devoted to Edward James, who once owned (and commissioned) so many of the well-known paintings and objects by Dali, René Magritte, Leonora Carrington and others without which the exhibition would be incomplete. But the display is puzzling, for there is only one illustration – in both exhibition and the accompanying catalogue-book – of the interior of Monkton. This is a photograph of the bedroom corridor, hung with a bright, wavy Italian decorative fabric leading to Paul Delvaux's *Les Belles de Nuit*. The other extraordinary rooms in the house, notably the dining room with upholstered walls which once contained two of Dali's celebrated Mae West Lips Sofas, are neither illustrated or even referred to. Why not?

Monkton House began life as a 'trianon' designed by Edwin Lutyens in 1902 on the Sussex estate of West Dean Park, the Late Victorian mansion bought and enlarged by Willie James, the wealthy big-game-hunting crony of King Edward VII. When Edward James inherited his fortune, he set about transforming Monkton as well as creating extraordinary interiors in his flat in Wimpole Street in London. Much that he did reflected the influence of Dali. Lutyens' brickwork was rendered and painted purple and pale green; bamboo-like (salvaged) down pipes were applied, along with 'aprons' below the windows (a development of a Baroque motif); the front door was flanked by giant palm trees; and the chimneys were converted into weird vertical features – one of which indicated the day of the week rather than the hour.

All this was done by the architect Christopher ('Kit') Nicholson, son of William and brother of Ben, assisted by the young Hugh Casson. Nicholson was also responsible for replacing Lutyens's timber staircase by a sweeping Art Deco stair, worthy of a cinema, with a port-hole window half way up which looked into the giant fish-tank which dominated the bathroom behind. The story of Monkton is complicated, however, and other interiors were created by Norris Wakefield, then a young assistant to Mrs 'Dolly' Mann, the interior decorator. Wakefield worked closely with James and found much of the furniture as well as the fabrics which lined the walls. James's office, in a Regency style, was lined with the same blue serge fabric of which his suit was made; both drawing room and dining room had padded and quilted fabric walls, an inspired treatment at once resonant and erotic extrapolated from Victorian button-backed furniture. Upstairs, James's bed was a giant full-tester with palm tree columns, modelled on the funeral carriage that took the body of Nelson to St Paul's. Another bedroom had a glass ceiling like the night sky, with the heavenly bodies in the positions they were at the moment of his birth.

The interior of Monkton was enchanting, weird, extraordinary, eccentric, highly original and decidedly surreal. The effect of the wall treatments and the Surrealist objects – including Dali's 'Arm' chair, champagne cup lamps and lobster telephones – and was enhanced by the presence of unusual and witty pieces of real Regency furniture and such things as the carpet woven with the footprints of James's dog (which superseded a design bearing the footprints of beautiful, ghastly Tilly Losh, the ballerina he had scandalously divorced) as well as by the works of art on the wall. And, although it was unique, it was also wonderfully representative of its time for, under the umbrella of Surrealism, fashionable 'Vogue Regency'and even *avant-garde* Neo-Victorian was combined with Art Deco. It seems extraordinary that this astonishing creation is not celebrated in the V&A exhibition. What, rightly, is exhibited are drawings and a model for another project by James and Kit Nicholson, a bailiff's house formed out of façade of James Wyatt's Pantheon in Oxford Street, taken down in 1938 and for which a new home was sought by the newly founded Georgian Group.

The Pantheon project came to nothing because of Edward James' departure for the safer side of the Atlantic in 1940, where he later created another architectural fantasy at Xilitla in the Mexican jungle. But Monkton survived intact as a secret Surrealist wonder until his death in 1984. The Trustees of the Edward James Foundation then decided to dismantle it and sell up. Recognising the importance of Monkton both as a Surrealist creation and as a period piece, the Thirties Society (now the Twentieth Century Society) and SAVE Britain's Heritage mounted a campaign, strongly supported by English Heritage, to preserve Monkton and open it to the public. In our report, Mark Girouard wrote that Monkton was 'a dream expressed in three dimensions… witty, creative, captivating… a little masterpiece which is also the most original and personal creation of its founder'. But we failed. The Foundation argued that opening the house was impractical and went ahead with the sale. Twenty-one years on, aspects of this affair remain troubling. Why were the Trustees in such a hurry, giving us so little time to raise the necessary money? Did they really need the cash to support the arts and crafts college James had established at West Dean? Why was Monkton cleared of most of its contents just before the chairman of English Heritage, Lord Montagu, went down to see it? Why was furniture also sold from West Dean which Edward James had expressly wished to be retained?

It was as if the Trustees disliked their late benefactor, who was certainly a peculiar and difficult man. Was it revenge for his notorious remark that he didn't leave his fortune to West Dean so that middle-class women could learn to make corn dollies? I do not know. What I do know is that had Edward James's ensemble not been broken up, Britain could now boast not only the finest collection of Surrealist art in the world but also, in Monkton, one of the most eccentric, revealing, enchanting and – yes – subtly representative architectural creations of its time.

July-August 2007

Guinness isn't Good for You

B rave New Worlds have a way of looking rather shabby and sad before too long. Between the two world wars, an exciting future seemed to be represented by the growth of London to the west and north-west. New, wide arterial roads, first mooted in 1909, were laid out to cope with the massive expansion of motor traffic, and along the Great West Road new factories were built, reflecting the growth of light industry that made the South-East prosperous when the old heavy industries of the North were in deep recession. The best were the 'fancy factories', the Art Deco-cum-Egyptian buildings designed by Wallis Gilbert & Partners, of which the most celebrated was the Firestone Factory. 'The Great West Road looked very odd,' thought J.B. Priestley in 1933. 'Being new, it did not look English. We might have suddenly rolled into California.' And what could be more modern than America, and Hollywood?

More interesting was Western Avenue, laid out from Acton in 1922-27 in the direction of Oxford. With new semi-detached houses lining the dual-carriageway and a smart new Underground station and modernistic shopping parades at Park Royal, it developed into a linear exemplar of inter-war British architecture – especially as there was the Hoover Factory, another Wallis Gilbert fancy factory, further out at Perivale. But the most impressive structures along what became the A40 were the three big monumental brick blocks rising on the north side on an eminence at Park Royal. This was another industrial complex, but one producing a product much more necessary and vital than vacuum cleaners, fire extinguishers, razor blades or car tyres. It was the new brewery – the first in England – run by Arthur Guinness & Co. of Dublin. 'My Goodness! My Guinness!' went one of the many striking and witty contemporary posters issued by the firm, but an equally good advertisement was this generous and magnificent industrial landmark.

The Guinness Brewery at Park Royal opened in 1936. The consulting engineers who designed it were Sir Alexander Gibb & Partners, but the external appearance was entirely due to the consulting architect, Sir Giles Gilbert Scott – fresh from his triumph in industrial architecture at Battersea Power Station. As at Battersea, Scott humanised the vast masses without denying their sublime industrial character by facing the steel structures with conspicuously fine brickwork and minimal 'jazz modern' trim. Equally important, he made the three different principal blocks – Malt Store, Brewhouse and Storehouse – rise to the same 100 foot height, despite varying in width and exterior treatment on falling ground, which gives the total ensemble a powerful visual presence. As at Battersea and at Bankside Power Station – now Tate Modern – Scott made utilitarian structures into great architecture – on Ruskinian rather than Classical principles. And now it is all to be demolished, to be replaced by a business park.

The Scott buildings have already been partly obscured as a landmark by the tawdry modern office block erected in front by Diageo, the multinational conglomerate which now owns poor old Guinness (no family members have been on the board since the Ernest Saunders–Distillers scandal of the 1980s). Brewing on the site will cease later this year, and all the 1930s structures demolished. How can this be, when, surely, they must be listed, as is Battersea Power Station and most other creations by the great designer of Liverpool Cathedral, the House of Commons and the red telephone box? The trouble is that, after much lobbying and despite expert advice from English Heritage and others, Diageo secured a Certificate of Immunity from listing, having argued that statutory protection would inhibit their operations and so endanger local employment. 'We act sensitively, with the highest standards of integrity and social responsibility,' announces the Diageo website. Yet, rather than stay, Diageo is closing the brewery and is indulging in mere speculative development, thus rendering the Certificate of Immunity (which expires in 2008) ethically unjustifiable if legally valid. No serious attempt has been made to see if the brewery buildings can be re-used while, with growing consciousness of the 'embodied energy' in built structures, demolishing such superb masonry seems to me wicked.

The imminent, scandalous fate of the Guinness Brewery is symbolic of the general decline of Western Avenue. What was, in the 1930s, one of the largest and most important industrial areas in Britain was seriously depressed by the 1980s, threatening many of the buildings despite the growing appreciation of inter-war architecture. At least the Hoover Factory has secured a new life as a Tesco supermarket, unlike the poor old Firestone Factory, which was demolished by its owners, Trafalgar House, over a bank-holiday weekend in 1980 in anticipation of listing. Elsewhere, much has changed and is changing. At Western Circus, close to the London County Council's humane and impressive Old Oak Common estate, the large cinema and attendant shops which once defined the road junction have been swept away, leaving an incoherent space. A little further out, a small factory of sub-*art nouveau* character which always intrigued me as it bore the unlikely date of '1916' has been replaced by a much larger and far less interesting commercial block. No longer is Western Avenue an instructive study in inter-war development; it is now a sad, uninteresting, polluted motorway, choked with traffic.

The worst destruction, however, has occurred between Western Circus and Gipsy Corner, a stretch of the arterial road once lined by typical but rather interesting detached and semi-detached houses in various styles: Tudor, Georgian and modernistic. This transformation is the subject of a remarkable book, a combination of suburban history and sociological reportage, called *Leadville: A Biography of the A40* (Picador, 2000). Between 1995 and 1998, the author, Edward Platt, visited and interviewed many of the occupants of the houses along the road, all of whom were threatened with eviction to enable a scheme to widen the A40. The area had certainly declined since its heyday, but what is fascinating is that while some houses were lived in by squatters, others were still owned by families who clung to the suburban dream of the 1920s and 1930s despite the torrent of traffic that poured past their front gardens. No matter: all were ruthlessly moved on by the authorities, who then smashed up perfectly good houses to make them uninhabitable.

And then, in 1998, for political reasons, the Highways Agency changed its mind, abandoned the plans for more fly-overs and underpasses and decided to increase capacity by less extravagant means. The evictions and demolitions had been largely unnecessary. Mr Platt interviewed one of the road planners responsible; essentially unrepentant, he still looked to a glorious motorised future. 'It's just a shame that elections come when they do. Had it all happened a year earlier, then we might not have demolished the houses by that time, but it's very easy to use hindsight. Unfortunately, at the time, it was considered the best thing to press on – to implement the policies as soon as possible.' But the damage was done. Western Avenue is now largely devoid of interest or even of suburban coherence – at least for the motorist. Underpasses now burrow past the interesting sections, like Park Royal, and the first characteristic landmarks are now to be seen out at Perivale: the jazzy colourful façade of the old Hoover building and the more sober Myllet Arms opposite, designed by E.B. Musman, *doyen* of roadhouse architects.

All this may be historically interesting, but I suspect that few readers will sympathise with my lament for Western Avenue, and even they may be surprised that a non-motorist can look with sympathy at an environment created in the 1920s and 1930s as much by the motor-car as by London Transport. One explanation for this is not only have I the privilege of being chairman of the Twentieth Century Society but I am also writing a book about inter-war architecture. But what should concern us all is that this story exposes the failure of Britain's planning and historic building legislation. Swathes of perfectly sound, ordinary buildings have been swept away for no good reason while the finest piece of architecture in the area – the work of a great artist and one of the best examples of 20th century industrial architecture in Britain – cannot be protected and re-used because of a flagrant misuse of the already dubious system of granting certificates of immunity from listing. It is an indication that politicians consider that commercial development is more important than the preservation of fine architecture.

And there is more. What has happened and is happening to Western Avenue constitutes a consistent degradation of the environment sanctioned by the authorities. This degradation is visual, but it is also material. If, as we surely all must, we worry about climate change, then the encouragement of more road traffic and the destruction of existing masonry structures

– potentially useful masses of embodied energy whether or not of architectural merit – is irresponsible and wrong in principle. Surely politicians and bureaucrats should learn to think more holistically, more intelligently? As for me, I will lament the fact that, in future, my Guinness will not emanate from those magnificent brick blocks at Park Royal but will have to be imported from Dublin – thus wasting more energy as well as wasting those millions of special $2^3/_8$ inch Wellington facing bricks separated by $^5/_8$ inch flush joints of carefully tinted mortar. Nobody is building walls like these any more.

August 2005

[The Guinness Brewery was duly demolished.]

Keeping an Open Mind

An open mind is an empty mind, insisted one master at school while another assured us that to change your mind is to show that you have one. I have long been haunted by these two contradictory precepts, but as I get older the more I favour the latter approach – especially with regard to architecture. First impressions of buildings are often superficial or misleading and it can take time to understand them and their designers' intentions. This is particularly true – for me – with more recent architecture, as I have often had to change my mind about buildings I once hated.

As chairman of the Twentieth Century Society, I find myself defending buildings which I detested (and didn't really *see*) when, decades ago, I first became architecturally aware and I was enthralled by my first love, the 19th century. Often it is a matter of rejecting easy prejudice to try and understand the aims of architects within the limitations of their time and the straightjacket of modernist ideology. Sometimes – as with that uncompromising master of reinforced-concrete, Ernö Goldfinger – I have come genuinely to admire structures I once saw as brutal, insensitive intrusions. Even so, my changing mind can only go so far. I couldn't, for instance, really sympathise with the defence of that concrete brute in Portsmouth, the Tricorn Centre, nor do I care about any alterations proposed to Lloyds of London, that naïve, posturing intrusion into the City, by its longsuffering users. After all, the middle decades of the 20th century produced more than the usual proportion of cheap, arrogant mediocrity, and it took time for the Modern Movement to try and care about context.

A stimulus to changing my mind was sitting on English Heritage's Post-War Listing Steering Group which was set up to make a careful thematic survey of more recent buildings to see which ones merited protection. This sensible initiative was launched by the government in 1992 at the Commonwealth Institute in Kensington, That strikingly unusual structure which, with its large tent-like copper-clad hyperbolic-paraboloid roof, had been built in 1960-62 to the designs of Robert Matthew, Johnson-Marshall & Partners and had already been listed – at Grade II* – in 1988. It is therefore not a little ironic that the Institute's Trustees now propose to demolish the building and that this proposal is reinforced by a nefarious suggestion that it should be 'de-listed'.

Many regard the Commonwealth Institute with affection because they recall visiting exhibitions about exotic countries and cultures there as schoolchildren. As for me, my qualified admiration for the building is undermined by the knowledge that it only exists because of the scandalous demolition of the old Imperial Institute in South Kensington in 1957. A colourful and flamboyant exercise in the eclectic style Goodhart-Rendel called *bric-à-brac*, it had been designed by T.E. Colcutt (architect of the Wigmore Hall and the Palace Theatre) and built in 1887-93. In the post-war, post-Colonial climate, however, the Institute had become a dowdy embarrassment and its magnificence was swept away – apart from the rather Spanish campanile – in favour of the dreary modernist buildings of Imperial College. This was one of the catalysts for the founding of the Victorian Society in 1958.

Well, the Imperial Institute has long gone, so it is no use me blaming the Commonwealth Institute for its disappearance. After all, its very different design was intended to express the nature of the independent nations of the diverse new British Commonwealth rather than British imperialist grandeur. And we should look after what we now have, but the Trustees argue that the building impedes its educational work. There are certainly things wrong with it. Not only was it experimental but it was built on the cheap and the roof has long caused problems. In 2000, the government, no longer wishing to subsidise this inadvertent legacy of Empire, gave the Institute a farewell present of £8.5 million, half of this being intended for repairs. But while some repair work was done, two years later the building was abandoned. Last year a listed building application for demolition was rejected by the Department of Culture, Media & Sport.

If the Commonwealth Institute is a problem, what should happen is clear: the merits and failings of the building should be aired at public inquiry, but before permission to demolish a listed building is granted it must also be put on the open market. But, of course, the Trustees would do better if they put a cleared site in Kensington High Street up for sale rather than one occupied by a problematic 1960s structure and, scandalously, the government is now trying to make this possible. A letter signed by Tessa Jowell, Secretary of State for, of all things, Culture (plus Media and, all too obviously, Sport) and Margaret Beckett, Foreign Secretary, to the Secretary of State for Communities and Local Government proposes a special Bill to de-list the Commonwealth Institute as 'the risks to the Trustees could be substantially reduced if the building were de-listed'. The government is arguing that the Commonwealth Institute is a special case because it is a charity with international responsibilities, but if charitable status is allowed to overrule our historic building legislation, then it is not just a 1960s building which is threatened, for no listed almshouse by, say, Wren would be safe. Such is the current British government's attitude to architectural heritage.

Fortunately, I have *not* had to change my mind about another 1960s building in Kensington: one which is not (now) in any danger. I always quite liked the building for the Royal College of Art on Kensington Gore as its tall dark mass balanced Norman Shaw's block of red-brick 'Queen Anne' flats on the opposite side of the Albert Hall. It was a modern building with good manners, therefore. And now I admire it as a powerful rectilinear composition of dark concrete and purple brick, with an embattled skyline created by the rooftop studios. Ian Nairn, in that inspiring book, *Nairn's London* – which had much to do with forming my architectural consciousness back in 1966 – wrote that 'It is the opposite of a firework; it smoulders through to your consciousness with quiet intensity' and he contrasted it with 'the glacial complacent emptiness' of the new Imperial College buildings nearby.

The RCA building is the work of H.T. Cadbury-Brown. Born in 1913, 'Jim' Cadbury-Brown, like the late Sir Denys Lasdun, belonged to the generation of modernists who began to build just before the Second World War. It was a generation for whom, after the war, the battles had already been won and, often in reaction against the 'white' architecture of the 1920s, was able to be less constrained and more free in its approach to architectural problems. In 1959 – when he was working on the RCA design – Cadbury-Brown gave his presidential address to the Architectural Association on 'Ideas of Disorder' and called for 'individual variation and self-expression to balance the frightening regularity of life'. He had worked for Goldfinger in the 1930s, but the disciplines he had learned were, surprisingly, tempered by the influence of dance, 'placing rhythm at the core of architecture'.

Happily, this elegant and sophisticated architect is still with us and his interesting and undervalued work is being celebrated in an exhibition at the Royal Academy of Arts. It is accompanied by a catalogue with essays by three perceptive historians of modern British architecture, James Dunnett, Alan Powers and Elain Harwood, who explore, amongst other things, Cadbury-Brown's half-way position between Modern and imitative contextual. It is also interesting to learn that one stimulus towards architecture was seeing a house by C.F.A. Voysey and that he once called for 'enrichment' in architecture, as found in 'the scale, the vigour, the self-confidence' of Victorian architecture. Perhaps that is one reason why the RCA block is so powerful and so appropriate in its essentially Victorian surroundings.

However, although Cadbury-Brown was able to express the still fresh ideal of the Modern, as Dunnett puts it, in a 19th century context, he failed a decade later with proposals to extend the RCA to the west. For this involved the demolition of houses in Queen's Gate, including one by Norman Shaw, and attitudes were changing; the listing of the houses, together with the opposition of the Victorian Society, defeated the expansion scheme. Listing could therefore be seen as the enemy of progressive architecture, but thirty years on the same legislation came to Cadbury-Brown's aid, for the listing (at only Grade II) of his building in 2001 helped prevent an inappropriate and insensitive expansion scheme by Sir Nicholas Grimshaw to build in the space between the college and the Albert Hall. This was surely right. The listing of buildings of architectural merit should pander neither to the prejudices against the modern (to which I once adhered) nor to the selfish imperatives of institutions or government.

November 2006

[The Commonwealth Institute survives and is now being converted for use by the Design Museum. Jim Cadbury-Brown died in 2009 and I stepped down as chairman of the Twentieth Century Society in 2007.]

Robert Byron

Robert Byron, who was born a century ago this month, died in February 1941 when the ship taking him to Persia to be a war correspondent was torpedoed in the North Atlantic. Had he survived, it is highly unlikely that he would be around today to celebrate his one hundredth birthday, but he probably would have become better known along with those other remarkable writers of his brilliant generation – John Summerson, James Lees-Milne and John Betjeman – who did so much to encourage interest in British architecture after the war. As it was, his achievement was largely forgotten and he was for long best known as a travel writer because of his remarkable book, *The Road to Oxiana*, describing his journey to Persia and Afghanistan in 1933-34. Only now, since the publication in 2003 by John Murray of James Knox's splendid biography, can the productive richness of Robert Byron's short life be fully appreciated.

There are at least two good reasons for remembering Byron today – other than for his frequent walk-on parts in the well-documented, incestuous saga of the Evelyn Waugh circle. One is the power and vitality of his writing in conveying the character of great architecture – whether the monasteries of Athos, the ancient brick burial towers of Persia or the modern buildings of Edwin Lutyens. It was, indeed, the special number of the *Architectural Review* devoted to New Delhi – published in January 1931 and entirely written and illustrated by Byron – which really inspired me to visit India and see the Viceroy's House for myself. He recognised that, far away from home, something extraordinary had been achieved – and so uncharacteristic of official architecture in its imaginative excellence: 'Here is something not merely worthy, but whose like has never been. With a shiver of impatience [the traveller] shakes off contemporary standards, and makes ready to evoke those of Greece, the Renascence, and the Moguls.' Lutyens – who Byron considered 'the genius of our age' – had 'accomplished a fusion between East and West, and created a novel work of art'. Unfortunately, 'The majority are deaf to all but the 'rights of man' – whether to give or to withhold them. They forget that one of those rights is beauty. This at least the English have given. And for this at least the English will be remembered.' In that, he may have been more percipient than he could have realised at the time.

Byron's view of Lutyens as a 'humanist' was strongly coloured by Geoffrey Scott's defence of the Classical tradition, and of Italian Baroque, in his book *The Architecture of Humanism*. But it is important also to appreciate that Byron saw Lutyens's interpretation of the Classical language as conspicuously *modern*. Viceroy's House is not a composition of flat walls ornamented with traditional detail – the simplistic Georgian manner which so many of our New Classicists today fail to get beyond – but a dynamic composition of massive horizontal layers, each given a slope, or 'batter'. The whole building is composed on what Byron called 'a faintly pyramidal principle' which creates a 'feeling of movement in mass'. In this extraordinary building, he thought, 'we behold this dynamic quality, while enfleshed with sufficient severity and on a sufficient scale to make it effective, combined with a scenic employ of colour, a profound knowledge of shadow-play, and the most sensitive delicacy of moulding, pattern and ornament... The Viceroy's House at New Delhi is the first real justification of a new architecture which has already produced much that is worthy, but, till now, nothing of the greatest.'

This 'new architecture', of course, was very different from the planar, Continental modernism which was already making strong inroads in Britain. Byron was not a crude 'traditional-ist' but he questioned the claims of this new movement. In his 1932 book on *The Appreciation of Architecture*, he illustrated an ancient brick wall at Merv, now in Turkmenistan, which, 'might almost be mistaken, at a casual glance, for a modern smelting-works instead of a mediaeval fortification. Not that this need imply any particular merit. But it may prove to those whose admiration for industrial forms amounts to mania that the architectural excellence in such forms (when it exists) is not so exclusively the gift of machinery as they imagine.' A few years later he pointed out in the *New Statesman* the real nature of so-called Functionalism about which, even today, so many architects and critics remain in denial: that it was not an inevi-table, absolute response to social conditions and structure – 'Of course the modern architect has a style... A more pronounced style... never decorated the earth.'

The second good reason for remembering Byron is for his skill and effectiveness as a polemicist. He was a master of passionate invective – something we need more of today when most architectural critics do little more than paraphrase press-releases and so encourage the pernicious cult of the architectural superstar. The reputation of Sir Herbert Baker has never really recovered from Byron's repeated assaults, not least his dismissal of the pierced stone screens on the Delhi Council Chamber as 'though fixed by clothes pegs on a line. Here are not only pants, but petticoats, camisoles, night-dresses, and even tea-gowns.' Byron's masterpiece in this vein was his pamphlet – which began as an article in the *Architectural Review* – on *How we celebrate the Coronation* (of George VI). It was a catalogue of destruction, cynicism and barbarism, and he caused outrage by naming the villains: 'The Church; the Civil Service; the Judicial Committee of the Privy Council; the hereditary landlords; the political parties; the London County Council; the local councils; the great business firms; the motorists; the heads of the national Museum – all are indicted, some with more cause than others, because of some more decency might have been hoped for, but all on the same charge. These, in the year of the coronation, 1937, are responsible for the ruin of London, for our humiliation before visitors, and for destroying without hope of recompense many of the nations most treasured possessions; and they will answer for it by the censure of posterity.'

The context for this polemic was the foundation of the Georgian Group that year in response to the loss of many of the finest 18th century buildings in London over the previous two decades: Devonshire House, Chesterfield House, Waterloo Bridge, the Adelphi, and the Foundling Hospital, as well as the threat to others, not least Carlton House Terrace. The actual founder of the Group was the writer Douglas Goldring, but it was Byron, as deputy-chairman, who really got the society going – and noticed. There was much to fight for: a Wren church (All Hallows', Lombard Street – in the event demolished two years before the Luftwaffe began to assist the redevelopment of London); Norfolk House in St James's Square (demolished by Rudolph Palumbo, who secretly bought it from the Duke of Norfolk: 'When noblesse ceases to oblige, it is not surprising that richesse should do likewise'); one side of Bedford Square ('it seems at times as if the English were really as mad, as gross and as intolerant of art and foreign culture as their foreign detractors pretend').

The threat to Brunswick Square (since gone) provoked a B.B.C. radio discussion in which Byron gave a memorably eloquent and poignant defence of Georgian architecture; it commemorates, he said, 'a great period, when English taste and English political ideas had suddenly become the admiration of Europe. And it corresponds, almost to the point of dinginess, with our national character. Its reserve and dislike of outward show, its reliance on the virtue and dignity of proportion only, and in its rare bursts of exquisite detail, all express as no other style has ever done that indifference to self-advertisement, that quiet assumption of our own worth, and that sudden vein of lyric affection, which have given us our part in civilisation.' In this broadcast, Byron was opposed by an estate agent and a Member of Parliament, both arguing for the inevitability of change, and supported by John Summerson, to whom he afterwards wrote of the M.P., 'I can only wonder he isn't in prison.'

Byron led the new society for only two years before he resigned. Had he survived, he would surely have resisted Albert Richardson's attempts to make it a vehicle for promoting modern Georgian architecture – a mischievous heresy the Georgian Group is guilty of today when it awards a prize for a modern Classical country house. Byron understood that Georgian architecture matters not as an agreeable style but as historical and cultural artefacts. He also understood that conservation by itself is not enough and that politics had to be engaged with. Byron loathed dictatorships even more than he detested establishment vandals, and he spent much of his last, unhappy years trying to warn his appeasing countrymen about the sheer wickedness of Nazi Germany and the inevitability of the war to come. One can only speculate, were Byron alive today, on what he might say about our present government's complacent indifference to the threat of climate change or its complicity in the thuggery and cultural vandalism in Iraq. What is certain is that we need eloquent, passionate, fearless voices of protest, like that of Robert Byron, as much as ever.

February 2005

Cartoon History

'All the architecture in this book is completely imaginary, and no reference is intended to any actual building living or dead.' So Osbert Lancaster noted at the beginning of *Pillar to Post*, which first appeared exactly seventy years ago but has scarcely dated. This 'picture-book', augmented with further caricatures of domestic interiors published as *Home Sweet Homes* and with a few American examples, was later re-issued as *A Cartoon History of Architecture* and is one of the most influential books on architecture ever published – and certainly the funniest, because of its illustrations.

Osbert Lancaster – cartoonist, designer, architectural and travel writer, stage-designer, wit and dandy – was born in 1908. His centenary is being celebrated with an exhibition at the Wallace Collection, curated by James Knox, accompanied by a splendid book, *Cartoons & Coronets: The Genius of Osbert Lancaster*, which includes a wealth of his drawings, cartoons and stage-designs as well as an admirable biographical introduction by Knox. The story of Lancaster's life has been told before, not least in his own, captivating, two volumes of autobiography. Knox, however, not only presents new material but emphasises that although Lancaster belonged to a seemingly blessed and gilded generation – friends included John Betjeman and John Piper (with whom he collaborated on the Pleasure Gardens in Battersea Park for the Festival of Britain in 1951) – he was prodigiously productive and had a unique talent – no, genius – as a draughtsman and caricaturist.

But this column is about Architecture, and to concentrate on that is not to present a partial view as buildings fascinated and entertained Lancaster from an early age. After he came down from Oxford and had left art school, this was an interest encouraged by working on the *Architectural Review* in its prime in the 1930s, when Betjeman was assistant editor. And it was out of the enthusiasms of that time, expressed in the witty and elegant pages of the 'Archie Rev', that Lancaster's first books emerged.

The brilliance of *Pillar to Post* was that not only were types, and styles, of buildings caricatured and made familiar, but also that they were placed in context. Lancaster's architecture is never ideal but used and lived in – made human, as architecture should be. Not only is the essence of a style conveyed, but the building is depicted with contemporary people in appropriate attitudes, drawn with his deceptively simple and naïve line. So a monk with a mop and bucket stands under a Decorated Gothic arch, and a sun-worshipping, pipe-smoking progressive intellectual lies on the roof terrace of his 'Twentieth-Century Functional' house. Lancaster's figures – as in the celebrated 'Pocket Cartoons' that he contributed to the *Daily Express* for forty years – are both funny and acutely observed. Lancaster, a natty dresser himself, had a sharp eye for clothes, loved uniforms and caught the precise fashion of the time.

In this book and its sequels, Lancaster not only illustrated architectural styles but he dissected and labelled them – often defining sub-styles that nobody had cared to notice before. In fact, he contributed more to the vocabulary of architectural history than any writer before or since – more, even, that Thomas Rickman, who taught us to distinguish Mediaeval Gothic work as 'E.E.', 'Dec.' or 'Perp.' It was Lancaster who christened that fancy red-brick, gabled manner derived from Norman Shaw as 'Pont Street Dutch'. But it is with 20th architecture that he came into his own. Lancaster identified 'Bankers Georgian', 'Curzon Street Baroque' and 'Pseudish' – a particularly clever name for that white-walled sub-Spanish Colonial manner with bright green or turquoise pantiles on the roof. And it was Lancaster who classified the sub-divisions of what is still the essential English domestic manner, that is, half-timbered Neo-Tudor: 'Wimbledon Transitional', 'Stockbrokers Tudor', 'Aldwych Farcical' and 'By-Pass Variegated'. Such terms are now indispensable.

The satire is in both drawings and in his accompanying irreverent texts. And sometimes the message was a powerful one. Famously, he drew two almost identical stripped-Classical colonnades, one 'Third Empire', the other 'Marxist Non-Aryan', making the point that the totalitarian states of Hitler and Stalin had much in common. He played the same trick with his similar drawings of 'Park Lane Residential' – the blocks of American-style flats that proliferated in the 1930s – and the simpler 'L.C.C. Residential' – working-class housing blocks – noting that 'they too look like pickle-factories, but quite good pickle-factories; not, it must be admitted, owing to any particular skill on the part of the architect, but solely to the fact that there has not been sufficient money to waste on Portland stone facings and other decorative trimmings'.

Lancaster also satirised town-planning, or its absence – being unsure which had the more destructive effect on towns and cities. *Progress at Pelvis Bay*, published in 1936, was his first book and depicted in words and pictures the rise and subsequent architectural degradation of a seaside resort. 'By means of the numerous carefully chosen illustrations the reader is enabled to follow the various architectural changes that have taken place and to realise with what diligence the authorities have striven to avail themselves of all that was Best in contemporary Art.' In reviewing what pretended to be a municipal brochure, Betjeman wrote that 'My only fear for this wonderful book is that some town councils may get hold of it and take it literally.' The idea was developed in *Drayneflete Revealed*, a would-be town history and guide, published in 1949. In addition to the caricatures of local antiquities, monuments and paintings in Drayneflete Castle, the seat of the Earls of Littlehampton (whose current Countess, Maudie Littlehampton, would become the star of the Pocket Cartoons), the genius of this book is the series of drawings, made from the same vantage point, depicting the changes to the imaginary town over time, all observed in minute and telling detail.

The last drawing, of 'The Drayneflete of Tomorrow' shows a 'Cultural Monument scheduled under National Trust' surviving on roundabout in a rebuilt modernist town. It was an all too accurate evocation of what contemporary planners were proposing for Coventry, Plymouth, Bradford and elsewhere. By this time – as with many of his generation – Lancaster's optimism about Modern Architecture was being dissipated while, as he confessed, 'I no longer find nineteenth-century Gothic so invariably funny as I once did' and followed Betjeman in admiring the work of such as Butterfield and Pearson. Increasingly, he became a force on the side of preservation, campaigning against 'speculative builders, borough surveyors, government departments and other notorious predators'.

One memorable battle was in 1972 over the proposed new Home Office building overlooking St James's Park. After its knighted architect had claimed it would be largely hidden by trees, Lancaster wrote to *The Times* wondering whether 'any architect in recorded history from Vitruvious [*sic*] to Colonel

Seifert [*sic*], engaged on an important public building on a prominent site, has ever before put forward the claim (one hopes justified) made by Sir Basil Spence... that his masterpiece will, when finished, be to all intents and purposes, invisible?'

Perhaps his happiest contribution to the cause of preservation, because both visual and funny, were the drawings exhibited at the 'Destruction of the Country House' exhibition at the Victoria & Albert Museum in 1974. Lancaster drew 'Great Houses of Fiction Revisited' to illustrate the way such buildings were now treated. P.G. Wodehouse's Blandings Castle was now used by the Ministry of Agriculture; Disraeli's Brentham in *Lothair* was crumbling behind barbed wire in the care of the War Office, while Jane Austen's Mansfield Park was now a girls' school. And here Lancaster had another swipe at his famous near-contemporary, for 'After the war a new dormitory wing, the work of Sir Basil Spence, was added... While the proportions of Wyatt's façade were carefully respected, no attempt was made to achieve any unconvincing pastiche and the result was immediately recognised as a forthright and welcome expression of twentieth-century ideals in a contemporary idiom.' Just what such typical clichéd drivel meant in practice was, again, mercilessly lampooned by this inspired architectural cartoonist.

October 2008

Betjemanic

A disconcerting aspect of getting older is encountering the centenaries of people one once knew. This year it is the turn of Sir John Betjeman, and his hundredth birthday is to be marked – amongst other events – by an exhibition at Sir John Soane's Museum in September. Given the location, this exhibition will explore Betjeman's relationship with architecture – a difficult thing to do in terms of objects and visual material as he was neither an architect nor an architectural historian. And yet his influence was immense, and this can probably best be illustrated through the many historic buildings he tried to save and through the once-despised examples of Victorian architecture whose appreciation he is often credited single-handedly with encouraging.

But how did he achieve such influence, so that – to his dismay – his name became inextricably associated with the most bathetic examples of 19th century design as well as the most glorious? This is, or was, 'a mystery of our times' as his friend Sir John Summerson once wrote (oh dear: I knew him too, and *his* centenary was two years ago). 'Betjeman has not written even one book about Victorian architecture nor ever to my knowledge promoted any serious general claims for its qualities. Yet his name has become an illuminant and a sanction; through him, kindliness toward Victorian architecture is permitted to thousands whose habits of mind would drive them in a quite other direction.'

At the risk of making this column even more tiresomely solipsistic, I can only try and answer that question through my own experience, for when I was a teenage schoolboy in South London, beginning to enjoy architecture, Betjeman was the person I most wanted to meet. Two things made him my hero. One was buying a copy of *First and Last Loves*, which introduced me to the recondite charm of Victorian churches and London's railway termini as well as to a pessimistic view of progress, although I found the long essay on 'Antiquarian Prejudice' confusing (and I still find it confused). And then there was the television play he wrote (with Stewart Farrar) which was broadcast on BBC 2 in 1965. Called 'Pity About The Abbey', it concerned a road scheme and redevelopment in Westminster which required the demolition of the great Mediaeval Royal church – not so very far fetched when you think of some of the more arrogant projects of the 1960s. This programme made a great impression on me and introduced me to the menaces who are with us yet: the blinkered road planner; the amoral, know-all civil servant and the venal, cynical architect sheltering behind the excuse of modernity and necessity.

Part of the fascination of Betjeman is the several methods he used to change taste. Kenneth Clark, in 1950, wrote of 'a generation influenced by the poetical insight of Mr Betjeman' towards the Victorian Gothic Revival, but this he achieved as much through his journalism as through his poetry. He wrote extensively about architecture for the *Daily Telegraph* throughout the 1950s and 1960s, as well as making many radio broadcasts – and it shouldn't be forgotten that he began the 'Nooks and Corners of the New Barbarism' column (to give it its full original title) in *Private Eye* in 1973. And then there was his success in using television to educate a wide public about unfashionable and often unloved buildings. Perhaps his best film – certainly the best known – is *Metro-land*, broadcast in 1973. In this he looked sympathetically at the Neo-Tudor suburbs of the interwar decades he had once despised as well as shuffling around grander houses by Voysey and Norman Shaw.

In broad terms, however, Betjeman's importance for British architecture is surely as a preservationist, as a resourceful and imaginative campaigner for buildings conventional taste dismissed. He was not always that. His early writings in the *Architectural Review*, imaginative and sometimes whimsical as they were, reflect his fashionable commitment to the Modern Movement with which he later became so disillusioned – indeed, he was an unlikely member of the radical MARS Group along with the likes of Berthold Lubetkin and Serge Chermayeff. But by the end of the 1930s he had come to admire and had befriended the aged church architect Ninian Comper, whose knighthood he was later instrumental in securing (which caused an entertaining *furore* at the RIBA as Comper advertised himself as 'Architect (unregistered)'). And in 1937 he became a founder member of the Georgian Group, although at that time Georgian architecture was widely considered to exhibit the same virtues as the modern.

Much of Betjeman's enthusiasm for more eccentric architecture, for the recondite and the unloved, as well as for English topography was directed into the series of *Shell Guides* which he edited. It was doubtless his proprietorial interest in that county series, which began in 1933, which made him resent Nikolaus Pevsner's soon indispensable *Buildings of England* series, which was launched in 1951. Betjeman's long and unpleasant feud with the 'Herr-Professor-Doctor', tinged as it was with crude xenophobia and jealousy, is something from which he emerges with little credit, although it has been used by some to justify their dislike of the modernism with which Pevsner is (so often wrongly) associated. No wonder that Pevsner had his revenge when, in his outer London volume describing St Cyprian's, Clarence Gate, he wrote that 'There is no reason for the excesses of praise lavished on Comper's church furnishings by those who confound aesthetic with religious emotions.'

Betjeman and Pevsner were, nevertheless, both instrumental in founding the Victorian Society in 1958 and were usually on the same side in the 'Vic Soc's' early battles: for the Imperial Institute in South Kensington (of which only Colcutt's campanile forlornly survives), for the Euston 'Arch' (murdered by that cynical philistine Whig, the Prime Minister Harold Macmillan), for the Coal Exchange in the City of London (whose demolition could so easily have been avoided), for Bedford Park (which was crowned with success); for Gilbert Scott's screen in Hereford Cathedral (now, at long last, on display in the V&A). But many of Betjeman's campaigns were his own, particularly those for churches he loved. One whose loss is unforgivable is St Agnes, Kennington, the influential masterpiece of George Gilbert Scott junior (father of the great Sir Giles whose work Betjeman came to admire after sniping at the 'restrained jazz' of Battersea Power Station). It had lost its roof in 1941 but could easily have been restored – and War Damage money was available. Instead, despite the protests of Betjeman and others, that most beautiful and haunting building was demolished by the Diocese of Southwark. When Betjeman published his *Collins Guide to English Parish Churches* in 1958, he dedicated it to the memory of St Agnes as well as Christ Church, Salford: 'fine churches of unfashionable date demolished since the war'.

There were many, many other buildings for which Betjeman fought, both publicly and privately, and most are mentioned in the third volume of Bevis Hillier's biographical trilogy.

And what is impressive is how he would go out of his way to help worthwhile campaigns for minor and sometimes obscure buildings – Hillier describes how he became involved in a fruitless campaign to save Lewisham Town Hall after he was written to by a thirteen-year-old schoolboy. Betjeman may have become a public institution, and often sometimes ridiculed as such, but he also performed a public service – selflessly. He was, however, sometimes diffident, even paranoid, about his status, as when he wrote to Summerson (whose detached, contrary coolness towards preservation dismayed his admirers) about British Railways' proposal to demolish both King's Cross and St Pancras Stations in 1966: 'It is no good my writing about Sir Gilbert and St Pancras in particular, because I have been so denigrated by Karl Marx [his name for the writer J.M. Richards], and the Professor-Doktor as a lightweight wax fruit merchant, I will not carry the necessary guns.'

But Betjeman did have the firepower, and he knew just how to aim it – as I discovered when, in 1974, he asked me to help his campaign to save Holy Trinity, Sloane Street. J.D. Sedding's great Arts and Crafts cathedral, just up the road from the scene of Betjeman's poem, 'The Arrest of Oscar Wilde at the Cadogan Hotel', was seriously threatened with demolition. The Rector and the Patron, Lord Cadogan, claimed the building was too costly to be maintained and proposed a new worship centre as part of a block of flats on the site – a development which would, of course, have benefited the Cadogan Estate. As well as badgering everyone concerned, Betjeman asked me to make some drawings of Holy Trinity to be sold by the parish to benefit its restoration, knowing full well that his offer would be declined. We then published them as *A Plea for Holy Trinity Sloane Street*, with Betjeman writing how 'After a long period of thought and prayer the Rector and congregation have decided that there is no way of retaining the present building as a centre of worship except by pulling it down...' The resulting publicity was very satisfactory.

I believe that today, thirty years on, Holy Trinity Sloane Street is still standing – cleaned, repaired and flourishing – only because of Sir John Betjeman. Can there be any greater contribution to British architecture than ensuring that good buildings survive to be enjoyed by future generations?

January 2006

Hawksmoor Redivivus

Architects' reputations are fragile things. Gilbert Scott, for instance, knighted for his great works, became a figure of fun within fifty years of his death when it was thought smart to laugh at the Albert Memorial. And what will the future make of those much lauded architectural peers of our own time, the egregious Lords Foster of Thames Bank and Rogers of Riverside? We can only speculate. But few reputations have oscillated so dramatically as that of Nicholas Hawksmoor. Beginning as the 'clerk' and trusted assistant to the great Sir Christopher Wren, his works were condemned for their 'fancy' by the pedantic Palladians and by the 19th century, when some of his buildings were maltreated, he was almost forgotten. Hawksmoor is missing from J.B. Philip's sculptured frieze of architects on the Albert Memorial while Wren and Vanbrugh are present. Today, however, he is rightly revered, and considered by some to have been a far greater and more original talent than his master while his surviving London churches are being lovingly restored.

The rehabilitation of Hawksmoor perhaps begins with the publication of a monograph in 1924 by H.S. Goodhart-Rendel, who complained that Fame had been 'especially unkind' to the architect; 'If a building of Hawksmoor's please, Fame credits it to Wren: if it fail to please, then Hawksmoor can have it.' Yet the most difficult and dangerous years for his creations came after the Second World War. Bombs gutted St John's Horsleydown behind London Bridge Station in 1941, and then its shell – along with the extraordinary steeple surmounted by an Ionic column – was demolished rather than restored. The magnificent gutted shell of St George-in-the-East, with its powerful tower, topped by Hawksmoor's version of the Octagon at Ely, would have gone the same way if the parish had not fought back against demolition proposals. In the event, a clever modern church by Arthur Bailey was built within the ruins in 1960-64.

At least those churches had been badly damaged by enemy action. Christ Church Spitalfields, of which Rendel had written that 'it remains doubtful whether of its date and kind there is any finer church in Europe', had survived the war unscathed, yet the Diocese of London could seriously propose its demolition in 1960. This great basilica just east of the City of London, fronted by the most weird and original of all Hawksmoor's steeples, haunted by the Gothic as well as by Antiquity, had long been neglected. In 1957, services were moved elsewhere and it might well have gone the way of St Luke's Old Street, which had its roof taken off in 1959. But the threat was averted. One consequence was the founding of the Hawksmoor Committee in 1961 by Elisabeth Young (now Lady Kennet) and others, to find money to secure the futures of both Christ Church and St Anne's Limehouse. The catalogue of the exhibition of drawings mounted the following year noted that 'The name of Hawksmoor, long neglected if never quite forgotten, now commands the devotion of a large number of architects, scholars and enthusiasts from many fields.'

Scholars there certainly were, the principal one being Kerry Downes, whose first monograph on Hawksmoor was published in 1959. Today, there are younger scholars like Anthony Geraghty and Gordon Higgott busily conducting research into what we can now call the period of the English Baroque, effectively demonstrating that Hawksmoor was almost certainly responsible for much of Wren's late work, like the domes at Greenwich, the west towers of St Paul's, and the ambitious designs for rebuilding Whitehall Palace. And there were certainly many enthusiasts prepared to explore what were then slightly intimidating and neglected parts of London to find and to wonder at those great East End fanes raised under the 1711 Act for building Fifty New Churches. Such explorations inspired Peter Ackroyd to publish his novel, *Hawksmoor*, in 1985. Although the author was accused by John Summerson of 'polluting the wells of truth' by presenting the eponymous architect as a most sinister figure, this brilliantly evocative book nevertheless encouraged the growing cult of Hawksmoor and focussed welcome attention on the disgraceful condition of several of his buildings.

That can no longer be said. St Alfege, Greenwich, damaged in the war, had been reasonably accurately restored by Sir Albert Richardson. Today, St Anne's Limehouse, that colossal prodigy in modern Docklands, is at last being properly looked after. But the restoration which best symbolises the rise of Hawksmoor's reputation is that of his masterpiece in Spitalfields. The Friends of Christ Church Spitalfields were formed in 1976 and organised concerts in the stripped out, sublime interior while the architect Red Mason investigated its original appearance. In the event, the planned restoration took decades and was completed only four years ago. The long-lost galleries have been replaced and the original form of the vast Portland stone pile restored. Perhaps the result is a little bright and new, but at least it has been done and finished: half a century ago, this awe-inspiring building, surrounded by dereliction, seemed doomed.

And then there is St George's Bloomsbury, the church with its Roman Corinthian temple portico which, although sited in a rather more familiar part of London, had also been long neglected. In my second column in *Apollo* (June 2004), I described the problems involved in the restoration of St George's being promoted by the World Monuments Fund, and argued that 'Any work by Hawksmoor surely deserves authentic reinstatement as far as is possible. In Bloomsbury, this surely means not only removing the later stained glass and recreating the stone-colour of the original interior but moving the altar back to where it belongs – and putting those gambolling lions and unicorns back on the steeple.' I am very happy now to be able to report that all this has been achieved.

First, the lions and unicorns 'fighting for the crown' (as the old nursery rhyme has it): these animated creatures had often been satirised, not least by Hogarth, and were finally removed in 1871. Now they are back. Wonderfully lively stone creatures, modelled by the sculptor Tim Crawley, have been incorporated at the base of the steeped spire. Perhaps they are just a little too big; no matter, a great London landmark and legend has been restored. More problematic was the treatment of the interior. St George's has the most complicated and perplexing of all Hawksmoor's church plans. Correct east-west orientation meant much to the architect, but the confined site in Bloomsbury was wider than it was long. Hawksmoor solved the problem by creating an axial, centralised galleried space under a square lantern, focussed on the communion table in an eastern apse, with the remainder of the site occupied by an additional north aisle to serve as a vestry. Unfortunately, in 1781, the pressure of population led to internal reorientation through 90°. Hawksmoor's magnificent mahogany reredos was moved to the additional north aisle and more galleries were added while some were removed.

Until a few years ago, the interior of St George's Bloomsbury was impressive yet puzzling. The elliptical arches on columns which Hawksmoor used to divide nave from aisles read as a series of transverse arches across the new axis from entrance portico to the altar. This looked well, yet was not at all what Hawksmoor intended. So, in the course of the restoration, after much debate, the reredos was moved back into the eastern apse. However, the resulting interior space remained incoherent. What was needed was the recreation of the original north gallery, balancing the surviving (altered) south gallery to enclose a centralised symmetrical space focussed on the reredos and dividing the worshipping area from that additional north aisle. This has now been done. As with other aspects of the interior, the detailed research conducted by Kevin Rogers established the original design of the gallery and the associated staircases and supporting timber piers (with an internal cast-iron core – a very early use of structural iron).

A magnificent restoration has now been triumphantly completed. For the first time in over two centuries, the cleverness and architectural coherence of Hawksmoor's interior can be appreciated. All that remains to do to redeem the reputation of this most imaginative and fascinating of architects is to put the galleries back in St Mary Woolnoth. Surely there is enough money sloshing around in the City of London to achieve that?

July-August 2008

[The restoration of St George's was begun by Colin Kerr of Molyneux Kerr architects in 2002 and completed by Inskip & Jenkins.]

Shakespeare in Stone

'Sir John Vanbrugh,' wrote Avray Tipping and Christopher Hussey in the introduction to their magnificent *English Homes* volume on the man and his school, 'provides the rare and stimulating spectacle of an original mind brought freshly to bear on architecture when already fully developed.' The lives of most great architects are not particularly interesting – they tend to be self-obsessed and workaholic, after all – but Vanbrugh's was extraordinary and endlessly fascinating. Soldier and herald, sometime prisoner in the Bastille as a possible spy, poet, playwright, wit and member of the celebrated Kit-Cat Club, he only turned to architecture later in life but with astonishing success – relying, of course, on the essential assistance of his long-suffering collaborator, Nicholas Hawksmoor. And although the subject of many books – indeed, his work has inspired a very distinguished and still growing literature – he still has the capacity to surprise. Surely the most exciting event in architectural history in recent years was the filling of a *lacuna* in Vanbrugh's biography in 1683-85 when Robert Williams discovered that he had been a 'writer' with the East India Company and had actually travelled out to India, to Surat.

This astonishing fact leaves architectural historians to speculate whether Mughal or Hindu influence might help account for the exotic strangeness of some of Vanbrugh's building in addition to debating whether he was an 'English Baroque' architect or really a Palladian like so many other Englishmen. The latter argument is, however, a trivial matter of semantics and taxonomy. Of course both Vanbrugh and Hawksmoor stole from Palladio as they did from other sources. What matters is that they handled those borrowings with a boldness and originality of which the English Palladians were incapable. Vanbrugh did not simply import villas from the Veneto; he created grand houses which responded to English traditions and conditions and which looked well in the (former) misty English climate, in which what matters is not sharp shadow but great masses and recessions. Vanbrugh's houses are telling, above all, in silhouette, and in this respect it is important that not only was he inspired by the Mediaeval but that he lived in a castle – that amazing tall brick house in Blackheath which does not have a single pointed window but yet has a castle-like air.

No wonder that his creations have long been and remain fascinating and compelling. Taste changes and silly pedants like Lord Burlington may have sniped at him, but Robert Adam was happy to acknowledge that 'Sir John Vanbrugh's genius was of the first class; and in point of movement, novelty and ingenuity, his works have not been exceeded by anything in modern times.' Even in the Victorian age he had his admirers: there are elements of Vanbrugh in Cockerell's work and, surprisingly perhaps, in Philip Webb's, and there he is on J.B. Philip's frieze of architects on the Albert Memorial along with Chambers and Wren (while Adam, Soane and poor Hawksmoor are absent). And since the beginning of the 20th century, Vanbrugh's status as the romantic dramatist of architecture has been unchallenged. His occasional influence on Lutyens is clear, while it can even be traced in the work of the New Brutalists – in parts of the Barbican, for instance – with their enthusiasm for the cyclopean and the Sublime.

Happily, Vanbrugh's works, like Hawksmoor's, are mostly accessible. Blenheim Palace and Castle Howard have long been open to the public – in the latter case long before the inaccurate use of Vanbrugh's first great creation as a backdrop for the *Brideshead Revisited* films further encouraged visitors. Grimsthorpe Castle, long secret, is now also open. And now the National Trust may at last acquire a Vanbrugh house in the shape of Seaton Delaval – and no better or more romantic pile could the Trust aspire to. No one surely forgets their first visit to the former home of the 'gay', cursed Delavals with its rusticated stonework and ruined hall, set in a bleak, stormy landscape near the North Sea coast somewhere to the north of Newcastle. Its survival is a miracle; fires gutted the west wing in 1752 and, more seriously, the whole of the castle-like central block in 1822. In her 1948 '*Vision of England*' guide to Northumberland, Ann Sitwell could write that 'The house is dead, doomed; only the tremendous outline remains of huge blocks of masonry superbly piled and placed... The workings of the coal seam are creeping nearer to its foundations and unless action is taken, time, weather and neglect may bring the house crashing down to its final ruin.'

But Seaton Delaval Hall still stands in all its lonely grandeur, although only the west wing is inhabited. Vanbrugh's (and Hawksmoor's) favourite bunches of massive rusticated Doric columns frame the entrance to the great hall, now a realised Piranesian fantasy of calcined stone and mutilated sculptures. Strangest of all Vanbrugh's creations, it is pure monument, pure romance, a Baroque castle, fantastic in shape: no wonder John Piper was drawn to paint it in 1941.

As Christopher Hussey wrote eighty years ago, 'We shall look in vain for any other buildings in England, of any period, that surpass, even equal, the rhythmic unity of Seaton considered as a symphony of masses. Beside it, St Paul's is comparatively lifeless, Hampton Court demure, and the Banqueting House, Whitehall, a scholarly pastiche.'

'Historians might write a hundred books on Vanbrugh,' writes Jeremy Musson in the latest, 'nothing really competes with the experience of looking at his buildings in context...' True enough, but for those of us who do not live in Blenheim Palace or near one of his buildings it is nice to have books of photographs of them on our shelves. Best of all is the sumptuously illustrated volume on *The Work of Sir John Vanbrugh and his School 1699-1736* with which I began, the only one in the *English Homes* series devoted to a single architect. But that book, published in 1928, is now rare and expensive, so it is a great boon to have Musson's new work on *The Country Houses of the John Vanbrugh*, the latest in Aurum Press's admirable *Country Life* archive series. This reproduces many of the images taken with large plate cameras by *Country Life* photographers almost a century ago, and it is interesting to compare how they look in each. In the Aurum book they are sharper, with more detail, but might seem rather grey when compared to the half-tone plates with their deep blacks and rich tones in the 1928 book. Why should this be?

It is also interesting to compare this engaging book with Vaughan Hart's *Sir John Vanbrugh: Storyteller in Stone* also published this year (by Yale University Press). This is a scholarly and fascinating study which investigates the meaning of the forms and symbols Vanbrugh used in his buildings, but visually it is disappointing – with many of the illustrations being little better than colour snaps characterised by what was once eschewed in any serious architectural book: converging verticals. New colour photographs, by Paul Barker, were also commissioned for Musson's book, but, fine as they are (taken with a proper camera with what used to be called a 'rising front'), I am not convinced they are really necessary. Vanbrugh's houses may be built of beautiful stone, but his architecture does not particularly lend itself to colour photography. It is the black and white image that brings out the powerful massiveness, the scale, the dramatic recession and projection, the boldness of the detail and the thickness of the walls in the incomparable, uniquely English buildings created by the fascinating man who was described by Sir John Soane as 'the Shakespeare of architects'.

January 2009

[Seaton Delaval was indeed bought by the National Trust later that year.]

The Destroyer

'All that is vile, cunning and rascally is included in the term Wyatt,' once wrote Augustus Pugin, whose bicentenary we celebrate this year. Next year marks the two hundredth anniversary of the dramatic death (in a coach accident) of his *bête noire*, the architect James Wyatt. On visiting Lichfield Cathedral, young Pugin was dismayed to find that 'the whole church was improved and beautified about thirty years ago by the late Mr Wyatt. Yes, this monster of architectural depravity – this pest of cathedral architecture – has been here; need I say more?'

Poor Wyatt has long had a bad press and an ambivalent reputation. To some extent this is owing to bad luck, as so many of his buildings have been destroyed – including two of the finest and most famous. The remarkable interior of the Pantheon in Oxford Street, that 'stately pleasure dome' which opened in 1772 and made the young architect's reputation (he was born in 1746), was gutted by fire within twenty years. And

Fonthill Abbey, that celebrated, astonishing Gothic folly built for William Beckford notoriously collapsed in 1825 soon after its owner sold it. Wyatt's own much admired London house and office in Foley Place has also disappeared, as have many of his country houses and, not least, the unfinished palace he designed for King George III at Kew.

Wyatt's unhappy treatment by posterity was partly his own fault, however. Through characteristic inertia, he never got around to producing the book of his own designs he had planned to rival that published by his jealous rival Robert Adam. And because he could never say no to any opportunity, he made the disastrous decision to accept the appointment of Surveyor General and Comptroller of the Office of Works in 1796, an office for which he was totally unfitted owing to his complete inability to run an office or manage his own or anybody else's finances. The result was that the Office of Works descended into chaos and corruption. After his death, the Prime Minister, Lord Liverpool, remarked of Wyatt that he was 'A man of the most considerable talents as an architect, he was certainly one of the worst public servants I recollect in any office...' Wyatt was buried in Westminster Abbey after a send off that was only rivalled amongst architects by the funeral of Sir Gilbert Scott, but he died bankrupt. As his estate had to pay money back to the government, his unfortunate widow was left destitute. Yet, having built up a considerable practice and reputation, having worked for the richest and grandest in the land and enjoyed the personal favour of the king, he ought to have left a fortune.

Now, at long last, justice has been done to this great and often unfairly maligned designer with the publication of a most splendid and handsome monograph by John Martin Robinson, who has long been interested in the whole Wyatt dynasty (yes, there's also Samuel, Charles, Matthew Cotes, Thomas Henry and Sir Matthew Digby as well as Jeffry Wyatt, who decided to call himself Wyatville when knighted for completing his uncle's work at Windsor Castle). It is an enthralling story, and James Wyatt emerges as a rather sympathetic, albeit a badly-behaved character. He certainly had charm, which he needed to cope with his many clients exasperated at his dilatory handling of a job and his disinclination to appear on site ('From the infamous Swine *nothing!*' complained Beckford; '...The heat and this eternal ridiculous tormenting by Bagasse [Wyatt] will make me go mad and throw up all the works.'). What is also clear is that Wyatt was a most accomplished and imaginative designer whose style, unlike that of his rival Adam or his (unlikely) friend Soane, continually developed.

Wyatt's early work was much indebted to Adam for interior decoration while his exterior treatments were more sober and grammatical, reflecting his admiration for the *Treatise on Civil Architecture* by Sir William Chambers. This combination may be studied at the Classical country house which Sir John Summerson thought his most important, Heaton Hall in Lancashire (whose current closure to the public by its long-standing owner, Manchester City Council, is a scandal). And then there are the buildings for the dead, the mausolea in landscaped settings which were almost the favourite building type of the British Neo-Classical architect. Wyatt designed several, the finest being that for Lord Darnley at Cobham in Kent (recently restored after severe vandalism) in which a domed interior is combined with a pyramid roof. What Dr Robinson also emphasises is Wyatt's fertile brilliance as designer for others: architectural ornaments for Mrs Coade, silverware for Matthew Boulton and furniture for Gillows; he was also adept in using iron. This is an aspect of his career which has hitherto been little documented but which reflects Wyatt's family links with the industrial culture of the Midlands during the Georgian Enlightenment.

A convincing case is made that Wyatt was the creator of 'the Regency Style'. Like many early 19th-century architects, he was certainly happy to work in several different styles

– not least Gothic. And here the problem with Wyatt arises. It certainly seems true that he took a more scholarly approach to Gothic detail than earlier architects while Fonthill was, in its way, revolutionary as it was amazing. But I cannot accept that, in his treatment of Mediaeval cathedrals, 'he was no more radical and interventionist in his approach than George Gilbert Scott and other Victorian restorers'. Nonsense: neither Scott (who was as respectful as he was scholarly) nor earlier architects like Hawksmoor or James Essex would conceivably have demolished the detached bell-tower or the chantry chapels at Salisbury or attempted to sweep away the Galilee Chapel at Durham (in both cases for the ineffable Bishop Shute Barrington). In applying Picturesque principles to ancient buildings and opening up vistas Wyatt was indeed reflecting the attitudes of his time – and then the times changed, charged with a new antiquarian and nationalist spirit. What was good taste became vandalism.

Wyatt's new Gothic buildings are another matter, however. Humphrey Repton wrote how, in them, he united 'modern comfort with antiquated forms' and 'introduced a style which is neither Grecian nor Gothic but which… may be called *Modern Gothic*'. Fonthill, alas, has long gone, but we still have Ashridge Park to suggest what Beckford's great folly must have been like. Begun for the Earl of Bridgewater in 1808, Wyatt devoted much time in his last few unhappy years to creating this grand example of 'Modern Gothic'. In it, as Dr Robinson suggests, he showed his 'great strength as an architect in the handling of external masses, and sublime internal spaces'. Ashridge is one of the great buildings of its time; the man who designed it does not deserve to be remembered merely as 'The Destroyer'.

September 2012

Slightly Subhuman?

Like Philip Webb, Sir John Soane is one of those British architects who has been unfortunate in the way posterity has treated his work. The greatest loss was the unforgivable destruction of the interior of his Bank of England in the 1920s, but his Law Courts at Westminster, his State Paper Office by St James's Park, Freemasons' Hall and the infirmary at the Chelsea Hospital have also all disappeared, whether by accident or design. Like Webb, Soane may have been highly regarded in his day, but taste moved against his personal, idiosyncratic style so that, similarly, many of his country houses have also perished or been mutilated. The great wheel of fashion having turned in his favour again, some of his interiors have been restored but, despite the modern cult of Soane, Pell Wall for instance remains a ruin.

All of which makes the recent restoration of Moggerhanger Park in Bedfordshire the more remarkable and praiseworthy.

When I first saw it over thirty years ago, it was a sad thing, serving as a hospital and mutilated with fire escapes. Today it looks like a country house again, and contains what must be some of the most extraordinary and exquisite interiors in England. All this is really due to the skill and commitment of one architect, Peter Inskip, who has known and cared about Moggerhanger since childhood as he lives nearby. Inskip has argued, convincingly, that the house is much more important than has usually been recognised. Soane became very friendly with his clients, two generations of bankers called Thornton, and worked at the house from 1790 until 1812. In the course of several building campaigns, he converted a modest pre-existing house into a much grander one, and in doing this he tried out many ideas he put into execution elsewhere.

More important is that Inskip managed to persuade others that Moggerhanger deserved respect and a full restoration. After the hospital disappeared, planning and listed building consent were actually granted for demolishing the stables and kitchens (with their amazing tall stepped chimneys) and for building fourteen houses in the grounds originally landscaped by Humphrey Repton. Most fortunately, however, Moggerhanger was instead acquired by the Centre for Contemporary Ministry, a Christian educational charity, as a training and conference centre. This was not inappropriate as the original client, Godfrey Thornton, was a cousin of William Wilberforce and a member of the Evangelical 'Clapham Sect'. Such organisations, however, are not normally much concerned with historic buildings. Inskip's genius was not only to persuade this Christian charity that it now owned a building of serious importance but also that restoring it properly was not incompatible with its mission. It is a most cheering and optimistic story: the Moggerhanger House Preservation Trust was established and, with aid from the Heritage Lottery Fund and others, the house has been restored (although more needs to be done and, naturally, more funds are required).

Thanks to the copious documentation at Sir John Soane's Museum, Inskip has not only restored the interior spaces but recovered lost elements in the design, like the internal oculus next to the staircase hall and the shallow dome over the entrance hall – a space now enlivened with rich, tantalising authentic graining. Stolen chimneypieces have been remade, lost columns reintroduced and the subtle, pale wall colourings repainted. Perhaps the most remarkable and memorable room is Mrs Thornton's dressing room, a complex oval space where the window to the verandah widens beyond shelves, where there is charming painted decoration and the architectural elements are enhanced with gilding and black lines; as Inskip remarks in his article on the house in the *Georgian Group Journal* for 2004, this is 'Soane at his very best'.

It is when one looks at the outside of Moggerhanger that doubts begin to emerge – not about the quality of the interior or the worthiness of the restoration project, but about Soane's ability as an *architect*. Not only are the walls somehow insubstantial – idiosyncratically detailed planes of stuccoed brickwork – but the elevations are simply ungainly. Some of the oddness may stem from the fact that the original house was successively enlarged and modified, but the semi-circular Greek Doric porch is not integrated into the composition while the spacing of the first-floor arched windows is irritatingly irregular. This rhythm is carried up into the raised centre-piece above the entrance but, with the outer windows coming so close to the sides, this feature looks tentative, awkward.

Moggerhanger, it seems to me, bears out the memorable analysis in Sir John Summerson's great study of *Architecture in Britain: 1530-1830* in which he argued that 'Soane never achieved real confidence and authority, even in his own style. There is always a temperamental factor, expressing itself in a sense of deflation, as if all *mass* had been exhausted from the design. This is partly due to awkward proportions […]. This deflationary tendency belongs peculiarly to Soane and makes his buildings, for all their feeling and invention, slightly sub-human. His architecture never commands; it shrinks into itself and nervously defines the spaces which it encloses.' So very true.

Of Soane's genius in the handling of light and in the organisation of interior space, in his ability to dissolve wall planes, there is no doubt. This is one reason why he has such a high reputation among modernist architects. But when it comes to the organisation and expression of mass, of weight, he was singularly deficient – even if the Regency was an age that valued lightness of touch. Compared with others who reinterpreted the Classical legacy with originality and, sometimes, eccentricity – Hawksmoor and Lutyens, for instance – Soane's work can seem insubstantial; there is no joy in the weight and texture of stone, piled up upon the ground. That necessary gravity seems only to have been attempted in his unexecuted formal designs – for triumphal bridges and royal palaces – where he used the full panoply of the orders, often in rather a pedantic way. Originality came with abstraction, but something else was lost in Soane's search for the economical and the ideal.

Soane's reputation is a curious thing. He enjoyed a very successful career, and he was knighted for his many official commissions, but the suspicion remains that he got many jobs because of his efficiency and his ability to deliver within estimates (certainly a great virtue). He was admired by the profession towards the end of his life, but that was because he was so devoted to it and was instrumental in the eventual foundation of the (Royal) Institute of British Architects. He was, of course, a difficult man – prickly and paranoid, as Gillian Darley's recent biography makes clear – but the fact remains that he had few imitators in his lifetime, and no successors. The Victorians, of course, had no time for his architecture. Only in the early 20th century was Soane's work taken seriously again, although that couldn't save the Bank of England. It appealed to those architects, like Raymond Erith, who wanted to develop and modernise well-tried traditions, but perhaps his happiest (as well as most ubiquitous) legacy is Sir Giles Scott's design for the GPO telephone kiosk.

More recently, of course, Soane has supplanted Hawksmoor as the modern architect's architect, partly, of course, because of the abstraction of his work and his brilliance in playing with light-sources, but also because the modern architect likes to bang on and on about *space* rather than be interested in form and mass. So was Soane modern before his time, to use that tired and pointless old *cliché*? One way in which he certainly did anticipate today's vain and self-important knighted practitioner was in his obsession with his reputation and place in history, collecting and saving almost every scrap of paper that came out of the office and, finally, by leaving his home and office to the nation, by Act of Parliament, as a museum to instruct and to be admired by posterity.

As far as I am concerned, Soane is without peer as a designer of interiors, as an organiser of spatial volumes in an intriguing and ingenious manner, and as the creator of novel detail. He was also a designer of impressive practicality and sense. But I cannot help having doubts about his current superstar status as an architect, and wonder whether, if it were not for the existence and survival of Sir John Soane's Museum to entertain and delight us, we would now just regard him as another good, if sometimes eccentric, Late Georgian architect, like George Dance junior, James Playfair, Thomas Hopper or Thomas Harrison. Discuss.

August 2006

[In Apollo *for May 2013 I argued that Soane's contemporary and sometime rival, John Nash, was a greater architect and one who left a more important legacy.]*

God's Architect

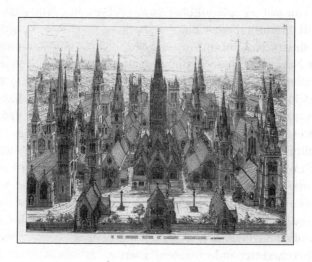

The frieze of architects on the podium of the Albert Memorial is a fascinating index of contemporary taste. While Vanbrugh is there next to Wren, Hawksmoor, Adam and Soane – all highly regarded today – are absent. Among the Victorians, Cockerell and Barry are represented, along with Pugin, who stands at the corner, dressed in a strange robe and looking away from all the others. But he is only there at the insistence of the designer of the memorial, Sir Gilbert Scott, whose own head is placed discreetly behind the figure of Pugin 'to whom I desired to do all honour as the head of the revival of mediaeval architecture and in many respects the greatest genius in architectural art which our age has produced... He was our leader and our most able pioneer in every branch of architectural work and decorative art...' Scott owed much to Pugin's example, so his ambition was 'to appear as his disciple, and to do him all the honour he deserves and which there is a strong tendency to deny him'.

This last remark might seem to confirm the perception that, until recently, Pugin has not been granted the recognition he deserves. Although he assisted Charles Barry in creating the New Palace of Westminster and was largely responsible for the design of that great national landmark and symbol, its Clock Tower, it is true that the established architect was anxious to suppress notice of his dependence on the younger man (who was only paid a pittance). After some years of difficulty, Pugin's Mediaeval Court in the Great Exhibition of 1851 was a triumphant success, yet only a year later, worn out, ill and mad, he died in his home at Ramsgate at the age of forty – and then his pathetic end was eclipsed by the death of the great Duke of Wellington in the same night in the same county. However, although he was an outsider, both because of his character and his fervent Roman Catholic faith, and was unfairly dismissed by Ruskin, Pugin was never really forgotten. As far as J.D. Sedding, the architect of that Arts & Crafts 'cathedral', Holy Trinity, Sloane Street, Chelsea, was concerned, 'we should have had no Morris, no Street, no Burges, no Shaw, no Webb, no Bodley, no Rossetti, no Burne-Jones, no Crane but for Pugin'.

Nor was he eclipsed in the 20th century, although he was often absurdly misinterpreted (not least as a theoretical pioneer of modernism). Pugin was taken very seriously in Sir Kenneth Clark's seminal study of the Gothic Revival (1928) and he was the subject of the first of the few post-Victorian biographies of Victorian architects to be published (by Michael Trappes-Lomax in 1932). More recently, he was the subject of a major exhibition at the Victoria & Albert Museum. And then, in 2007, Rosemary Hill's biography of this extraordinary man not only broke out of the introverted world of architectural history to become a best-seller but to win three prizes as well as being chosen as Radio 4's Book of the Week.

Pugin's bicentenary falls this month – he was born in London, to an English mother and a French father – on 1 March 1812. But that event cannot be marked by the laying of a wreath on a tomb in Westminster Abbey, as happened last July to celebrate the 200th birthday of his disciple Scott [see below]. Pugin was not buried there with the other great Victorians who received that accolade. Instead, he was placed in the chantry chapel he had created in St Augustine's Church in Ramsgate. He lies in a vault beneath an effigy of himself in a monument designed by his architect son Edward. The surrounding floor is covered with encaustic tiles, obsessively bearing his monogram and invented crest, a martlet, while above is a stained-glass window depicting both the life and work of his patron saint, St Augustine, and Pugin himself with his three (successive) wives. It is appropriate, not least as Pugin had done so much to encourage the revival of both making tiles and proper stained-glass.

Pugin had known Ramsgate since he was a boy, and he moved there permanently in 1843. He had bought land on the West Cliff overlooking the sea and he immediately began work on building his own house in that simplified and secularised Gothic that became the model for countless Victorian villas. Soon he was planning 'a flint seaside church' in the Kentish manner to rise next door. Inside, the plan is intriguingly asymmetrical and all of plain stone rather than gaudily decorated like Pugin's famous church at Cheadle. Both these seminal Gothic creations, along with a cloister, school and other buildings, were depicted in a bird's eye perspective he made in 1849: *A True Prospect of St Augustine's*. In it, this ideal Catholic community, this 'little town', sits, as Rosemary Hill has written, 'peacefully amid the fields, demonstrating the ideal harmony of Christian art and life. It is the self-contained world of a book of hours, translated to the 19th century'. Later, in 1860, a Benedictine monastery, designed by his son, began to rise on the land Pugin had bought opposite the church, thus completing his dream.

In fact, Pugin had an ambivalent and far from harmonious relationship with the rapidly expanding seaside town. St Augustine may have landed in Thanet but Pugin found it 'a most barren spot for Catholic ideas in *these days*'. Indeed, his ideal was regarded with suspicion and hostility by the many Low Church Protestants in the town, especially during the 'Papal Aggression' rumpus in 1850. Nor would the future be serene for Pugin's very generous legacy; what his biographer rightly describes as 'one of the most important groups on nineteenth-century buildings in Europe' only survives today after considerable vicissitudes.

Pugin's house, The Grange, was subsequently altered by Edward Pugin. Later, it was bought and further spoiled by the monks who, in 1991, sold it to a most unsuitable couple who, amongst other things, sawed Pugin's kitchen dresser in half prior to trying to sell it. Mercifully, after much controversy and thanks in part to the Pugin Society, the house was acquired by the Landmark Trust which has carried out an exemplary restoration, bringing it back to the state it was in at Pugin's death for us to experience and enjoy. As for the church which cost him a fortune, Pugin made sure that it was not to be given to the diocese until it was finished (in the event, without its spire), fitted out and furnished just as he wanted, for he had bitter experience of interference by clergy and patrons. In the event, the church was taken over by the monks who, in 1970, decided to re-order the chancel, move the screens to which Pugin attached such importance, destroy his altar and banish the tall tabernacle (now in Southwark Anglican Cathedral). Then, in the last few years, the monks tired of running the church and the parish priest in Ramsgate, resenting the fact that visitors came to see Pugin's creation, decided to close it for worship.

The future, however, is now much brighter. The monks have moved away and a new parish priest is enthusiastic about the building and about Pugin. The Friends of St Augustine's Church have been formed to raise funds to restore it. There is surely no better way to celebrate the bicentenary of that great man and inspiring designer than to care for his last, beautiful and ideal church.

March 2012

Midland Grand Hotel

'It is often spoken of to me as the finest building in London,' recorded Sir Gilbert Scott with typical self-regard in his autobiography about the hotel he had designed in front of the Midland Railway's new terminus in London; 'my own belief is that it is possibly *too good* for its purpose...' By that he meant that his extravagant essay in modern Gothic offended against the Victorian belief in propriety, for such a rich treatment might well be considered inappropriate in a mere commercial building; as Scott's severe critic, that mediocre architect J.T. Emmett, put it, 'an elaboration that might be suitable for a Chapter-house, or a Cathedral choir, is used... for bagmen's bedrooms and the costly discomforts of a terminus hotel'.

Such moral concerns do not trouble us today. Surrounded by cheap concrete and tawdry finishes, the former Midland Grand Hotel impresses by the sheer quality of the materials and craftsmanship as well as by its fantastic, romantic skyline:

granite, wrought iron and the best and best-laid Midland red bricks are combined with superbly carved and enriched Ancaster stone. Visitors express amazement that, less than half a century ago, so magnificent a structure could seriously have been threatened with demolition. But so it was. The vicious prejudice of taste that led to the easy dismissal of anything 'Victorian' combined with that sadly ubiquitous inability to see beyond the soot and dirt to the beauty and quality of the architecture underneath meant that, in the 1960s, British Railways could cheerfully propose to make both St Pancras and King's Cross Stations go the way of Birmingham New Street and Snow Hill, Birkenhead Woodside, Nottingham Victoria, Bradford Exchange, Glasgow St Enoch and more: the list is as long as it is depressing.

I first saw inside Scott's secular masterpiece in 1966. A visit had been organised by the Victorian Society to see inside the threatened building which was then called St Pancras Chambers, for the hotel – hopelessly inadequate when it finally closed in 1935 – served as railway offices. Inside, the tall spaces were cut up by partitions and covered in drab paint, but what remained impressive, amazing, was the grand staircase – still with its original carpet as well as the painted decoration – rising and dividing under a glorious ribbed vault. All this was to be reduced to rubble under the plan to replace both 19th century termini by a new station – like the miserable rebuilt Euston up the road.

The Victorian Society, founded eight years earlier, was determined that the Midland Grand would not go the way of the Euston 'Arch' and argued that it could perfectly well become an hotel again; the architect Roderick Gradidge demonstrated how the necessary modern services could be introduced into the solid 19th century structure. Such is the power of myth that it is now generally believed that St Pancras was single-handedly 'saved' by John Betjeman. The Poet Laureate certainly did his best to aid the preservation campaign, but it was the whole Victorian

Society, led by its chairman, the great historian Nikolaus Pevsner, who, in 1967, succeeded in defeating British Railways by persuading the late Lord Kennet, then Parliamentary Secretary to the Ministry of Housing & Local Government (and that very rare thing: a politician who was civilized, and *cared*) to upgrade St Pancras from III to I.

Thus thwarted, British Rail then assiduously neglected St Pancras, emerging from a quarter-century long sulk only to try and destroy the splendid timber ticket office which, today, is the dominant feature of what is today the Booking Hall Restaurant. This vandalism was again resisted by the Victorian Society, this time at public inquiry. Salvation for the Midland Railway's terminus finally became possible in the 1990s when the stupendous train shed by the engineers W.H. Barlow and R.M. Ordish – the largest span in the world when opened in 1868 – was chosen as the Eurostar terminal for Channel Tunnel trains. That made the restoration and modernisation of Scott's now abandoned hotel a serious commercial possibility. Trains to Paris and Brussels started leaving St Pancras four years ago and the hotel has at long last reopened this May.

The refurbishment of the Midland Grand – now renamed the St Pancras Renaissance, operated by Marriott – carried out by RHWL with Richard Griffiths Architects, is both very clever and superbly executed. Only the bottom two floors – containing the restored original restaurants – are now in hotel use. The upper floors of this huge building (Scott originally designed it even taller, and had to lop off a floor) have been converted into private apartments. To make the enterprise viable a new five-storey sound-proofed hotel annexe – the West Wing – has been built alongside the train shed in Midland Road. Here the new red-brick elevations, which harmonise with Scott's modern Gothic without copying it, are hung from a steel frame. The connection between the new and old parts of the hotel is the reception area which has been created in the former cab road adjacent to the old Booking Hall, still covered by the original iron and glass roof. This road had been designed to plunge down under the station and re-emerge between the platforms for cabs to pick up arriving passengers. Scott's hotel, placed in front of the train shed, was therefore originally penetrated by two giant arches, crossed by internal metallic bridges. These remain: the right-hand arch now allows access to the station; the left-hand one is the hotel entrance, leading to a space which, appropriately, still has an 'external' character.

Intelligence and care also distinguishes the treatment of the old Midland Grand. It is probably a mercy that the building was not made back into an hotel back in the 1960s, as the conversion would not, then, have been done so sensitively. Thanks to Harry Handelsman, whose Manhattan Loft Corporation is the developer of the building, original details, cornices and mouldings have been restored or recreated with immense care while surviving examples of the original painted decorative schemes have been applied over new fireproof paint. A stone Gothic screen in the old entrance hall off the Euston Road was destroyed in an accidental fire during the work; this has been immaculately recreated. As for the grand staircase, now cleaned and restored, with appropriate new light fittings installed and a new carpet woven to the pattern of the old, it is simply one of the most glorious spaces in London. Clearly this superb restoration has been a labour of love.

Grand hotels, by their nature, are semi-public buildings so their architecture matters. I have now completed a trilogy of articles about recent restorations of magnificent 19th century hotel buildings (the Savoy was in *Apollo* last January and the Pera Palas in Istanbul in March) and there is no doubt that the St Pancras hotel is the most important of the three architecturally. Its closure, long neglect, near destruction and now triumphant restoration and reopening reflects changing attitudes to Victorian architecture over the last century. Back in 1966 I could scarcely have hoped that not only would St Pancras survive but that it would one day be generally regarded with such respect, and affection. Attitudes to its designer, George Gilbert Scott, have also changed. No longer sneered and laughed at, his stature continues to grow, and it seems only right that his 200th birthday is to be celebrated on 13 July in Westminster Abbey where he is buried. He really was one of the great Victorians.

May 2011

The Second Greatest Briton?

This year sees not only the centenary of the birth [1906] of Sir John Betjeman but also the bicentenary of a very different individual, the great engineer Isambard Kingdom Brunel. The lives of both are being celebrated with some fanfare. Both perhaps represent different aspects of Britain's self-image (however false): Betjeman, the avuncular, cuddly poet and preserver of things and places beautiful; Brunel, the dynamic, inventive and individualist creator of the new – 'The man who built the World', 'In love with the impossible', to quote the subtitles of two recent new books – who died, worn out, at the age of 53. Certainly, though he was never forgotten, Brunel's heroic status has risen dramatically since the publication of Tom Rolt's biography in 1957; in 2003 BBC television viewers voted him second only to Sir Winston Churchill as the 'Greatest Briton' (even though he was, of course, like Pugin, half-French). Such, in these mediocre, timid and shameful times, is our need for heroes.

Brunel's achievements were certainly heroic. He built the finest railway in the world (the Great Western, from London to Bristol) as well as engineering other lines both at home and abroad. He was also responsible for three pioneering ships: one the first steam-powered vessel designed to cross the Atlantic, another the first iron-hulled, screw driven ship, and a third the largest ship in the world for half a century (the *Great Western*, *Great Britain* and *Great Eastern* respectively). And then he designed the noble bridges which are still doing their job after a century and a half, notably the beautiful brick elliptical arches over the Thames at Maidenhead, and the great wrought-iron spans across the Tamar at Saltash. It is also worth remarking that Brunel could make mistakes and that his failures were also on a heroic scale and hugely expensive (for others): the magnificent but doomed Broad Gauge, the grossly over-optimistic use of atmospheric traction on the South Devon Railway, and that last ship which, as Steven Brindle rightly concludes, was 'his ultimate triumph and his greatest folly'.

What is disturbing about the bicentenary celebrations is that we are being treated to yet more uncritical, gushing hero-worship. For there was a dark side to Brunel, as Adrian Vaughan first explored in his revisionist biography published in 1991. This bold engineer was arrogant and dictatorial, treating individuals – whether contractors or assistants – with contempt; not a few he bankrupted. He found it difficult to collaborate with others, and could not brook disagreement. He was a doctrinaire believer in *laissez-faire*, impatient of any regulations or official interference, even though experiments and the way he conducted operations could lead to loss of life. Perhaps this ruthlessness was essential to get things done, but I do wonder if his personal qualities are quite what we really ought to celebrate today. Not that you would learn anything of this from, say, the recent *Brunel: in love with the impossible*, a book of essays (some good) which seems to have been published largely as a public relations exercise on behalf of the city of Bristol.

What particularly interests me is Brunel's relationship with architecture. And I find it extraordinary that it still seems generally to be believed that he designed every bridge, every tunnel portico, every station, every building – everything, in fact – on the Great Western, right down to the fine details. Clearly this was not physically or humanly possible, workaholic as Brunel was. Of course he had an impressively well-developed architectural sensibility while in the first few decades of the 19th century – when it sometimes seems it was impossible to design anything ugly – the roles of engineer, surveyor and architect overlapped as the professions were not rigidly defined as they came to be later. Even so, like every other railway engineer, Brunel delegated, passing sketches to assistants to work up into detailed designs. Adrian Vaughan came up with some of the names: William Westmacott for Temple Meads Station while the architect J.H. Gandell assisted elsewhere on the Great Western. Vaughan has also shown that his unjustly overshadowed engineer father, Sir Marc Brunel, worked on both the Clifton Suspension Bridge and on the powerful detailing of the Wharncliffe Viaduct at Hanwell. Then there is the case of the Hungerford Suspension Bridge, where the City of London architect, J.B. Bunning, was responsible for the Italianate towers designed to harmonise with the style of the adjacent Hungerford Market.

Given the scale of current Brunelmania, it seems to be strange that so little attention is paid to this footbridge, for it was a remarkable and beautiful structure right in the heart of London; perhaps it is because it had such a short life. The Hungerford Bridge – 1,352 feet long – was flung across the Thames to Lambeth partly to try and revive the ailing fortunes of the Hungerford Market from which it sprang. This market was itself a most remarkable and elegant thing, a shopping centre on two floors, stretching all the way from the Strand to the unembanked Thames at Hungerford Stairs – near the blacking factory where Dickens had worked as a boy. It was a noble Classical structure, built of stone, granite and cast-iron, and was designed by Charles Fowler, who was also responsible for the market buildings in Covent Garden. It opened in 1833: an event marked by a balloon ascent by the celebrated and disaster-prone aeronaut, George Graham.

The Hungerford Suspension Bridge was first proposed two years later and eventually completed in 1845. It was Brunel's first wrought-iron structure, and consisted of a footway 14 feet wide running from the upper terrace of the market into the warehouses and brick terraces on the South Bank. The central span was 676 feet long – a little shorter than that proposed for the Brunels' unfinished Clifton bridge across the Avon; the side spans were of 343 feet. To judge by contemporary photographs and images, it was a wonderful thing. But, although foot traffic increased after the opening of Waterloo Station in 1848, it was not enough to save the Hungerford Market. Both market and bridge were acquired by the South Eastern Railway in 1859 (the year Brunel died) to make way for its extension from London Bridge to Charing Cross; both these most elegant structures were destroyed in 1862 (except for the bases of the bridge towers, which can be seen today). The scale and brutality of the railway terminus and bridge that replaced them is clear evidence of the unhappy divorce between architecture and engineering which occurred after Brunel's day; the only boon was that the suspension chains were rescued and used to complete the Clifton Bridge.

The Hungerford Bridge was no ordinary bridge as the handsome Brunel-Bunning supporting towers incorporated an interesting innovation: the saddles to which the suspension chains were attached were on oiled rollers so that the load on the masonry was always vertical and the chains could move to compensate for unequal loads on the roadway. This worked. On the opening day in April 1845, 20,000 people paid the half-penny toll to cross the river in just one hour, and later that year the proprietors were told that 'on two or three occasions there had been between 14,000 and 15,000 persons upon it, and it remained perfectly unshaken' (although Brunel himself observed that the bridge had a pronounced swing in windy conditions). Four years later, when Prince Albert travelled by ceremonial barge from Whitehall Stairs to open Bunning's Coal Exchange in the City (that most remarkable structure of masonry and iron wickedly destroyed in 1962), the long central span was nearly empty while a large crowd gathered on one of the landward spans. In consequence, the saddles moved horizontally to allow the chains to be pulled down and, 'when the crowd had dispersed, they returned to their original position'.

All this is worth recalling because of what happened a century and a half later with the Millenium footbridge across the Thames to Tate Modern. Just a few days after this much hyped structure – a 'blade of light' – was opened to the public in June 2000, it had to be closed as movement of people across it made it wobble violently. It remained closed for almost two years while it was fitted with dampers – at great extra expense. Now what is interesting is that at first the architect Norman Foster was very happy to take the credit for the design of this surely rather ugly footbridge, but once it began to wobble it was all the responsibility of the engineers, the Ove Arup Partnership. What does that tell us about the relationship between engineering and architecture today?

September 2006

[For more on the Hungerford Bridge, see my article on 'The Hungerford Market' in AA Files 11, *Spring 1986.]*

The Spirit of Ernest George

The Annual Discourse at the Royal Institute of British Architects in 1979 was given by the American architect Philip Johnson, who exhorted the audience to 'build in the spirit of Ernest George'. The architects present must have been bemused: not only would they not have heard of that Late Victorian domestic designer but they would have had absolutely no sympathy for his highly eclectic work. Why Ernest George? Johnson was then in his Post-Modernist phase and was busy with his AT&T tower in New York – the so-called 'Chippendale skyscraper' – which so disgusted his doctrinaire modernist contemporaries. Finding himself staying in the Connaught Hotel in London, he had a view down Mount Street and he telephoned me to ask who was responsible for the engaging riot of elaborate gabled facades he could see, all made of cheerful red brick and terracotta. So I told him.

Mount Street is a good example of the quaint gabled variant of the 'Queen Anne' manner inspired by the Early Renaissance merchants' houses in the Low Countries and Germany which Late Victorian architects thought urbane, colourful and eminently suitable for prosperous mercantile London. Osbert Lancaster famously categorised the style as 'Pont Street Dutch' in the 1930s and he noted how the 'more remarkable features of the new style were a fondness for very bright red brick, a profusion of enrichments in that most deplorable of materials, terracotta, and a passion for breaking the skyline with every variety of gable that the genius of Holland had produced and a good many that it had not'. Ernest George was a masterly exponent of this highly picturesque manner, assiduous at reinterpreting the ample contents of his sketchbooks that he brought back from his regular Continental tours.

There were two offices in the 1880s that a bright young aspirant architect would want to work in. One was that run by the famous Richard Norman Shaw, the other was George & Peto. It is said that there was a standard printed letter, 'Mr Norman Shaw presents his compliments to Lord....... and regrets that owing to pressure of work he is unable to accept his commission', on which his pupils would mischievously add that 'Mr Ernest George... will be very pleased to do so'. But George was just as prolific as Shaw, and his clients just as rich and grand – if conservative. George once explained that, 'the client for whom we build dreads seeming startlingly modern with his new house... he would rather it should seem to belong to the past' (while having every modern comfort). Amongst George's many large country houses was Batsford Park, built for the 1st Baron Redesdale, in which the Mitford sisters spent some of their early years.

The list of distinguished architects who came out of the Ernest George office is impressive. The most celebrated was Edwin Lutyens, but there was also Herbert Baker, Guy Dawber and many of the best Arts and Crafts architects. It is also worth noting that two of his pupils were women – Ethel and Bessie Charles – who went on to become the first two women members of the RIBA. In all, it seems unjust that George should have become rather eclipsed by Shaw and comparatively forgotten, but this state of affairs has now been rectified with the publication of a fine monograph by Hilary Grainger, magnificently illustrated with new photographs by Martin Charles, our best architectural photographer.

Ernest George was not just an ingenious planner and a master at artful composition; he was also a notable artist. Unlike many busy practitioners, he was responsible for his own perspectives and was a most accomplished painter in watercolour. He also took up etching, and his sketches of picturesque scenes on the Continent were much admired by John Ruskin. Yet he was reluctant to exhibit his watercolours, lest he be thought of as a painter rather than an architect. For him, architecture was 'the happiest of callings... We may not gain credit for great originality, yet in each essay there is an effort at invention and creation; and there is the after pleasure of realising our schemes – however imperfect – on a nice big scale; a result so much more tangible than that enjoyed by the painter or even the sculptor'.

Perhaps the best place to study Ernest George's talents is Harrington Gardens in Kensington where there is a row of substantial town houses built in the 1880s, each wildly different from its neighbour – the antithesis of Georgian regularity and, in the words of the *Survey of London*, 'the extreme point of Victorian architectural individualism'. As far as Hermann Muthesius, that astute German chronicler of *Das Englische Haus*, was concerned, these were 'among the finest examples of domestic architecture to be seen in London'. The most celebrated is No. 39, a house which, with its multiple-stepped gable and rich decorative embellishments in terracotta, looks as if it has strayed from Ghent or Dantzig. It was built by W.S. Gilbert, creator, with Arthur Sullivan, of the Savoy Operas, and paid for, apparently, with the profits of *Patience*, the operetta which satirised the contemporary Aesthetic Movement whose influence is, ironically, so evident in the opulent and ingenious interior.

Gilbert's house is, to some extent, a personal fantasy, but he had chosen the best architect to realise it – Muthesius noted that 'the dominant mood of these houses is almost romantic, fantastic'. Ernest George was, however, a practical architect who insisted on high standards of craftsmanship. His urban facades, richly allusive and hugely enjoyable, enhance rather than deaden the streets in which they stand. And one reason they do this is that, with his pictorial approach, George understood the importance of colour. Like many of his contemporaries, he was anxious to introduce colour to the dirty, smoky streets of Victorian cities and his typical and best buildings combine fine red brick with the orange-brown of that most underrated of building materials, terracotta.

Inspired by Italian Renaissance examples, the mid-Victorians began to revive terracotta. It had the virtue of being washable in addition to weathering well, and could be moulded to make fine architectural detail and sculpture. It was used on the first buildings of the South Kensington Museum – now the V&A – and on the Albert Hall, on the elaborate buildings of Dulwich College and Alfred Waterhouse made the Natural History Museum almost entirely out of ceramic blocks. As Hilary Grainger observes, 'George employed terracotta with the sensitivity of an artist. It could have appeared hard and brash...' but in his hands the effect is charming. And then, in the 20th century, perhaps because of the lavatorial associations of ceramic materials, it went out of fashion – as the Osbert Lancaster quote above suggests.

Happily, it is now beginning to enjoy another revival as a welcome and long-overdue alternative to grey concrete; the new extension to the Holborne Museum in Bath by Eric Parry, for instance, is faced in a (blueish) ceramic material. Whether they realise it or not, some architects do now seem to be building in the spirit of Ernest George.

July-August 2011

[Martin Charles, whose superb photographs – particularly of Victorian buildings – enhance many publications, died in 2012.]

Forgotten Prophet

The reopening of the expanded Whitechapel Art Gallery has rightly attracted much attention and was celebrated in the April issue of *Apollo*. But what was striking was how very few of the authors of articles in non-specialist publications mentioned the name of the designer of the original building which opened in 1901: Charles Harrison Townsend. It is not, after all, as if his creation is in any way commonplace. With its giant entrance arch placed off-centre on its terracotta façade which is ornamented with Arts and Crafts foliage in relief and rises into two strange towers with flush pinnacles, it is, in fact, extraordinary. Half a century ago, Sir Nikolaus Pevsner could describe it as a 'façade without any borrowed motifs of the past, as original as any Art Nouveau on the Continent'.

This omission may simply be due to the ignorance of most journalists, but it surely also reflects how architecture is marginalised in British cultural life. For years, mention of new buildings in the press would name the client and the contractor as well citing the cost and the name of the dignitary who declared it open while ignoring the identity of the poor architect. It is as if people imagine that the shape and appearance of a building somehow emerges by default or by a mysterious process which does not deserve comment. Architects (at least until the recent emergence of knighted and ennobled superstars) were not thought very important; other arts are valued more. It would surely be shaming today not to have heard of, say, Aubrey Beardsley or Oscar Wilde or Edward Elgar, but ignorance of the name of their contemporary Harrison Townsend is somehow acceptable.

Yet Townsend's was clearly a remarkable talent, and his work was of European importance. That was the context in which Pevsner placed him in his classic study of *Pioneers of Modern Design*, in which he wrote that Townsend's designs of the 1890s 'are without question the most remarkable example of a reckless repudiation of tradition among English architects of the time'. Similar in spirit to the experimental modern buildings of the Art Nouveau, they were certainly noticed and admired by Continental contemporaries. The German architect and critic Hermann Muthesius, author of *Das Englische Haus*, considered him to be one of 'the prophets of the new style'.

Townsend died in 1928, a year after Muthesius and the same year as the one *fin de siècle* progressive British architect that, these days, even journalists have heard of: Charles Rennie Mackintosh. Townsend, born the year of the Great Exhibition, was rather older than both of these other two men yet he designed little of consequence before the 1890s. Nor did he produce much of interest after about 1905 when British architecture changed direction and became more conservative, leaving him and like-minded designers, like Voysey and Mackintosh, out on a limb and suddenly looking rather old-fashioned. Townsend's eminence rests on a handful of buildings designed during those few heady years either side of 1900.

Two are ecclesiastical: a charming little church at Blackheath in Surrey and a much bigger church at Great Warley in Essex where he collaborated with the Arts and Crafts metal-worker William Reynolds-Stephens. But what really matters are the three cultural institutions he designed for unfashionable parts of London, one of which is the Whitechapel Gallery.

First came the Bishopsgate Institute, which opened in 1894 on a site close to Liverpool Street Station on the edge of the City of London. It was intended for use by people working and living nearby. Townsend had won a limited competition for the building because of his skill as a planner, for the site was extremely awkward. It was long and thin, and consisted of house plots and back yards stretching eastwards from bustling Bishopsgate into Spitalfields, then one of the most deprived and depraved parts of the capital where the Jack the Ripper murders had recently taken place. On this site, Townsend contrived to arrange three entrances, a library and several meeting rooms connected by a long corridor together with a surprisingly large Great Hall, 'for the benefit of the public to promote lectures, exhibitions and otherwise the advancement of literature, science and the fine arts'.

The internal spaces are nicely detailed but utilitarian, as are the small exposed side and rear elevations which use a simple round-arched manner in red brick and terracotta. Architecturally what tells is the show front in Bishopsgate, 'one of the most original buildings of its date in London', to quote Pevsner again. The style, as with so much work of the 1890s, is essentially free Tudor and may have been inspired by the frontispiece of 16th century Brereton Hall in his native Cheshire (interestingly, Townsend provided an introduction to a new edition of Joseph Nash's *Mansions of England in the Olden Time* published by *The Studio* in 1906). But although Townsend's façade also has twin polygonal towers, the details are very different and very weird, such as the shafts emerging from their ogee tops and the raised bar between the towers above and across the high-pitched roof – where does this come from? And progressive as he may have been, he never forgot the necessity for integral ornament to symbolise and humanise. Much of the external terracotta is moulded into a dense tangle of leaves and branches illustrating the Tree of Life. But what is evident above all, particularly with the giant entrance arch resting on pairs of small squat columns, is Townsend's deep interest in Romanesque art – an interest which may have been encouraged by his evident admiration for the Neo-Romanesque work of the great American architect H.H. Richardson.

These influences are also clear in Townsend's third cultural building, the Horniman Free Museum in the south-east suburb of Forest Hill which opened in 1901 – the same year as the Whitechapel Gallery. The building and its contents were a gift to the London County Council by the tea importer and Liberal Member of Parliament, Frederick John Horniman, who had already opened to the public the large ethographical collection he had amassed in his own house nearby. Horniman chose Townsend as his architect, and the resulting building demonstrates both his originality and eccentricity. He again provided a show front facing London Road, this time in stone rather than terracotta (the utilitarian brick side elevations are almost shockingly disappointing). A large blank façade surmounted with a segmental pediment reflecting the shape of the gallery behind is relieved by a large mosaic frieze by the artist Robert Anning Bell. But what attracts attention is the tall landmark clock tower placed at the lower corner of the site. This is modelled with Townsend's typical heavy rounded forms and its base is pierced by two of his big heavy rusticated round arches – one of which was the main entrance, at the top of a flight of stairs. The top-lit galleries on two levels were utilitarian, but ornamented with more Trees of Life and with pilasters treated in a manner that makes them seem Art Nouveau.

Whether or not it is owing to his fascinating but thoroughly practical architecture, all three of the institutions designed by

Townsend continue to flourish. The Horniman Museum has also expanded, first with a library and lecture hall added in 1910 by Townsend himself and more recently, in 2000-02, with further galleries and a shop, a café and a new entrance facing Horniman Gardens to the west (though I am pleased to report that the original entrance remains in use). These clever, unusual but harmonious buildings were designed by Allies & Morrison. Now it is the Bishopsgate Institute's turn. It is hugely cheering to discover that the building has been well looked after and that it continues to perform its intended function, that its rooms and library are much used and that it now houses an important historical archive about the East End of London. Now money is being sought for a 'Renewal Project' to improve it, to create a new archive store and café, and to open up the blocked skylight over the Great Hall. It is a very good cause.

June 2009

[The Bishopsgate Institute's Renewal Project was carried out.]

Spence's Charm

Coventry Cathedral was surely the last modern building in Britain that people actually queued to see inside. I recall going there as a schoolboy with my parents after it was consecrated in 1962 and standing in a long line that snaked between the walls of the old blitzed Cathedral next door. The popular appeal was, of course, partly polemical, for the new Cathedral was a much publicised phoenix that had risen from the ruins of the city devastated by the Luftwaffe during the Second World War. But there was also curiosity to see what a modern cathedral might be like, for this was the first truly public building belonging to the controversial 'New Architecture' completed since the Festival of Britain, in which one of the successes was the Sea and Ships Pavilion designed by the same architect: Sir Basil Spence.

Even before his death in 1976, Spence had a somewhat ambivalent reputation. Ambitious, energetic and immensely charming, he was also pompous and prickly. Big jobs seemed to fall effortlessly into his lap. But the reason why he was regarded with suspicion, and sniped at, by many in his own profession was that he was not seen as truly Modern with a capital 'M'. In fact, he can almost be regarded as a pioneer Post-Modernist. He seldom indulged in either the light, planar aesthetic of steel and glass, nor in the aggressive ungainliness of the New Brutalism while Coventry, his undoubted master-piece, was often dismissed as a compromise: a rich, modernist aesthetic applied to a traditional plan and conception, reliant on symbolism and works of art. And that, of course, was precisely its success and its strength. Spence had managed to produce a building which satisfied his clients, the Anglican clergy, and please and intrigue the public while being evidently Modern.

Critics tend to prefer architects who are principled innova-tors in the privileged and rarefied compound of the profession, remote from an uncomprehending and ignorant public – architects, like civil servants, always know best, after all. But Spence knew both how to charm and please his clients and the public; while convinced of the merit of his designs, he knew that architecture is an impure and messy business and that to get a building built requires compromise. Like Sir Giles Scott – who, after his competition win, he supplanted as the new Cathedral's architect – he was subtly attuned to popular taste. He was also interested in the colour and texture of masonry and in mass, in the sculptural power of built forms – some-thing he may have learned from his brief time in the office of Edwin Lutyens working on New Delhi as well as from the later work of Le Corbusier.

The centenary of Spence's birth has been celebrated with a large travelling exhibition – in Edinburgh (Spence was a Scot, although actually born in Bombay), London and Coventry – as well as with publications and conferences. Does Spence deserve all this fuss? Surely, yes. Not only was he responsi-ble for several major public buildings, he also did more than any other architect to make modernism acceptable, or at least comprehensible, to a wider public. This he achieved through the buildings themselves and by what might be regarded as self-promotion through lectures, public events and films. He became – and certainly regarded himself as – a familiar and famous public figure.

The exhibition consists of material from the architect's archive recently given to the Royal Commission for the Ancient and Historical Monuments of Scotland. On show are drawings and models as well as films of Sir Basil smoothly explaining his work. But it is dominated, above all, by his perspective drawings. Spence had fatal charm, both in the flesh and on paper. He drew like an angel. From the very beginning of his career he was executing slick and engaging colour perspectives for other architects and, having developed his real talent as a painter, he continued to produce large, ravishing 'artist's impressions' – in oils and *gouache* as well as watercolour – of his buildings to captivate his clients. His assistant and later partner, Anthony Blee, recalls that 'if they wanted to be reminded of what Basil had in mind for them, when travelling with them in a train or plane he would grab the nearest piece of paper (on several occasions this would be a BOAC airline sick bag) and he would rattle off a quick sketch using a felt pen with astonishing fluency and graphic clarity'.

Sometimes, one fears, he seduced too much, for some of the built designs fail to live up to his painterly vision. But what is also impressive is the range of work that the Spence office(s) produced: not only a cathedral and churches but an airport, a foreign embassy, a parliament house, a university, commercial offices, exhibition buildings, a barracks, country houses and public housing. Most remain in use although a few buildings have been demolished – the fate of the creations of so many architects working in the mid-20th century. Perhaps the greatest failure was the pair of reinforced-concrete long high-rise housing blocks in Hutchesontown built as part of the (disastrous) redevelopment of the Gorbals in the 1960s. Here, for once, Spence adopted a powerful Brutalist aesthetic. They look magnificent in early black & white photographs – typically, Spence charmed the Glasgow Housing Committee by telling them that 'on Tuesdays, when all the washing's out, it'll be like a great ship in full sail!' – but were not much fun to live in and they were blown up, in a squalid public gesture, in 1993.

Other than Coventry, perhaps Spence's greatest success was the University of Sussex, where he succeeded in giving that trendy new university a suitably modern image which was also congenial. He adapted the rough Corbusian aesthetic of shallow concrete arches – as at the Maison Jaoul – for seaside Sussex, creating powerful shapes while removing the pejorative associations of a 'red brick university'. Equally impressive is the Chancery for the British Embassy in Rome – the replacement of a building blown up by Jewish terrorists in 1946 – which is a richly textured and modelled modern *palazzo* faced in travertine and raised up above elegant gardens. It was Spence's response to a sensitive site next to Michelangelo's Porta Pia and one which succeeded in pleasing the Italians. Less successful perhaps was the Cavalry Barracks in Knightsbridge with its highly controversial residential tower looming over Hyde Park. Oddly, the officers' mess was placed at the summit, and it is good to learn that it is true that it contains a specially strengthened large lift to take a heavy 'drum horse' up there on certain special occasions.

Such jobs indicate that, by the 1960s, Spence was an establishment figure. He was knighted and was awarded the Order of Merit – and it was rather pathetic that, at the end of his life, he dwelt on his honours when his design for the exterior of the Home Office tower in Queen Anne's Gate was widely and loudly criticised. Indeed, there was a less attractive side to Spence. In his second volume of memoirs, *Echoing Voices*, John Harris recalls how when there was a vain attempt to secure his archive for the RIBA Drawings Collection, the Past President of the RIBA brusquely announced his arrival to the receptionist as 'Sir Basil Spence, Royal Gold Medallist'. On another occasion, when a deputation went to see him in his home and office in Canonbury, he declared that 'Of course, I am the greatest architect in Britain' and then went on to claim that, for his wartime bravery, he really deserved the Victoria Cross.

No matter. Spence should be judged by his buildings, and the best of them are some of the best of their time. Above all there is Coventry Cathedral, where Spence's inspired compromise seems all the more convincing and moving as time passes, full of resonant symbolism. And what also deserves respect here is that Spence commissioned seriously good works of art which are an integral part of his overall concept – not just the great tapestry by Graham Sutherland and the sculpture by Jacob Epstein but also the powerfully colourful abstract stained glass by John Piper and Lawrence Lee, the etched figurative glass by John Hutton, the carved lettering by Ralph Beyer and the rest. Not only is it the last modern building the public queued to see, it is also the last great work of the Arts and Crafts movement.

September 2008

[Spence did not in fact supplant Giles Scott as the latter had resigned in 1946 after his design was criticised by the Royal Fine Arts Commission. Amongst other publications, Basil Spence: Buildings and Projects *by Louise Campbell was published in 2012 and an English Heritage Blue Plaque was placed on Spence's home in Canonbury the year before.]*

Knight's Tale

Nostalgia and progress are not necessarily contradictory. The year 1838 saw the opening throughout of that modern wonder, Robert Stephenson's London & Birmingham Railway as well as the first crossing of the Atlantic by a steamship. It was also the year when the cut-price coronation ceremony for Victoria was regarded as such an insult both to the new young queen and to tradition that the 13th Earl of Eglinton announced he would stage a grand aristocratic tournament, open to the public, at his Ayrshire seat. The following summer, therefore, it was possible for the curious to pass through the new Greek Doric portico at Euston Station, travel by train to Liverpool and then take a paddle steamer to Ardrossan and then walk or ride the few miles to Eglinton Castle to witness one of the most extraordinary spectacles of the 19th century. Others got there by steam train on the first section of the Glasgow, Paisley, Kilmarnock & Ayr

Railway from Ayr to Irvine which had only been open for a matter of weeks.

Thanks to these much improved methods of transport, some hundred thousand visitors converged on Eglinton Castle at the end of August 1839. What then occurred was described and explained by Ian Anstruther in his book, *The Knight and the Umbrella*, published in 1963. What was intended was an authentic re-enactment of a Mediaeval tournament, with jousting on horseback. Armour and other necessary accoutrements were largely supplied by Samuel Pratt, an enterprising Bond Street dealer who catered for the growing interest in things Mediaeval. At Eglinton – a rather feeble Neo-Gothic castle built by the Earl's father – a grandstand and tents had been designed by the antiquary and architect, Lewis Nockalls Cottingham. And, as well as the knights, there was a Queen of Beauty in the shape of Lady Seymour. The Lord of the Tournament was, of course, Eglinton himself, 'In a Suit of Gilt Armour, richly chased; on a barded Charger – caparisons, &c. of Blue and Gold'. He had spent some £40,000 on the event, although it was not the tournament that eventually bankrupted his family (today there is nothing left of Eglinton Castle).

Unfortunately – though not surprisingly to anyone familiar with the climate of the West of Scotland – things did not go according to plan. As the umbrella in Anstruther's title suggests, on the afternoon of the first day the heavens opened. The tents collapsed under a torrential downpour; knights and squires, grooms and horses slithered in the mud as the castle grounds rapidly became a quagmire. Thousands of spectators struggled home drenched to the skin. In consequence, the Eglinton Tournament is often dismissed as a fiasco. It certainly had its comic side: it was laughed at in *Punch* magazine (itself a new invention) and mercilessly satirised by the artist Richard Doyle. But this is not the whole story. In fact, the sun came out the following day, jousts were conducted and the final Mediaeval banquet and ball was a great success.

More to the point, the Tournament was not an isolated phenomenon. It was part of a much larger historical shift: the whole revival of interest in the Middle Ages encouraged by antiquarianism and the Romantic movement. The novels of Sir Walter Scott (*Ivanhoe* especially); the many paintings illustrating chivalrous themes; Newman and the Catholic movement within the Church of England; the rebuilding of Windsor Castle by Victoria's wicked uncle, George IV, to make it look more Mediaeval; and, indeed, the whole Gothic Revival in architecture all lay behind Lord Eglinton's jamboree – which had a serious purpose. As Rosemary Hill, Pugin's biographer, has remarked, 'to take a steam train to a Gothic tournament was to enter fully into the spirit of this particular age'. As for Pugin himself, busy trying to return England to Mediaeval Catholicism by covering the land with churches, he thought the tournament a little silly and old-fashioned – like the ramshackle Mediaevalism of George IV's extravagant coronation in 1821 when, for the last time, the King's Champion, in armour and mounted, had appeared in Westminster Hall.

1839 was also the year when both Daguerre and Henry Fox Talbot announced the invention of photography to the world. Of course there are no photographs of the Tournament, but, fortunately, the event was recorded in a lavish book, *A Series of Views representing the Tournament held at Eglinton Castle...*, published in 1843. These lithographs were made by James Henry Nixon and illustrated processions of all the protagonists in full heraldic detail as well as the actual jousting. Recently, the exciting discovery has been made of most of Nixon's original watercolours. These have been carefully restored and exhibited by the London firm of Abbott & Holder. Most commendably, this collection has been kept together and the Yale Centre for British Art hopes to acquire it. The pity is, perhaps, that despite the best efforts of Abbott & Holder, these precious historical documents have not found their way into a Scottish archive (although, at the time of writing, efforts are being made in Ayrshire to mount a bid for them). But the sad truth is that modern Scotland is not comfortable with the pioneering Romantic origins of Scottish nationalism, with MacPherson's 'discovery' of the poetry of Ossian, with the novels of Walter Scott and his role in stage-managing George IV's visit to Edinburgh in 1822, with the revival of tartan and the vogue for visiting Staffa and the Highlands, even though all this made Scotland and Scottish culture of European fame and significance.

It is not just the Scots who are blinkered, however, for all Britain now seems to have lost a sense of the deep importance of Mediaevalism in national life. Five years before the tournament, the Palace of Westminster had been destroyed by fire and Parliament, conscious of history and wishing to express its own origins, decided that its replacement should be Gothic or Elizabethan in style. A few years later, Pugin would resume helping Charles Barry to create what is surely the finest Gothic Revival secular building in the world. Today, the ignorant and stupid dismiss this great work as 'Mock-Gothic', thus misunderstanding not only the nature of architectural style but also its symbolism. For Gothic always meant something. For Pugin it was the national, Christian style. For Lord Eglinton, Mediaevalism was aristocratic and Tory (he refused tournament tickets to Whigs as well as to a socialist like Robert Owen). But to the politicians who had recently passed the Great Reform Bill, Gothic could represent the origins and development of British parliamentary democracy.

Today, that democracy is rather tarnished, what with the recent scandal over the expenses of Members of Parliament. Many now seem to think the institution should be radically modernised. But neither toning down the rich pageantry of Pugin's interiors nor dressing the Speaker in a lounge suit rather than knee breeches will address the real problem, which is the venal mediocrity of so many of our elected representatives. Indeed the facile proposals now being aired suggest an alarming lack of understanding of how our liberties are vested in traditions and institutions. The nation and its elected representatives were rather wiser during the Second World War, when the Gothic Revival building and Pugin's clock tower was not just a famous London landmark but a symbol of hope and democracy to the world in desperate times. After the destruction of the House of Commons by bombing in 1941, Parliament decided that the chamber should be rebuilt to exactly the same configuration as before, and in the same style: Gothic. It was in this debate that Winston Churchill made his celebrated observation that, 'We shape our buildings, and afterwards our buildings shape us.' The 13th Earl of Eglinton would surely have understood, and sympathised.

September 2009

[Because of their cultural importance, the application for an export licence was deferred and East Ayrshire District Council purchased the watercolours for Dean Castle, Kilmarnock, with assistance from the Art Fund, the Heritage Lottery Fund, the Barcapel Foundation and the National Fund for Acquisitions.]

Dreaming Towers

The principal landmark in the city of Bristol is the colossal Gothic tower that stands at the top of Park Street, the straight street lined with regular stone terraces that climbs from the old city centre up towards Clifton. The tower rises four-square, with massive corner buttresses framing large Perpendicular Gothic windows, before breaking back at high level, with pinnacles and rich blank tracery, to become an octagonal belfry. It is a form similar to that of the Boston 'Stump' – the lighthouse-tower of the Lincolnshire parish church – or the crossing tower of St Ouen in Rouen, although it is certainly a copy of neither. As it is flanked by lower buildings also in a Late Gothic style, many visitors to Bristol assume that it is the city's cathedral but it is not – Bristol Cathedral, part Mediaeval and part Victorian, stands rather less conspicuously at the bottom end of Park Street. This great vertical feature, 215 feet high, is the Wills Memorial Tower of Bristol

University, raised in memory of its first Chancellor, and is less than a century old.

University College Bristol became Bristol University exactly a century ago, in 1909. Instrumental in this elevation was the Wills family, the wealthiest of the Nonconformist commercial dynasties who flourished in the city in the later 19th century. Now George and Henry Wills gave the new institution a visible focus. This last great secular Gothic Revival building, containing a vast vaulted entrance hall and staircase leading to a Great Hall, was paid for with the profits of an activity which is now widely regarded as socially unacceptable, for the Wills brothers ran the Wills Tobacco Company, manufacturer of cigarettes. The tower was designed in 1912 but work on it ceased during the First World War and it was only completed in 1925. (One of the men who worked on it, as a plumber, was the late Harry Patch who, when he died earlier this year at the age of 111, was the last surviving British soldier who had served in the trenches).

Soon after the Wills Tower was topped-out in the presence of King George V, its newly-knighted architect was awarded an honorary degree by the University. 'As long as the great bell tolls in its lofty tower,' proclaimed the Vice-Chancellor; 'as long as that Lantern of the West stands to symbolise the light radiating from this centre of learning, Sir George Oatley's fame must stand secure.' But it does not. Oatley (1863-1950) is hardly known outside his native Bristol. This is partly owing to the character of the man himself. Indifferent to worldly honours and fame, this modest, retiring and devout man believed that his talent was God-given and directed – his biographer, Sarah Whittingham, quotes Oatley writing that, 'I have been deeply & solemnly conscious all through that I was being borne along by a power entirely above & beyond anything of my own.' He could almost be seen as Pugin's perfect Christian architect except that while he designed churches and other University buildings in the Gothic style, he also designed Edwardian Baroque banks and loved the Georgian architecture of the city.

But the real reason for the comparative obscurity of Oatley's work outside Bristol is that his towering masterpiece was out of its time. Many historians and architects, in their blinkered, historicist way, do not know what to make of it. The more ignorant assume that if a 20th century building is not Modern in style, it cannot be significant, but this is to ignore what actually happened. The Gothic Revival carried on right through the century, of course, but only for churches (the great crossing tower designed by Sir Giles Scott and completed in 1941 above his vast cathedral at Liverpool is comparable with Oatley's). A few secular Gothic buildings had been raised around 1900, such as the John Rylands Library in Manchester and the Middlesex Guildhall in Westminster (now disgracefully mutilated internally to convert it into England's Supreme Court), but by 1925 such a full-bloodied expression of the decorative richness of Gothic was completely out of fashion. A few buildings in Oxford and Cambridge were designed in a polite, abstracted Tudor to harmonise with the ancient buildings in those universities, but the important new academic buildings were usually Classical and, later, Modern. The Wills Tower is unique – in Britain, that is.

As with earlier provincial university buildings in the style, such as those at Glasgow by Sir Gilbert Scott, the choice of Gothic at Bristol was partly motivated by the desire to emulate England's ancient universities at Oxford and Cambridge. And this was a form of academic snobbery which had contemporary resonances on the other side of the Atlantic (as well as in the Antipodes). Almost exactly contemporary with the Wills Tower is another tall Gothic university tower which rises to an octagonal pinnacled summit: the Harkness Tower at Yale. It is the most dominant feature of the Harkness Memorial Quadrangle built in 1917-21 (which also sports a smaller tower modelled on that of the parish church of Wrexham in England where Elihu Yale is buried). Paid for by Edward Harkness (with money from oil rather than tobacco), this new set of buildings marked Yale University's adoption of 'Collegiate Gothic' and over the following two decades a series of residential quadrangles and other university buildings were built in a manner closely inspired by the old colleges of Oxford.

Almost all of these were the work of Harkness's own architect and Oatley's near contemporary, James Gamble Rogers (1867-1947), who had not hitherto been particularly committed to Gothic. Indeed, it is likely that much of the design work at Yale was carried out by assistants hired for the purpose, notably Otto Faelten. Nor was Yale the first North American university to go in for a romantic, Neo-Oxbridge architecture. Gothic had long been used for academic buildings and there are earlier, and arguably better examples of Collegiate Gothic at Princeton, such as the Graduate College of 1913. This was designed by Cram, Goodhue & Ferguson, the firm founded by the Bostonian architect and writer Ralph Adams Cram who, with his passion for European Mediaevalism, really can be seen as a true disciple of Pugin. But it was Rogers who became most closely identified with the style and who, having secured a monopoly of architectural patronage at Yale, carried on with it well into the 1930s.

It cannot be claimed that James Gamble Rogers was the most accomplished of Gothicists. He was conservative and pragmatic, and his Harkness Tower, closely inspired by the Boston Stump but with an excessive inwards batter, seems confused and ungainly compared with Oatley's robust erection in Bristol. And the finest building at Yale associated with Rogers is surely the Sterling Library, which was originally conceived in a monumental, abstracted Gothic manner by Cram's brilliant former partner, Bertram Goodhue before his untimely death in 1924. But Rogers's other Yale buildings, with their careful use of rugged, irregular stonework and other sophisticated devices to create an impression of instant antiquity, have great charm, work well and create a strong visual identity for Yale. They are very much of their time, and do not deserve the abuse heaped on them by those who wish that the university's benefactors had brought in Frank Lloyd Wright or another progressive designer instead.

This is the last of a triptych of articles about aspects of the Gothic Revival. If there is a common argument in them it is that the revival and adoption of the Gothic style, whether in the 18th, 19th or 20th century, always means something – and something which deserves to be taken very seriously.

November 2009

[A comprehensive illustrated monograph on Sir George Oatley: Architect of Bristol *by Sarah Whittingham was published in 2011. The restoration of Horace Walpole's Strawberry Hill was discussed in the author's article in* Apollo *for October 2009.]*

Englishmen's Castles

Neo-Tudor is the style that the English still love to hate. Superior modern architects delight in sneering at it, especially its ubiquitous 20th century suburban manifestations. 'The man who builds a bogus Tudoresque villa or castellates his suburban home is committing a crime against truth and tradition', announced Anthony Bertram in his 1935 book, *The House: A Machine for Living In*; 'he is denying the history of progress, denying his own age and insulting the very thing he pretends to imitate by misusing it'. Yet the style obstinately remains popular.

From John Nash's enchanting Neo-vernacular cottages at Blaise Hamlet at the beginning of the 19th century to Sam Wanamaker's and Theo Crosby's recreation of the Globe Theatre on Bankside at the end of the 20th, the ideal of the Tudor past has been important in English architectural culture. It informed some of the finest houses of Norman Shaw, Philip

Webb and Edwin Lutyens, after all. But it is the 20th century expression of this taste, as adopted by the builders of the new suburbs between the world wars, that has damned it. In his description of that half-timbered style he labelled 'Stockbrokers Tudor', Osbert Lancaster wrote of being 'a little unnerved at being suddenly confronted with a hundred and fifty accurate reproductions of Anne Hathaway's cottage, each complete with central heating and garage' and how 'all over the country the latest and most scientific methods of mass-production are being utilized to turn out a stream of old oak beams, leaded window panes and small discs of bottle-glass, all structural devices which our ancestors lost no time in abandoning as soon as an increase in wealth and knowledge enabled them to do so'.

But so what? As with any style of architecture, what matters is whether it is used well or badly. 'Mock-Tudor' the architecturally illiterate call it but it is as valid a style for reinterpretation as any other (and, after all, so much building today is essentially 'Mock Modern'). The trouble is that few historians have bothered to look at such houses despite the fact that millions of them were built in the 1920s and 1930s, preferring to concentrate on the handful of flat-roofed, Neo-Corbusian villas illustrated in the architectural journals. Admittedly many were standardised, run up by builders from pattern books. That a few token beams are still often attached to the new brick boxes run up today by the house builders testifies to the enduring appeal of Tudor imagery, though such houses seem bleak and banal when compared to even the most pedestrian examples of inter-war 'by-Pass Variegated' (to use Lancaster's evocative terminology). But some architects managed to build in Neo-Tudor with conviction, accomplishment and wit, and their work deserves attention.

One recent house, which has attracted much publicity, seems to me to be in a great tradition in its individualism and eccentricity. At the beginning of this century, Mr Robert Fidler of Honeycrock Farm at Salfords in Surrey secretly built a dream house for himself and his family – Tudor in style, of course. Secrecy was required as he did not have, and knew he would not get, planning permission for a new dwelling in a semi-rural area (although Surrey is so full of half-timbered and tile hung houses, ancient and modern, that the late Roderick Gradidge called it the 'Surrey Style'). And secrecy was achieved by building the house behind 40 foot high walls of bales of straw covered with blue tarpaulin.

For a number of years, the Fidlers lived in their house despite little daylight being able to penetrate its leaded-light windows. Then, in 2006, Mr Fidler took down the haystack to expose his triple-gabled, stone, brick, tile and timber creation – arguing that as it had stood for four years without eliciting any objections, it was lawful. But Reigate and Banstead Council, with the pedantic malevolence typical of the bureaucratic mind, argued that there were no objections because the house could not be seen and that as it was only finished when the cocoon of straw bales was taken away, the four year rule did not apply. Mr Fidler was ordered to demolish his house, a decision upheld two months ago in the High Court. This may be lawful but it does seem cruel, given the number of mediocre new housing developments for which this and other local authorities grant planning permission as a matter of course.

In the extensive press coverage, journalists presented the case as an Englishman's home being his castle, an individual versus the planners, but the offending house was inevitably and patronisingly dismissed as 'mock Tudor', the style of 'Middle England'. It seems to me, however, that Mr Fidler's house is rather well designed and well built. More to the point, the three half-timbered gables and other aspects of the design make it a more than competent essay in a continuing English tradition – in what might be regarded as the characteristic style of the 20th century. The carefully textured irregular masonry, of brick and rubble stone, achieves that picturesqueness found in such 1930s Tudor fantasies as Tudor Close at Rottingdean while the conversion of two round concrete grain silos into miniature castles like Martello Towers by facing them in stone and brick and adding battlements seems to be a piece of inspired pragmatism. As it is a much more interesting and, I suspect, better constructed and more comfortable house than most being built today, with or without the aid of a trained architect, I very much hope it survives. Indeed, Mr Fidler's castle was conceived and built in that tradition of bloody-minded individualism typical not only of such revered Arts & Crafts architects as C.F.A. Voysey but of wonderful Tudor eccentrics like Ernest Trobridge.

Ernest Trobridge (1884-1942), the 'Visionary of the Suburbs' as a new exhibition about his work at Brent Museum describes him, was one of the inter-war Neo-Tudor architects whose name is known. A devotee of the teachings of the philosopher and mystic Emanuel Swedenborg, he was an idealist and an eccentric. Most of his work is to be found in the developing north-western London suburb of Kingsbury where, after the Great War, he built half-timbered houses using green elm. He had developed his own patent system of 'compressed green wood' construction as an economical way of solving the housing problem, although few were in fact built. He also advocated the use of thatch for economy. Some of his houses are quite extraordinary, with wildly irregular fenestration and covered by undulating all-embracing thatched roofs which almost seem to be alive. The closest parallel is some of the more eccentric rural works of Dutch Expressionism of a few years earlier, though it is not clear if there is any connection. Later Trobridge designed small artfully-planned blocks of flats at Kingsbury, vaguely reminiscent of Gaudi's work, which sport battlements and external staircases. His last design, of 1938 when war seemed imminent, was for semi-detached houses in Wembley with fortified, bomb-proof garages which he called the 'WAR-DEN'.

Because the imaginativeness and eccentricity of Trobridge's houses raised them above the conventional Neo-Tudor of the suburbs, he has long had a small but distinguished following. The great Ian Nairn noticed the castellated flats in Kingsbury and wrote, in *Nairn's London* (1966) that, 'Like most true follies, more than a joke and more than a whim: a real expression of the dreams of individuality which sent people flocking here in the 1920s along with the Underground'. The same flats also appeared in John Betjeman's wonderful television film about *Metroland* a few years later, although he evidently did not know the name of the designer. Trobridge was at last properly celebrated in 1982 when an exhibition about his work, assembled by Graham Paul Smith, was shown both in Oxford and Neasden. And now, over a quarter of a century later, he is being celebrated again in the London Borough of Brent. What we need now, perhaps, is more light shone on some of the other unsung heroes of inter-war Neo-Tudor, like Blunden Shadbolt, the master of 'New "Old" Houses' of extreme irregularity and contrived antiquity.

April 2010

[*At the time of writing, Robert Fidler's house still stands although several further appeals against the council's intransigence have failed. But he fights on: good luck to him.*]

Flogging Off the Silver

English churches – both new and old – are more than places of worship and more than works of architecture. They are also the homes of works of art and craft, whether magnificent sculptured funerary monuments of the 17th, 18th and 19th centuries, or the devotional fittings themselves which may have been designed and embellished by architects, designers, painters or sculptors. To quote the introduction of John Martin Robinson's book on *Treasures of the English Churches* (Sinclair-Stevenson, London, 1995), 'More than any other old buildings they are the tangible expression and receptacle of English history. They are treasure houses of wood carving, painting, sculpture, furniture, books, musical instruments, needlework, silver plate and stained glass. Moreover, all these things have the unique impact of works of art still used and loved, and form part of their original architectural setting rather than being isolated in a museum.'

Until comparatively recently, the notion of discarding and selling such objects was unthinkable. Church furnishings and monuments were regarded as integral parts of both the history and function of a church. Reredoses or pulpits might be replaced, but that was because of changes in taste or liturgy, and usually homes would be found for them in other churches. But times have changed, and the financial consequences of declining congregations combined with the increasing threat of theft have made parishes begin to look at their works or art and craftsmanship as financial assets – or liabilities. The ever pressing costs of maintenance and repair has encouraged incumbents to consider cashing in on the art market and selling some of their treasures, and a recent case of such asset-stripping has set alarm bells ringing. It happens to concern a 19th century church and is being energetically challenged by the Victorian Society, but the precedent it could set could damage churches of any date.

St Peter's Church at Draycott in Somerset is not particularly distinguished, although it is listed at Grade II. It was designed by C.E. Giles (not a name to conjure with) and consecrated in 1861. The building gets a brief, five-line mention in the *Buildings of England* volume, but Nikolaus Pevsner did not then know what we know now: that the most impressive object in the church, the massive Neo-Romanesque font, carved with figures illustrating the Ages of Man inspired by sculptures in the Ducal Palace in Venice, was designed by William Burges, that extravagant romantic Gothic Revivalist who created Cardiff Castle for the Marquess of Bute and designed the extraordinary Tower House for himself in Melbury Road in Kensington – 'massive, learned, glittering, amazing' as W.R. Lethaby described it. It turns out that the similarly massive and amazing font was given to the new church by the Revd John Augustus Yatman, the squire of nearby Winscombe, who was one of Burges's important patrons. This discovery was made only two years ago by a collector who chooses to remain anonymous when investigating the remarkable painted Neo-Mediaeval furniture commissioned by the Yatman brothers from Burges in the late 1850s.

So far, so good. But collectors being what they are, and the modern cult of Billy Burges among Victorian enthusiasts being what it is, our anonymous collector was not content with having identified the font but offered the parish £110,000 for it. What, however, is really shocking is that the vicar and church-wardens were tempted, arguing that taking the money was essential to meet the cost of emergency repairs, even though the roof had been repaired a few years earlier with financial assistance from English Heritage and the Historic Churches Preservation Trust. 'If we don't repair the church,' the Revd Stanley Price disingenuously claimed, 'the likelihood is it will close and then the font will be lost anyway. We are not going to let that happen', although he doesn't explain what the parish would have done if the anonymous well-heeled Burges enthusiast had not suddenly appeared out of the blue.

Fortunately, the Church of England has its own Faculty Jurisdiction system for controlling alterations to churches, and the sale was opposed not only by the Victorian Society but also by the Diocesan Advisory Committee and the Council for the Care of Churches. The parish, however, then petitioned the Chancellor of the Diocese of Bath and Wells, Timothy J. Briden, who, in an extraordinary judgement, while accepting that the font is a fixture in the church, allowed its removal and sale on the grounds of pastoral need. The Victorian Society is now appealing to the Court of Arches against the judgement, arguing that, amongst other things, 'Only in the most extreme case should a sale be allowed of an object which is not redundant and which is part of, or intrinsic to, the church. This is the more so where (as here) the object is the greatest contributor to the aesthetic and architectural value of the church.'

The Chancellor's judgement must dismay anyone who loves churches – whether as works of art and architecture or as sacred buildings (not that, *pace* so many modern clergy, the two are necessarily incompatible) – for, with such a precedent, what is there to stop a cash-strapped parish with a leaking church roof flogging their Rysbrack monument or stained glass windows by Burne-Jones? 'We are a forward-looking church,' platitudinously notes Mr Price, 'and the sale of a piece of our past will guarantee the work of the church in the future.' But will it? The judgement requires that if the font is not kept in the public domain by being purchased by a museum – and it must be hoped that no museum will come forward – then it must be offered for sale at public auction. And at auction the font may well sell for far less than offered by the anonymous collector, leaving Draycott church without the one object that makes it interesting, and so less eligible for grant aid in future.

But there is no deterring the determined asset-stripper who cares nothing for art and history. In this column for March 2006 I wrote at some length about the chapel designed by James Gibbs for Sir William Turner's Hospital at Kirkleatham in the old North Riding of Yorkshire, one of the grandest sets of almshouses in England. Here, the chairman of the Hospital trustees, Peter Sotheran, had already sold the pair of elaborate gilded and upholstered chairs which flanked the communion table and had his eye on the 'gilt wood chandelier of great splendour' given to the chapel by Chomley Turner in 1747. Very properly, Redcar and Cleveland Council decided that this was a 'fixture' and refused listed building consent for its removal and sale. I am sorry to report, however, that in a recent appeal judgement, the planning inspector, Keith P. Durrant, granted listed building consent because the chandelier was not original to the building and, in his opinion, 'proportionally and visually it appears out of kilter with the galleried space around it. That is in no small measure due to its ornate Baroque style compared with the predominant simplicity of the chapel's Palladium [sic] architecture'.

So never mind that it is beautiful and special and had hung there for over two and a half centuries. To reiterate, the

Hospital, together with the church and its Turner mausoleum, the former Free Grammar School and several unusual (and neglected) estate buildings and follies, constitute one of the finest ensembles of Georgian architecture in England. But Mr Sotheran claims that it is not the job of his charity to care for historic buildings, nor does he seem concerned with the intentions of donors who gave beautiful things to enrich the lives of the charity's beneficiaries. So he now proposes to revive a project to build bungalows for the elderly in the grounds. And to pay for these, what will he sell next? There is still the glass in the Palladian window in the chapel by Sebastiano Ricci…

The trouble with asset-stripping is that the assets are finite and the institution, church, chapel or whatever is impoverished for no obvious long-term benefit. That is, we are all impoverished and future generations are denied enjoyment of these things. So in conclusion, I can do no better than to quote from the verse written by John Betjeman in 1974 when he was campaigning to prevent the demolition of Holy Trinity Church, Sloane Street, by its Rector and patron, Lord Cadogan, on the grounds that they could not afford to maintain that glorious Arts and Crafts 'cathedral': 'You who your church's vastness so deplore/Should we not sell and give it to the poor?/Recall, despite your practical suggestion/Which the disciple was who asked that question'.

February 2008

[The following year the Court of Arches accepted the arguments of the Victorian Society and ruled that no compelling need to dispose of the font had been demonstrated and that, had removal been allowed, 'much of which adorns and adds interest, both historically and architecturally, to our churches would be lost to future generations.']

Nature Versus Culture

'The regard for conservation in its widest sense raises some very difficult issues, where cultural and nature conservation conflict...' So concludes an English Heritage leaflet explaining the problems generated by *Bats in Churches*. Far from being a holistic, enlightened, conservative respect for both the man made and natural worlds, held in balance, conservation is, indeed, full of internal conflicts and fraught with the often incompatible aims of particular pressure groups. And such conflicts can even occur within the same general area of interest. The Georgian Group, for instance, would like to see a fine house like Barrington Park in Gloucestershire restored to its original 1730s state and shorn of the later good but overweening wings which the Victorian Society is bound to defend. Who is right? Who decides? As for those who are concerned with the English countryside, as we all know all too well, the romantic conservatives who claim that hunting is part of a traditional rural way of life and those who purport to care about foxes could not detest each other more.

Potential conflict between architectural and nature conservation is illustrated by the case of St George's Bloomsbury. As I discussed in this column in *Apollo* for June 2004, this great church by Nicholas Hawksmoor is being carefully restored partly with the help of public money. Yet the public will not be able to admire the cleaned and repaired north elevation of the church as the view is obscured by two tall, straggly plane trees in the churchyard which, unfortunately, despite mutilation by pruning, probably have a century of life in them. So will the nature conservation officer for the London Borough of Camden allow the World Monuments Fund to remove these ugly trees, or even to replace them by carefully sited new young ones? No; absolutely not. Now I am all in favour of trees, and am alarmed by such catastrophes as the escalating destruction of the Brazilian rain forests, but trees live and grow and can be planted while a building by Hawksmoor is unique and irreplaceable. Besides, Little Russell Street is urban, not rural, and Camden is being ridiculous.

Then there are windfarms, which generate strong passions both for and against. Now wind turbines are big, obtrusive and, for some, frightening things that, when grouped together, can disfigure and trivialise wild landscapes – and the truly wild is becoming all the more precious and rare. On the other hand, if wind power can, in fact, reduce our dependence for electricity generation on burning fossil fuels (although this seems to be disputed), perhaps we should tolerate them. After all, they will not be permanent and in due course may well go the way of the electricity pylons which once seemed ubiquitous but may eventually become so uncommon that a few will have to be listed. There are many worse and more serious threats to landscapes than wind farms: yet more roads and motorways, enlarged airports, swathes of new housing, to name but three being so enthusiastically promoted by our blinkered government.

What seems clear to me is that anyone who genuinely cares about conservation, whether of historic buildings, endangered species or the countryside, should also be deeply concerned about CO_2 emissions and global warming and thus supporting any political means to try and ameliorate its evident causes. Nobody who is not in the pay of the oil industry or the United States government can surely have any doubt about the reality of climate change, and its potential, terrifying consequences. After all, well-meaning efforts to preserve for posterity a Mediaeval church or an avenue of oaks, say, are rather point-less if Britain is to be utterly transformed – culturally as well as physically – over the next century by rising sea levels, higher temperatures, the extinction of species, food shortages, irre-sistible pressure for immigration and social breakdown. We must hope that governments might take action, but altering the profligate and destructive way we live is also the respon-sibility of each and every individual. That is to say, knowing that jet airliners are major polluters, anyone who flies off for a cheap holiday by Ryanair or Easyjet to, say, Venice to admire the Tintorettos or to drool over Palladio is, if not stupid, a hypocrite.

But I begin with a slightly less momentous issue: the problem of bats. Now bats are nice, mysterious furry creatures who seem to have many influential friends. All bats in Britain are now pro-tected under the Wildlife and Countryside Act of 1981, which requires that no work can be done to buildings which might affect bats or their roosts without consulting English Nature. And English nature considers that bats are more important than buildings. Such sentimentality means, as the late lamented Auberon Waugh constantly complained, that it is illegal for a householder whose loft is infested with bats to try and protect his property by getting rid of the wretched creatures. Now bats may be furry but they are also filthy; they fly about cheerfully defecating and peeing anywhere and everywhere, and bat drop-pings, as well as being disgusting, cause pitting and staining to porous materials while bat urine is powerfully alkaline and dissolves wooden, metal and painted surfaces.

Old churches have become very popular with bats in recent years. Even if they roost in the roof, they tend to fly about the interior of the church, peeing. The damage they do is immense, and irreversible. Unless protected, Mediaeval brasses are pitted by their droppings, as are tomb slabs. Wall paintings can also be damaged as well as all the interior woodwork and seating being rendered filthy and unpleasant. Significant damage caused by bats in recent years includes that to the important murals of c.1100 in Clayton Church in East Sussex, and to the monuments and brasses in St Mary's Broughton, Oxfordshire. Another example is the brass to Sir Hugh Hastings, who died in 1347, at Elsing Church in Norfolk; in 1984 this was in perfect condition, with fragments of the original inlaid colouring surviving; today it is pitted, blotched and ruined thanks to legally protected *pipistrelle* bats. Great damage has been done to almost all the fittings and furnishings inside the Fitzalan Chapel at Arundel while many Mediaeval painted screens are at risk from urine drips eating through the pigments.

Yet, apart from covering up the most precious objects and monuments, parish councils can do little about these natural depredations. Indeed, on the standard form for applying for a Faculty for any repairs or alteration to an Anglican church (and almost all Mediaeval, country churches belong to the Church of England) there is a question about the possibility of bats being disturbed by the work. Surely our priorities are quite wrong here. Ancient churches are some of the most beautiful, precious and historically important buildings we possess, and the monuments and furnishings in them are, I must reiterate, irreplaceable. Bats, on the other hand, seem to have little difficulty in reproducing themselves and there would seem to be no real shortage of them.

Yes, some of the sixteen species of British bats are endangered (and one became extinct in 1990), but allowing our finite stock of Mediaeval churches to be spoiled is scarcely the best answer. As the English Heritage pamphlet observes, 'The decline in bat numbers has been caused by changes in agricultural practice resulting in a reduction of insect abundance and loss of pasture, deciduous woodland, and hedgerows, and by the loss of roosts in buildings and old trees...' It is not just bats who are affected by modern agricultural methods, which are a major factor in the general spoiling of the countryside and skewing the natural order of things. Surely legislative attempts to protect bats should begin with tackling the agricultural interest and not by being so cavalier with historic buildings. Other European countries would seem to be more sensible and have legislation which establishes a hierarchy of conservation priorities – and in Austria, for instance, culture comes before nature.

So what is an English parish to do if a church is colonised by these protected intruders? They are tenacious creatures, even without legal impunity. One suggestion is that an afflicted parish should go Anglo-Catholic, for bats are notoriously Low Church and hate the smell of incense, but I am sorry now to learn that this is a myth. Perhaps the best solution is to invite natural predators into the building, remembering the Iron Duke's succinct and wise advice to Queen Victoria to deal with the problem of bird droppings from the trees enclosed within the Crystal Palace in Hyde Park: 'sparrow-hawks, ma'am.' Owls?

July 2005

Gothic Revival

Obituaries are sometimes written too soon. Seventy years ago, Harry Goodhart-Rendel dated the death of the Gothic Revival – that vital national artistic movement he admired and understood so well – to the years in which the great central tower of Giles Scott's Liverpool Cathedral was beginning to rise. He was (for once) wrong, just as he was mistaken in stating that 'any hope for its future must be based upon its possible reappearance in a form so changed to suit changed methods of construction'. Proof of that is the completion of another Gothic cathedral tower, one that is rather smaller and less original than Scott's in Liverpool but which is nevertheless an extraordinary triumph – a triumph of traditional values and methods of construction as well as of resolution in the face of adversity, hostility and indifference.

Suffolk has been the unlikely setting for this architectural drama. The scaffolding is now coming down at Bury St

Edmunds Cathedral to expose gilded weathervanes and crocketted pinnacles, flint flushwork battlements and stepped buttresses on a tall tower which might well have been designed by John Wastell, the architect who, in the early 16th century, built the nave of the former parish church of St James, behind which once stood the huge abbey church containing the shrine of St Edmund. Built of Barnack stone using methods little different in essence from those Wastell must have employed, this new tower may well soon look as if it has been there for centuries. But its timeless serenity was only achieved after a struggle and because of the bloody-minded determination of two little-known architects who continued to believe in the pointed arch. The first was the late Stephen Dykes Bower, who was so unfashionable and out of his time in the *zeitgeist*-conscious 20th century that, despite having been Surveyor to Westminster Abbey, he has been largely written out of architectural history; the second is his sometime assistant, Warwick Pethers, whose name is conspicuous by its absence in all the literature about the Cathedral.

Dykes Bower was appointed cathedral architect in 1943, an inauspicious year. He was then already antipathetic to a modernist approach to church design, and as a student at the Architectural Association in the 1920s he had been unusual for his sympathy for the Gothic Revival as a living movement, even confessing an unlikely admiration for the work of Sir Gilbert Scott. Ironically, at Bury, he was obliged to demolish the chancel designed by Scott which had replaced an 18th century structure. Dykes Bower's task was to convert the Mediaeval parish church into a visibly convincing cathedral (its status had been elevated in 1914) by adding transepts and a much larger chancel (choir) as well as a new cloister and porch. And one day a tower might rise over the new crossing... Construction finally began in 1959. The new transepts and choir are all in a Late Gothic style, harmonious with the nave, but in a flat, spare manner, enlivened with flushwork, that is reminiscent of the work of some of Dykes Bower's Late Victorian heroes: Temple Moore and Walter Tapper. What is very much in his own style is the bright colouring of the roofs, for he was an artist who (unusually again) continued to believe in artistic unity and had no patience with antiquarian sentimentality or conservationist restraint.

Work stopped in 1970, leaving blocked arches in the incomplete north transept, only a few bays of the intended cloister and reinforcement rods protruding vainly from the stump of the crossing tower. The architectural climate could not have been more inimical to Dykes Bower's vision while a new Provost was hostile to money being spent on building. But he never gave up, and continued to dream, and design. Somehow, in 1990, a cathedral centre was completed – faced in brick rather than stone – to the north of the choir, with Dykes Bower as consultant. But what really got the building project going again was his own death in 1994 at the age of 91, for it emerged that in his will he had left £2½ million to the Cathedral (a fortune not made from architecture: he was one of four bachelor brothers, and the last to go). Now the cathedral authorities certainly didn't want to continue building, but money is always worth having and a bequest like that is not to be sniffed at… And then the National Lottery and Millennium Commission came into existence and it became clear that more necessary millions could be raised. A momentum slowly built up.

First, however, it had to be decided what was to be built, and who was going to be the architect in charge. Before he died, Dykes Bower had set up a trust for Bury and indicated that he wanted Warwick Pethers to continue his work. Pethers had also been a student at the A.A. but in a less tolerant decade, and he became disillusioned with the modernism he had been taught. After spending time in America, he had asked to work for Dykes Bower so that he could learn about alternative, traditional approaches to design. The problem was that he was not only unknown but inexperienced. But Pethers had the political skills necessary for successful practice, so he brought in a well-established firm of conservation architects with whom he thought he could work. And then he had to fight to make sure Dykes Bower's intentions were not betrayed.

First came the battle between advocates of a short tower and those who wanted a much taller tower over the crossing. There should have been no dispute about this, for Dykes Bower himself had prepared a design for a tall steeple in about 1962. This was unusual: a concave-sided pyramid roof supporting a high *flèche* rising above a Perpendicular Gothic square tower to create a profile curiously reminiscent of the Empire State Building. Possibly inspired by the Low Countries, this would have been 'a unique symbol for Suffolk' – but it had few admirers (and, I am now sorry to say, I was not one of them). It then emerged that Dykes Bower had also prepared sketch designs for a much shorter tower in 1980. In fact, he had only done this in order to secure estimates, but the short tower was supported by everyone – clergy, advisory committees, modern architects – who didn't really want anything built at all, and certainly nothing properly Gothic. This situation was resolved by the emergence of a new design for a tall tower, a scholarly essay in Perp. in the spirit of Dykes Bower, which won the support of the Millennium Commission and other funders.

This design was acceptable partly because it was attributed to Hugh Matthew, the architect who had assisted Dykes Bower on building the crossing back in the 1960s. In fact, it was entirely the work of Warwick Pethers (Matthew has designed the interior timber vault in the tall lantern which has yet to be installed). With this design eventually approved, Pethers and Matthew joined forces as the Gothic Design Practice and, after all the many and necessary consents had been secured, work finally began in the year 2000. But there were other battles that had to be fought. The new work at Bury has been a live experiment in traditional construction methods – particularly concerning what has become the esoteric cult of lime mortar as the traditional, flexible and longer-lasting alternative to rigid Portland cement. The new tower, north transept extension, chapel and cloister bays are all built of cut stone laid with lime over solid brickwork. This was the method used by the Mediaeval builders, but it frightens modern contractors and engineers as it doesn't easily conform with the many pedantic building regulations now in force. But Pethers somehow got his own way, and the new masonry is a joy to see – and touch; indeed, it is much better in quality than Dykes Bower's work.

This whole story is worth telling (albeit briefly here) as it shows how many obstacles there are to building something well in an unfashionable style (and architecture today is all about fashion). And it is quite extraordinary how one unknown architect has managed not only to see off the better-connected firm that tried to take over the job but also to outwit opposition from the cathedral authorities, the clergy, the parish, local grandees and the myriad of interfering advisory committees (the local climate of resentment against the whole project suggests that Trollope was writing about a perennial Anglican situation). In consequence, Bury St Edmunds has a proud landmark tower that completes the cathedral and is a worthy Millennium monument – an optimistic symbol of faith and continuity that cost a mere £12 million (rather cheaper than Blair's stupid Dome). Yet Pethers insists he would rather have built Dykes Bower's original scheme. Certainly his design for the tower is conservative rather than innovative, scholarly not conspicuously original. Its sources are clear: Wastell's Bell Harry tower at Canterbury, Lavenham and the new (19th century) tower at Long Melford designed by Dykes Bower's greatest hero, G.F. Bodley. Perhaps no more should be expected when the Gothic Revival has ebbed and is little understood (although the new north chapel and arcade, with beautiful mouldings dying into circular columns, suggests he does have a creative imagination). Pethers, however, is keen to point out that, thanks to the conservation movement and the more tolerant plurality of Post-Modernism, he has worked in a more sympathetic climate than that in which Dykes Bower struggled.

So will the Bury tower now, finally, mark the end of the Gothic Revival? I hope it is too early to say – there is still the four-sided cloister to complete, after all. And then what? I note that the crossing tower of Westminster Abbey remains unfinished... and the Gothic Design Practice has shown what can still be done – even in the 21st century.

May 2005

[Since 2005, a project to build something above the crossing at Westminster Abbey has come and gone while at Bury St Edmunds continuing provincial pettiness has resulted in Warwick Pethers being no longer employed – despite the success of his tower – and the cloister remains incomplete. There has, however, been the boon of the monograph on Dykes Bower by Anthony Symondson published in 2011 by RIBA Publishing in the English Heritage and Twentieth Century Society series on Twentieth Century Architects.]

Inspired Patronage

St Elizabeth's, Eastbourne, was consecrated by George Bell, Bishop of Chichester, in 1938. Designed by the local architects Peter D. Stonham, Son & A.R.G. Fenning and sited in a suburb of the Sussex seaside town, it is a large, gaunt brick Gothic building in that tradition of urban Anglican churches which Charles Booth once called the 'bare style'. Typical of its period is the way the upper parts of the walls step back above the buttresses before reaching a straight parapet. Unfortunately, this feature, together with poor detailing to the windows and the use of ferrous rods as wall ties, has led to structural problems due to water penetration. These are not insuperable, and the architect Nicholas Hills has proposed an ingenious solution which involves adding a new roof with generous overhanging eaves to throw the rain water off the walls. But this will be expensive: is it really worth doing?

St Elizabeth's may be a fine building, but it is not as distinguished as contemporary churches by, say, Giles Gilbert Scott
or Edward Maufe. Oddly enough, what most merits preservation is in the crypt, where there are murals by the German
Jewish refugee artist Hans Feibusch. These were painted in
1944 and represent the second commission he received from
Bishop Bell (the first being in St Wilfrid's, Brighton – a magnificent building by Harry Goodhart-Rendel since mutilated
by being converted into flats). Feibusch, who died in 1998 just
before his 100th birthday and who had served the Kaiser on
the Eastern Front during the Great War, had achieved notice
as a painter before he was forced to leave his native land in
1933. Later he achieved the distinction of being represented in
the Nazi exhibition of 'Degenerate Art' in Munich in 1937. In
England, his skill and sympathy as a muralist led to a remarkable number of church commissions. In London, for example,
there is the *Trinity in Glory* on the huge east wall of St Alban's,
Holborn, and the triptych in St Etheldreda's, Bishopsgate
(damaged but not destroyed by the IRA bomb).

In the admirable *Otter Memorial Paper* devoted to Feibusch
(edited by Paul Foster and published in Chichester), Alan
Powers writes that he was 'an artist who represents many
things which have been left out of conventional art history'.
Hence, perhaps, Nikolaus Pevsner's dismissal of his mural
in Chichester Cathedral: 'What is to be said? More modern in
style than most English paintings of this date [1951] and position, yet nowhere near a truly C20 religious expression.' But
what is a truly 20th-century expression? Certainly Feibusch
was an Expressionist in German terms, and his work can be
an acquired taste – especially because of his colouring. But he
was a superb draughtsman and he knew how to work with
architecture. His murals not only deserve respect, but they can
be powerful and moving. In the crypt at Eastbourne his subject
was *Pilgrim's Progress* and he painted it as a thanksgiving for
the welcome he had received in England.

Those murals deserve preservation as fine works by an underrated artist whose life in exile says so much about the terrible history of the last century. They might also be regarded as a memorial to Bishop Bell (1883-1958), who asked to meet Feibusch in 1940. Bell's ashes were discreetly interred in Chichester Cathedral so perhaps a memorial elsewhere might be appropriate – modest though Bell was. After all, he was perhaps the most impressive and saintly prelate produced by the Church of England in the 20th century, committed to ecumenism, reconciliation and social justice, and consistent in condemning tyranny. His principled and courageous stand against the saturation bombing of German cities and the refusal of the British government to distinguish between the German people and the Nazi enemy remains a redeeming bright light in a dark period (his speech on the subject in the House of Lords in 1944 is said to have cost him the chance of becoming Archbishop of Canterbury). This great, compassionate man was also remarkable as a patron of the arts, asking T.S. Eliot, for instance, to write *Murder in the Cathedral* as well as commissioning artists like Feibusch

Coincidentally, Bell's time at Chichester overlapped with that of another remarkably imaginative clerical patron of the arts, Walter Hussey (1909-85). Before he went to Chichester as Dean in 1955, he had been vicar of St Matthew's Northampton, for whose fiftieth anniversary he commissioned Benjamin Britten to write the cantata *Rejoice in the Lamb*. That was in 1943 and in the same year he secured the famous '*Northampton Madonna*' from Henry Moore. This sits in the north transept of the big, comfortable Gothic church designed by Matthew Holding. A few years later, this was joined by Graham Sutherland's searing *Crucifixion* in the opposite, south transept. Pevsner had no problem with these works, as they were unimpeachably *avant-garde*, remarking that 'The Moore is as peaceful as the Sutherland is violent.' But Hussey had the support of his congregation in installing them. As Giles Watson remarks, in his essay in the new *Oxford Dictionary of National Biography*, 'It was not a coincidence that this occurred amid 1940s austerity; Hussey's sacramental aesthetic, like that of Bishop Bell of Chichester, was nourished by a conviction that the vision of the artist, in conjunction with that of the church, was a weapon in the spiritual arsenal of "Christian civilization", essential for combating the cultural influence of totalitarianism.'

Hussey's legacy in Chichester is equally important and enduring. In addition to leaving most of his personal art collection to the Pallant House Gallery (the rest went to Northampton), he commissioned works for the Cathedral. In addition to the Feibusch mural, there was a window by Marc Chagall, another painting from Sutherland – *Noli me tangere* – and a tapestry by John Piper above the altar. Such names might imply that Hussey simply used the Cathedral as a sort of art gallery, but all the works he acquired had a definite symbolic and liturgical purpose while enhancing the architecture. Furthermore, he looked after the building with intelligence, putting back the 15th century Arundel Screen under the crossing, whose foolish removal a century earlier seemed to have precipitated the spectacular collapse of the central tower and spire in 1861.

This inspired and intelligent patronage by both Hussey and Bell is worth recalling not only because it was rare in its time (although the impulse and the taste were echoed in the contemporary creation of Coventry Cathedral) but because it seems without parallel in the Church of England, both before or since. To quote Pevsner (again) from the *Buildings of England*, writing in 1965 about the Sutherland, 'If it seems, as it is, too self-conscious, that is largely the fault of the inertia that has sat on the Church of England for a century, and still does in places less enlightened than Chichester.' For all the many and great merits of Gothic Revival churches, the controlling hand of Scott, Bodley or Pearson seems to have had little room for the independent, distinguished work of art. The exceptions, perhaps, are windows by Morris & Co. rather than sculptures or paintings. It was precisely this rigid control by the architect against which the Arts and Crafts movement rebelled, so that J.D. Sedding filled Holy Trinity, Sloane Street, with superb furniture and fittings by several different artists and craftsmen. Even so, there is no one object in that lovely interior that stands out as a great work of art in its own right. The only example I can think of from that period is the great mosaic mural by Frank Brangwyn in St Aidan's, Roundhay Road, Leeds.

And since?... Oh dear: that impulse to do something new seems to have become destructive rather than constructive, involving the throwing out of pews and pulpits in the cause of change and relevance rather than adding anything appropriate and distinguished. And then there is the problem that few artists seem to want their creations outside the established setting of the art gallery, and fewer still (of ability) seem interested in the life and work of the Church. There are exceptions, of course, but one in particular rather proves the rule. In 1987, at the instigation of Peter Palumbo, a large circular altar of white marble by Henry Moore, weighing over ten tons, was installed directly under the dome of Wren's famous church of St Stephen Walbrook (requiring the gratuitous strengthening of the floor where there were once box-pews). When reluctantly accepting the commission, the sculptor was apparently told to imagine the sort of altar on which Abraham attempted to sacrifice his son Isaac – which is not exactly what the rubrics of the Anglican Church envisage for the celebration of Holy Communion. The resulting stone – once appropriately described as looking like 'a ripe Camembert' – is therefore liturgically absurd. It is also visually destructive as it wrecks the tension between the centralised space created by Wren and the longitudinal axis focussed on the original reredos and Communion table in a City Church which, more than any other, deserves a full, coherent restoration.

Walter Hussey was never so foolish, or so concerned with the novelty and status of a work by a particular famous artist. Rather, he sought continuity while the objects he commissioned had clear purpose. 'Art of high standard can and should be offered to God,' he believed, 'and in the offering symbolise all that should be offered by mankind.' Good church furnishings therefore deserve respect, whether Victorian pulpits, Arts and Crafts metalwork, or murals by Hans Feibusch. And St Elizabeth's, Eastbourne, deserves help.

March 2005

[Although the parish has moved into the adjacent church hall, St Elizabeth's Church still stands, but in poor condition. Hans Feibusch's mural does not survive in the restored St Ethelburga's, Bishopsgate.]

Sell the Rubens

Returning to Cambridge as a research fellow some thirty years after I graduated, I find, of course, that some things have changed, and not always for the worse. But much remains the same and, unfortunately, this includes the result of what has always seemed to me one of the greatest aesthetic scandals of the last century, perpetrated during my time as an undergraduate. I refer to the mutilation of the interior of the east end of King's College Chapel to incorporate Rubens' 1634 painting *The Adoration of the Magi*. It may have been done during the year of revolutions, 1968, but the cavalier arrogance with which one of the supreme examples of English Perpendicular architecture – and surely one of the great buildings of Europe – was treated remains astonishing as well as shocking. And it is shocking that nothing has yet been done to undo the damage.

As few among the public who queue every day to hear choral evensong at King's can be aware of how the choir of the chapel used to and ought to look, it is worth rehearsing the story of this scandal again. It began in 1961, when Major A.E. Allnott, who had bought the Rubens two years earlier from the estate of the Duke of Westminster for a record £275,000, offered to give it to King's College. If ever a gift-horse was worth looking in the mouth this was it: the painting is huge – some 4.2 metres high by 3.2 wide – and there was nowhere to put it in the chapel. But one Fellow of King's was determined that the college should have it. Michael Jaffé, head of the University's new fine art department and future director of the Fitzwilliam Museum, who, in addition to being a powerful personality, could wield authority as an expert on Rubens.

Jaffé's first proposal, incredibly, was to hang the picture (which, being painted on wood, weighs some 15 cwt.) above the central opening in the chapel's glorious timber screen, installed in the time of Henry VIII. However, the architects Maguire & Murray were already employed by the college to rearrange the east end of the chapel and they strongly recommended that the Rubens be installed on an easel on one side of the ante-chapel. But when Jaffé, together with the Provost, Noel Annan, conspired that it should go in pride of place, on axis above the high altar, they resigned. They were replaced by the more accommodating Sir Martyn Beckett, Bt, a country-house architect whom nobody has ever accused of displaying sensitivity (and who, interestingly, was a kinsman of the notorious Lord Grimthorpe, the lawyer who despoiled St Alban's Abbey in the 1880s). In 1964, the existing timber reredos and the panelling connecting it with the choir stalls were stripped out; four years later the floor levels were lowered so that the Rubens could fit underneath the east window of the Chapel. It had been removed from its original frame and now was given fatuous blank wings to make a pseudo-triptych to give it a greater presence.

To achieve this dubious end, two whopping lies were told to both the college's governing body and the wider public. The first was that the new level floor from choir screen to the east end was a 'restoration' and that the *gradus chori* or step to the east of the stalls and the further steps to the altar were installed only in 1774. In fact, the history of the choir arrangements had been carefully charted in a report by Maguire & Murray (which was suppressed). The will of the college's founder, Henry VI, specified steps and stated that the high altar should be raised three feet above the choir floor. Even without documents, however, the physical evidence for the antiquity of the raised floor was clear: the stonework and plinths (since covered up by a new stone dado) indicated the original levels, and the two small doors which once opened directly off the sanctuary can today only be reached up flights of steps. But there is worse: when the sanctuary floor was dug up, it was found to rest on Tudor brick arched vaults – which were then destroyed. Human remains were also discovered, and lead coffins dating back to the 15th century. These had to be removed so the floor could be lowered (further proof that the original level was higher) but the workmen refused to continue until this was done properly and a service held. Even so, the college seems to have kept no records of the number and positions of these discoveries: so much for scholarship and truth.

The second lie was that the discarded panelling was 'Victorian and not of good quality' when, in fact, none of it was 19th-century and all of it was very fine. The reredos and flanking panelling had been installed in 1911 and was a scholarly and appropriate Classical design by the distinguished Arts and Crafts architect Detmar Blow, while the panelling between this and the choir stalls dated from 1678-79 and was the work of Cornelius Austin, who was responsible for the present canopies above the Tudor stalls. Removing all this means that there is no longer a continuous horizontal band of warm dark woodwork enclosing the whole choir. Worse, the exposed wall is bare and ugly, relieved only by large and grotesque modernistic candle sconces designed by Beckett. As the 15th-century architects of the chapel ensured that all the internal walls were articulated and ornamented by a pattern of shafts, panels and heraldic carving, the idea the lower walls of the choir were intended to be bare is simply ludicrous. The vaulting shafts and window jambs spring from a consistent level at the height of the stalls and clearly the blank walls below must have been intended for tapestry hangings if not for panelling. The present arrangement is barbaric, but it is not only an aesthetic disaster, as it fails in liturgical terms as well. A former chaplain of King's tells me he wanted to undo the damage done by Jaffé and Beckett as the white, bare walls create a barren gulf between the activity in the stalls and the remote, semi-secularised high altar, which is further diminished by now being too low.

So what should be done? As the protagonists in this scandal are now dead, the answer is clear: the Rubens should be sold. It has no historic connection with the chapel and, besides, King's needs the money. The college is no longer the exciting, trendy institution it was perceived to be in the 1960s and is now running a defecit of over £1 million a year. Last November, sensationally, the bursar was suspended. Now I am a buildings man and no expert on flat art, but it seems to me that selling the Rubens would be no loss. Its colouring is not in harmony with that of the glorious Flemish stained glass and Reynolds thought the painting 'a slight performance', while the Emperor Joseph II declined to purchase it after it had left its home in a convent in Louvain. Even so, as Rubens' *Massacre of the Innocents* was sold for £49.5 million two years ago, it ought to fetch a decent sum. A proportion of the proceeds could then make the college solvent again while the rest should be spent on restoring the original floor levels and putting back the panelling – which is apparently still in store at the yard of Rattee & Kett, the Cambridge contractors.

The question is: can King's be shamed into behaving decently? Back in 1966, Provost Annan actually had the gall to tell a concerned Royal Fine Art Commission that they were 'entitled to do as they like' with this magnificent building, this monument of European importance, and disregarded the opinions of the likes of Nikolaus Pevsner, John Piper, Henry Moore and Kenneth Clark. In truth, King's College has shown itself in recent years to be unfit to be the custodian of the celebrated chapel – the shop designed in a crude Gothic manner which today obstructs and disfigures the ante-chapel is a further disgrace. But it is not too late to make amends: the Rubens should go.

May 2004

[Unfortunately, the wretched Rubens is still in place and no attempt has been made to repair the results of the vandalism of the 1960s in King's College Chapel. In fact, the delinquent, irresponsible college has made matters worse. Hoping nobody would notice, in 2006 it conducted a shabby, back-street sale of many interesting artefacts given to the college by benefactors. These included the two mag-nificent tall brass candle standards designed for the Chapel in 1871 by George Gilbert Scott junior to harmonise with the 16th century bronze lectern and which stood in the choir until 1964. Their present whereabouts is unknown.

This article generated more correspondence (entirely in favour) than any other I have contributed to Apollo. *One congratulatory letter came from the late Hugh Montefiore, the former Bishop of Birmingham, who at the time of 'the ridiculous reordering of the Chapel' was Vicar of Great St Mary's: 'I remember the row I caused by criticising the reordering on theological grounds in our monthly letter, and this got into the papers. I pointed out that King's Chapel was living up to its reputation as a humanist temple by removing the cross from the altar, and substituting on the East wall that picture of a myth.']*

A Tomb for a King

The recent, extraordinary discovery of the remains of Richard III – England's last Plantaganet King, killed at the Battle of Bosworth Field in 1485 – presents an intriguing design opportunity. The defeated king is to be reburied not in York, as some have urged, but in Leicester where his body was originally taken and buried, and his final resting place is to be Leicester Cathedral. Modern Yorkists have been snobbishly disparaging about this, objecting that it is modern and unworthy. It may have been given cathedral status in 1927, but the former parish church of St Martin is in fact a Mediaeval building, although much restored and enlarged in the 19th century. And – unlike York Minster – it would benefit from a striking modern intervention such as a royal tomb – or tomb chapel, perhaps.

The Richard III Society has already published a design for a table tomb for the slain monarch: a traditional concept ornamented with the white rose of York and the cross of St Cuthbert and its flat top relieved by an inlaid brass plaque and a coat of arms. But this is surely rather dull and simply not ambitious enough. The model for such a thing is obvious – a majority of England's kings and queens are interred in or under elaborate tomb chests on the top of which lie an effigy of the monarch, usually accompanied by his consort. And most of these, from Henry III to Elizabeth I, are in Westminster Abbey. The most magnificent is that of Henry VII – the first of the Tudors who defeated Richard III at Bosworth – set in the centre of the glorious Perpendicular Gothic chapel that bears his name, surrounded by a glorious metal screen and bearing gilt bronze effigies of the king and his queen modelled by the Italian sculptor Pietro Torrigiano.

After Elizabeth, this tradition faltered, largely owing to England's turbulent history in the 17th century. Projects for tombs – including that of Henry VIII – remained unexecuted or incomplete. And then, after the burial of Queen Anne in Henry VII's Chapel at Westminster, monarchs were laid to rest at Windsor. All the Hanoverians ended up in the Royal Crypt in St George's Chapel, but none of them – not even George III after his 60-year reign – is commemorated by a fine funerary monument. The tradition of table tombs and effigies was, however, revived by Queen Victoria following the death of her beloved consort, Prince Albert, in 1861. She built the Royal Mausoleum at Frogmore in Windsor Great Park to contain tomb chests bearing the figures of Albert and, eventually, herself, modelled by Albert's favourite sculptor, Carlo Marochetti. The whole conception of this mausoleum, designed by the obscure A.J. Humbert, is Germanic, and Michael Hall tells me that the inspiration for the effigies was not the ancient royal tombs at Westminster but the mausoleum built at Herrenhausen outside Hanover in the 1840s by Victoria's 'wicked uncle' Ernst Augustus, the penultimate King of Hanover, to house tomb chests with effigies of himself and his queen.

Another recumbent effigy of Prince Albert is placed on the cenotaph in the chapel at the east end of St George's Windsor which Victoria made into the Albert Memorial. But this chapel is now dominated by the tomb of the Duke of Clarence, the unfortunate eldest son of the future Edward VII, who died in 1892, a monument clearly inspired by the tomb of Henry VII and surely the finest example of royal patronage in recent centuries. It was created by the sculptor Alfred Gilbert – he of 'Eros' in Piccadilly Circus – who gave traditional forms a mysterious, *art nouveau* character and surrounded the effigy of the prince with exquisite small figures. If a mere heir to the throne who was, by all accounts, dim and useless, was given a tomb of this magnificence, surely Richard III deserves more than a table tomb. After all, the tradition of sculptured effigies continued well into the 20th century, for there are white marble recumbent figures of Edward VII and Queen Alexandra (by Bertram Mackennal) and of George V and Queen Mary (by William Reid Dick) to be seen in St George's Chapel.

Given the exhaustive, almost indecent, analysis of Richard III's skeleton with its twisted spine by the University of Leicester, it would surely be possible for a good sculptor to make a suitable effigy – after all, many Mediaeval effigies were not, in fact, accurate portraits. But then the vexed question of style has to be addressed. The figures on the tomb of Henry VII can be seen as the dawn of the Renaissance in England, but the tomb of the king he destroyed should surely not be in that style. It should rather be Gothic, Perpendicular Gothic, the vigorous, national English style of Richard's time. But who could design such a thing? We now have a small number of competent modern Classical architects, but their attempts at Gothic are feeble. Perhaps the only person capable of doing convincing Gothic today is Warwick Pethers, the architect responsible for the magnificent crossing tower which now rises above Bury St Edmunds Cathedral [see *Apollo* for May 2005, above].

It may be, however, that a rather less traditional approach might best succeed. The last monarch to be buried in St George's Chapel Windsor is George VI. He lies, under a plain ledger stone inspirited by that for Henry VI, in a new chapel added to the exterior of the building, tucked between the projecting Rutland Chapel and the north choir aisle. Built in 1967-69, it was designed by George Pace with Paul Paget and, by being in the abstracted and stylised rectilinear Gothic manner that Pace made his own, it succeeds in being at once modern and traditional while being a discreet addition to the great Mediaeval building. Interestingly, in explaining his design, Pace wrote how 'When Alfred Gilbert was designing the Duke of Clarence tomb for the chapel he said – "I am determined to treat the whole work in such a way that its general appearance should be that of Gothic yet devoid of the slightest evidence of imitation".' An addition in this spirit would greatly enhance Leicester Cathedral.

As for the tomb itself, a striking modern solution is suggested not by anything in Britain but in Prague Castle where, in the 1920s, that great genius, Joze Plečnik, demonstrated how traditional forms can be creatively and sympathetically adapted in an historic setting. Within the castle is the Mediaeval Cathedral of St Vitus, only finally completed in 1929. Soon afterwards, in 1934-35, the royal mausoleum under the nave floor was recast by the architect Kamil Roškot (not a pupil of Plečnik but of the Czech modernist Josef Gočar) in a manner which reflects the progressive outlook of the newly established Republic of Czecho-Slovakia. Beneath a low vault, covered in mosaic, new tombs were made for the old Bohemian kings which are very different in character to the elaborate monuments in the cathedral above. Some are simple and severe monoliths of granite, relying on surface and chamfer. But most impressive is the new tomb of Karel (Charles) IV, the King of Bohemia, later Holy Roman Emperor, who began the cathedral in 1344. It is of metal, streamlined like a futurist military tank, with further interest given by applied heraldic blocks. This tomb is extraordinary, unprecedented and yet dignified and suitably imperious. If the proposed new tomb of Richard III were to be as bold and imaginative, the much-slandered and abused Plantaganet king would be well honoured and Leicester Cathedral made much more interesting.

April 2013

The Empty Plinth

If the King had had his way, the public space in front of the National Gallery would be William IV Square rather than being named after Nelson's great victory over the Franco-Spanish fleet. Like so much in England, this urban focus – in fact an irregular pentagon rather than a square – was created by accident rather than design. Trafalgar Square is a consequence of the removal of the old Royal Mews combined with the contemporary street improvements being carried out by that sole, sympathetic genius in the history of English town planning, John Nash. It was Nash who proposed putting a public building on the north side of the cleared space, but it was Charles Barry who levelled the sloping site leaving a terrace to the north. And only in 1838, with Victoria a year on the throne, was the new square proposed as the site for the long-overdue memorial to England's naval hero.

The erection of William Railton's colossal and overscaled

Corinthian column set the military tone to Trafalgar Square (but how reticent London is about our victories compared with complacently militaristic Paris, with only Trafalgar and Waterloo nominally commemorated). Generals Havelock and Napier followed, along with Admirals Jellicoe, Beatty and Cunningham. But Le Sueur's statue of Charles I, the first equestrian bronze in England, was already there, on the site of the ancient Charing Cross. And the eastern of the two granite pedestals placed symmetrically at either end of the North Terrace was immediately filled by an equestrian statue by Francis Chantrey of that preposterous but magnificent royal patron of the arts (and of Nash) King George IV (a sculpture originally intended for the Marble Arch when it stood in front of Buckingham Palace). This left the other pedestal for, presumably, a future Royal Personage but it has remained empty for over a hundred and sixty years.

Only recently has the Empty Plinth become a focus of concern and attention, being used in consequence for a series of temporary, attention-seeking modern sculptural gestures. The latest is Marc Quinn's naked marble figure of 'Alison Lapper Pregnant'. As a polemical public statement about perceptions of deformity and the triumph of the human spirit over severe disadvantages it is admirable (although, as many have now pointed out, we already had a sculpture of a disabled person in Trafalgar Square in the shape of the one-armed, one-eyed sailor on top of that column). But as a work of sculpture, a work of art, it is lamentable and it is a mercy that, like the earlier pieces, it will occupy that plinth for only eighteen months. There is, however, a new sculptural proposal for the square which is to be permanent: a statue of Nelson Mandela on the North Terrace in front of the National Gallery. This has generated much controversy and is currently the subject of a public inquiry, as the project is opposed by both the City of Westminster and English Heritage.

All these recent proposals say much about modern Britain

and, in particular, about our unease with our Imperial past. But whatever the sins of the British Empire – and there were many – it existed, and Trafalgar Square, like much else, is an inescapable, tangible expression of our history. Some, however, would like to atone for, or defuse, that past by altering the square. In particular, Ken Livingstone, Mayor of London, a strong supporter of the Mandela statue who pushed through the naïve and gratuitous new flight of steps which replaced Barry's sheltering retaining wall, has proposed removing the statues of Havelock and Napier. An inscription on the plinth of the latter insists that it was largely paid for by the subscriptions of private soldiers; nevertheless, the Mayor can cheerfully admit that, 'I have not a clue who two of the generals are or what they did' – a statement which may well say more about Mr Livingstone than about the importance of those distant men. Both, of course, were instrumental in the British acquisition of the Indian sub-continent (Napier being the ostensible author of that celebrated telegraphic pun: 'Peccavi' – 'I have Sind') and so have a pregnant relevance to the state of the country today.

There is no doubt that Nelson Mandela is a towering and inspiring figure who deserves permanent commemoration in London, not least as the Republic of South Africa was once part of the British Empire. Whether a public space dedicated to British military victories is the right place for it is another matter – even if the South African Embassy is on the east side of the square (English Heritage arguing that the statue should be placed, if anywhere, on the pavement in front). Ian Walters, the sculptor of the figure, insists that 'The North Terrace is the most fitting place in which this statue can express the universal recognition of Mandela's great humanity.' But the main objection to his nine-foot high figure in a loose shirt is that it is a stiff, naive and mediocre piece of work. Although public sculpture, like war memorials (which I discussed in this column last June) are increasingly popular and seem to be proliferating in indirect proportion to the greatness of Great Britain, sculptors seem to have forgotten what statues are for: that they are not just portraits but should also be symbolic, commemorative works of art, of high seriousness and significance. As Glyn Williams, professor of sculpture at the Royal Academy, said in evidence to the inquiry, 'An important public memorial needs a stronger sculptural sense rather than mimetic rendering. The work must be timeless if we are to take it seriously.'

We have been here before. In the late 1920s there was controversy over the equestrian statue of the late Field-Marshall Douglas Haig intended for Whitehall, with his widow and others objecting that Alfred Hardiman's model didn't look like the man. As the *Architectural Review* commented at the time, the objectors were wrong because the statue was intended not as a private but a national monument, and, 'For such a monument the symbol of the *equestrian state* is required, and it is essential that the statue be symbolical, and not the portrait of a gentleman on the portrait of a horse.' In the event Haig – who insisted to the last that cavalry was not rendered obsolete by the machine gun and the tank – got the statue he deserved in Edinburgh Castle: a ludicrously gauche portrait on a realistic horse. In Whitehall he is commemorated by the work of art he didn't deserve: a taut, sophisticated, authoritative composition on a carefully designed plinth (by Roland Pearce). And if a callous brute like Haig is commemorated by so superb a sculpture, how much more does Mandela deserve something exceptional. The problem is finding a sculptor alive today who could do what is needed.

The statue of David Hume in the Royal Mile in Edinburgh suggests that Alexander Stoddart might be able to, for he is a brilliant, misunderstood sculptor who achieves the necessary symbolic authority by working in the Neo-Classical tradition: Hume is not in contemporary dress but is depicted in a toga. Perhaps there are others, but they have certainly not been allowed to practice in public in London where the statues raised in recent decades suggest a total collapse of artistic standards. There is Mountbatten in Horse Guards Parade, a pompous, stiff figure with a pair of binoculars (by Franta Belsky) standing on a plinth which is simply an up-ended shoe-box, painfully unintegrated with tiers of steps – it could almost double up for a monument to Enver Hoxha in Tirana. Then there are the two airmen outside St Clement Danes. The first was a belated recognition of the contribution of Hugh Dowding, the head of Fighter Command – a national hero if ever there was one as he undoubtedly saved Britain in 1940. But the pure purpose of this monument was undermined when, after lobbying by justifiably aggrieved Bomber Command survivors, he was joined by another stiff figure in RAF uniform depicting yet another callous military leader in the shape of Sir Arthur 'Bomber' Harris.

Both naively realistic statues are by Faith Winter; both stand on embarrassingly crude Classical plinths. And the embarrassment is compounded by comparison with the Gladstone Memorial which stands nearby, for Hamo Thorneycroft's commanding robed figure stands on a tall plinth (by John Lee) which is enlivened by complex mouldings and four allegorical groups on lower pedestals. The sad fact is that not only are most modern British sculptors incapable of realising the symbolic and monumental, they also have forgotten the importance of the plinth, for a well designed pedestal is integral to a sculpture's success. Most modern sculptors, indeed, dispense with the plinth altogether, seeing it as somehow elitist. Ian Walters wishes to place his Mandela on a low plinth to make it 'more accessible', pretentiously arguing that 'the accessibility of the statue to the public, and the freedom to touch and stand against it is essential...' But not only does a plinth have an artistic purpose, raising a statue symbolically as well as literally, but it serves a functional purpose, as earlier generations understood. In Glasgow, for instance, the bronze statue of the late share-trading socialist, Donald Dewar, in crumpled suit, stands almost on the ground in Buchanan Street and so encourages the public to exercise the freedom to vandalise and regularly to break his spectacles.

So what should happen to that Empty Plinth in Trafalgar Square? There is surely only one answer. When the time comes, it should support a statue of the present Queen, who would be more appropriately commemorated on a horse than her nearby great-great-great grand-uncle. Furthermore, a monument to the monarch in whose reign the Empire was dismantled would also complete the square historically and symbolically. There would be no more frivolous posturings by fashionable conceptual artists, and that would be that. But who on earth could make such a thing?

December 2005

[In the event, the Mandela statue was placed in Parliament Square.]

A Canova for Today

I recall the late Sir Denys Lasdun once being asked if he could contemplate a work of sculpture being associated with his National Theatre in London. His reply was revealing: yes, he said, a Henry Moore placed... at the other end of Waterloo Bridge. Such is the gulf between the modern architect and the modern sculptor: neither employs a language of form that can contemplate integration. It is a state of affairs so different from most of architectural history; the Mediaeval cathedral, the Baroque church almost relied on the sculptor or carver. That great 20th century English architect Charles Holden thought that it was the hand of the artist that raised building to architecture (and he managed to persuade the young Moore to carve on his London Transport headquarters). And it was his partner, Lionel Pearson, who worked with that very great sculptor, Charles Sargeant Jagger, to produce the most moving and powerful of war memorials in London, the Artillery Memorial at Hyde Park Corner.

The modernist divorce between the sculptor and architect can also be seen in the vexed question of the plinth. In the 19th century, public statues stood on architect-designed, carefully proportioned plinths. Today, the embarrassingly mediocre statues we raise to heroes stand either on crude shoe boxes or, more likely on nothing at all. They are intended to look real, as if waxworks in bronze – as with the proposed figure of Nelson Mandela proposed to stand in front of the National Gallery (which, fortunately, London has so far been spared). A plinth, of course, would raise such a figure from naïve realism to being something idealised, that is, a *monument* – as well as introduc-ing an inescapable element of unfashionable elitism. When statues are mere waxworks, they are on our own level (and so much easier to vandalise). As Alexander Stoddart has written, 'Modern liberalism demands that statues be at least plinthless', and he also observes that 'All statues are made of sculpture, but few sculptures attain the status of statuary.'

Sandy Stoddart is my mentor in matters of sculpture. He is a self-confessed 'doctrinaire Neo-Classical sculptor' of – these days – extraordinary accomplishment and sophistication. He was the most impressive individual I encountered during my time teaching in Glasgow: not only a brilliant sculptor but also an artist, an eloquent and inspiring writer, and a power-ful polemicist (not for nothing was he once one of the late Ian Hamilton Finlay's notorious 'St Just Vigilantes'). He is also an heroic figure, for he has had to struggle to produce public monuments in the face of the indifference or contempt of the modern art establishment and most of the official funding bodies. As his heroes are Canova, Bertel Thorvaldsen, G.F. Watts and Jagger, he is dismissed as reactionary, irrelevant. Fortunately you can see his work in places like Paisley (statue of Witherspoon, the founder of Princeton University) and Kilmarnock (double-statue of Burns and his publisher) as well as in Edinburgh, where there is his seated figure of David Hume in the Royal Mile (soon to be joined by one of Adam Smith) and the recent monument to Robert Louis Stevenson – all rich in allusion and symbolism. And all of them on proper plinths.

What is particularly remarkable is that, as a sculptor (and as a philosopher), Stoddart is self-taught. He was a student at the Glasgow School of Art in the 1970s but, as he describes in a recent autobiographical essay (which ought to be compulsory reading in all art schools), the fashion then was for 'culture-free constructivism on the one hand, object-free conceptualism on the other… You found a railway-sleeper, preferably one rather the worse for wear, then wrapped it in a coil of barbed wire. Onto the barbs you hung a series of, say, smoked mackerel – the better through which to appreciate the 'spatial relationships inherent in the intervals between wood, tar, and metal'.' (I am sorry to find that the GSA does not seem to have much more respect for real skill today and declines to acknowledge Stoddart as one of its distinguished alumni in its prospectus.)

After having done 'a pop-riveted construction which had been a hit at a tutorial', intimation of what sculpture could be came from confronting the plaster cast of the Apollo Belvedere which had survived in the Mackintosh building, despite it being 'a great comfort to be gathering the knowledge of exactly how reprehensible such items of antique art were. Imagine if, on the contrary, these objects represented a paradigm of goodness! What a pickle we would all be in, for they would be so hard to emulate and deeply troublesome to make.' But revelation came with a visit to that strange and resonant polychromatic museum building in Copenhagen designed by Bindesbøll to house the work of that Danish national hero, Thorvaldsen. Stoddart was there to do research for a never-to-be-completed thesis and, confronted by the plaster figures and busts by the Neo-Classical sculptor, he was silenced – and knew what his life's work must be.

It was far from easy to produce works of art that were resolutely unfashionable in style, conception and purpose. It is good to know, however, that he was first helped by an architect (an intelligent modernist, indeed), David Page of Page & Park, who asked him to execute statues to go on the parapet of the Italian Centre in Glasgow, a development of new and restored buildings. This was the commission which launched Stoddart as a serious public sculptor. Since then he has occasionally but very successfully collaborated with other, rather different architects. One is John Simpson, who asked him to model the plaster friezes in the entrance hall of the new Queen's Gallery at Buckingham Palace – where the remarkable generic bronze bust of the Queen that greets the visitor on the stairs is also Stoddart's work. And soon there will be an esoterically satirical 'mitigated' herm of Priapus, 'the deity of Gardens', outside a Simpson building in St Vincent Square, for which the typically elaborate and learned programme by Stoddart would take up more space than this column.

And now he is working with another sympathetic architect, if on a rather unlikely commission. This is an isolated private Roman Catholic chapel in North Britain which, last year, secured the Georgian Group's annual award for the best new building in the Classical tradition. The architect is Craig Hamilton, one of the most intelligent and sophisticated of the so-called New Classicists working today, one able to reinterpret precedents with knowledge and conviction. His chapel is an exquisite little building, impeccably detailed, which has echoes of Neo-Classicists like Dance, Soane and Cockerell inside but has an entrance façade that plays games in the manner of Michelangelo. And sculpture is an important part of the whole conception – all of it by Sandy Stoddart, and the several devotional images commissioned reveal his own wide and deep knowledge of the history of sculpture.

In the tympanum of the entrance door is a bronze bust of St Rita of Cascia (to whom the chapel is dedicated) in the

Neo-Florentine manner of Adolf von Hildebrand. In the apse are two framed marble reredos panels in a Neo-Classical Anglo-Italian manner 'somewhere between Canova and Flaxman'. In the vestibule is to be a figure of St Augustine of Hippo, over life-size in marble, which is Hellenistic in style but pays homage to Thorvaldsen's figure of Christ. Other works will show the influence of, amongst others, Andrea Della Robbia, Alfred Gilbert and Jagger. All this – what he calls a 'confessional accumulation' which explores the debt of Christianity to Antiquity – is perhaps surprising for a sculptor whose primary model has hitherto been Greece seen though the work of his Neo-Classical heroes. But this has been not only an unusual but a disturbing commission for an artist who, as he confesses, thought that his Scots Presbyterian background would keep him detached and so safe from any 'spiritual bruises'.

That, of course, is his problem, but it is extraordinarily interesting, and cheering, to see two accomplished and learned artists – one a sculptor, one an architect – working harmoniously together with a shared respect for tradition. Both have created a true work of architecture in which we can see, in Stoddart's words, 'antiquity and Christian function coming into congress with one another'.

March 2007

[Stoddart has since been appointed Sculptor in Ordinary to The Queen in Scotland, and, amongst other works, has been responsible for the monument to James Clerk Maxwell in Edinburgh. On my last visit to the Queen's Gallery, I was disappointed to find that Stoddart's generic portrait bust of HM the Queen was not on display: it should be as it is a brilliant work.]

Too Many Memorials

It is now sixty years since the end of the Second World War, yet as memories fade and the number of those who can remember the conflict decreases, the number of new war memorials being commissioned grows and grows. Recently, memorials to the dead of the Commonwealth, of Australia and to non-human casualties have all been erected and, later this year, memorials to the Battle of Britain and to serving women of World War II are to be unveiled. A visitor to Blair's Britain might suppose that, far from believing in 'forward, not back', we are instead wallowing in past glories. But the real problem with these memorials is not that they are an expression of our national self-justifying obsession with the defeat of Nazi Germany as our last great moment in history, but rather that most of them are so embarrassing, so aesthetically mediocre.

In terms of art, the catastrophe of the Great War took

place at just the right time. The Edwardian Classical revival had reached a peak of sophistication so that architects could produce austerely monumental structures whose forms resonated with the European tradition and so had meaning. Above all there was Edwin Lutyens, who, by his 'Elemental Mode' seen in the Cenotaph in Whitehall and in the many cemeteries and memorials created by the Imperial (now Commonwealth) War Graves Commission, set a high standard in dignity and meaningful restraint without resorting to crude religious or patriotic symbolism and imagery. His Memorial to the Missing of the Somme at Thiepval in France is surely the greatest as well as the most moving expression of 20th century British architecture. Today, however, that tradition, if not dead, is certainly misunderstood as architects have not been trained in a visual language within which they can work with sculptors. Despite the fine examples all around, attempts at designing even a decent pedestal can be painfully crude – the statues of Mountbatten or Bomber Harris are more worthy of Tirana or Pyongyang than London – while the lettering is often as stiff and conventional as the standard, awful work of modern monumental masons.

The best of the recent monuments is the set of gate-less 'Memorial Gates' erected in Constitution Hill to the memory of five million volunteers from the Indian sub-continent, Africa and the Caribbean who fought for Britain in two world wars. The first design, by Liam O'Connor, was, however, a crude, stiff essay in the Xerox-Palladian Prince of Wales school of Classicism and what has been built was greatly improved by looking at the proposal by the architect John Simpson who, intelligently, looked to the best precedents; that is, to the 1920s memorials of Lutyens and Herbert Baker. This shows in the finely modelled pylons; the flanking little Indian temple, or *chattri*, is more fussy, however, and not as good an essay in the style as Baker's memorial at Neuve Chapelle to the poor Indians who died in the filth of the Western Front.

There is, of course, no reason why memorials should be in the Classical manner. Surely it is possible to design a modern, abstract memorial of suitable dignity and poignancy? This was certainly achieved in Maya Lin's Vietnam sunken folded wall of names in Washington D.C., a concept echoed in the new Australian War Memorial at Hyde Park Corner. This is an irregular wall curving around the bottom end of the traffic island which, discordantly, is in dark grey granite rather than the Portland stone used for the neighbouring Wellington Arch and the Artillery Memorial, and which, for no obvious reason, has water dribbling down one end of it. The design seems arbitrary and contrived; sloping granite blocks line the inside of the curve and are reminiscent of that distressing sight of old tombstones uprooted and stacked around a churchyard wall to facilitate the motor-mower. The best aspect of it is the clever lettering, with the big names of battles made legible by widening the smaller inscriptions of place names where necessary.

This memorial also manifests another unhappy modern trait: vanity. The Cenotaph is, very properly, unsigned; it speaks for itself. But this memorial is flanked by ugly plinths recording the names of its creators – Tonkin Zulaikha Greer, architects, and Janet Laurence, artist – as well as the circumstances of its dedication in 2003. But would the dead, will posterity, care that it was dedicated in the presence of two unpleasant warmongering prime ministers (Howard and Blair) in addition to the Queen? Even worse, in this respect, is the new Animals in War memorial in the centre of Park Lane, for here half the back of its curving stone wall is covered with large inscriptions recording the names not only of David Backhouse, the designer and sculptor, and the carvers, Richard Holliday and Harry Gray, but also a long list of trustees and donors. As for the animals, who 'had no choice', they are represented by free-standing bronze figures of mules, a horse and a dog wandering though a gap in the wall and by a giant carved frieze reminiscent of a plate in an illustrated edition of *The Jungle Book* which depicts a camel, elephant, bullocks and other creatures. The sentiment behind this memorial may be admirable, but the result is pure *kitsch*.

There is more of this sort of thing to come. On the Victoria Embankment, one of Bazalgette's granite plinths (a ventilation shaft for the District Railway) is being made into a Battle of Britain Memorial by having a modish diagonal Deconstructivist slice cut through it (architect Tony Dyson) and having long, bronze relief friezes by Paul Day fixed to its walls. These are in a sort of 3D super-realist style depicting pilots scrambling for action and giving Jerry a good hiding. The importance of that conflict for Britain and Europe and the heroism of those pilots certainly cannot be exaggerated, but do the events of 1940 really have to be recalled quite so literally? I am afraid these sculptures just remind me of the cartoon strips illustrating the improbable adventures of 'Paddy Payne, Fighter Pilot' which I read in the *Lion* comic as a schoolboy. The objection to this work is not that it is figurative but that it is so childish and lacking in subtlety. It should be contrasted with the 1914-1918 Artillery Memorial at Hyde Park Corner where the carved friezes and standing bronze figures by C.S. Jagger – surely the greatest British sculptor of the last century – are at once modern and traditional, starkly realist and yet stylised, and depict suffering, stoicism and the horror of war with a dignity and lack of sentimentality which make the whole into great art. Jagger knew what war was really like, after all.

How are the designs for these vulgar new memorials which are threatening to trivialise London chosen? We may not have a Jagger, or a Lutyens, living today and standards may well have fallen, but there are nevertheless alternatives. Michael Sandle, for instance, is a sculptor who (like Jagger) is able to stylise and dignify machines and incorporate them into architecturally satisfying conceptions, as he has demonstrated in his Malta Siege Bell Memorial and his recent Seafarers' Memorial (whose bow emerges from a building on the Lambeth Embankment).

Or there is the possibility of modernist abstraction. To my surprise, the recently unveiled National Police Memorial by the Citadel in the Mall (designed by Foster & Associates with the artist Per Arnoldi) turns out to be a fine and dignified thing. It is like a 1950s architectural concept: a miniature solid glass skyscraper (or giant tombstone?) counterpoised against a black granite box (which conceals a ventilation shaft for the Jubilee Line). And there are no vainglorious inscriptions, just its name and purpose: 'honouring those who serve' (along with another saying 'Dry Riser Inlet'). These alternatives are important as, with the modern secular concern with memorials (its healthy expression being a new concern to look after older ones) and the press's and television's obsession with constantly reliving the Second World War, there can be no end to worthy possibilities for national commemoration. (I was going frivolously to suggest the cats killed in the *Blitz*, but what about those bravest of men, the bomb-disposal experts?)

There is one more memorial being unveiled soon, whose siting has caused some controversy. This is the Women of World War II Memorial, which will now consist of a bronze pylon on a granite base (who by?) with sculptures by John W. Mills of different uniforms hanging on pegs around the sides to symbolise the many tasks performed by women during the last war (a sculptured group which was to sit on top has been wisely abandoned). Originally to be sited in front of the Air Ministry building instead of the diminutive statue of Sir Walter Raleigh (now exiled to Greenwich), it is now to be placed in the middle of Whitehall. Right and proper, if belated, as is the purpose of the memorial, this seems wrong. Although evidently vaguely inspired by the Cenotaph, this 22 feet high object will surely conflict with the delicate scale of Lutyens's masterpiece which, after all, is now hallowed as the national memorial to *all* the British dead of *both* world wars. Originally erected as a temporary structure in 1919, that elegant pylon, seemingly so simple and yet so sophisticated in design, somehow resonated so powerfully with the grief of millions that it was permanently re-created in stone the following year. And so complete a memorial is it that, after another terrible world war, there was nothing else that needed to be done but to add two more dates: 1939-1945. Enough was enough.

June 2005

[Michael Sandle's magnificent Malta Siege Bell Memorial is sited on the southern ramparts of Valletta.]

The War Goes On

It is now 92 years since the First World War ended and 65 years since the Second. After the First, it was boom time for architects, sculptors and letter-cutters as there was a huge campaign of memorial building to commemorate the vast human loss. After the Second, often little more was done than to add two more melancholy dates and an extra (shorter) list of names on existing memorials. But then, after an interval of almost half a century, came another wave of memorial building in London which has given us, amongst others, the recent Women of World War II memorial in Whitehall, the Australian and New Zealand memorials at Hyde Park Corner, the Animals in War Memorial in Park Lane and a number of statues to military commanders. The artistic quality of these artefacts (as I discussed in *Apollo* for June 2005) unfortunately varies from the mediocre to the frankly embarrassing.

Why there should be this apparent public demand for more war memorials, which the planning authorities seem reluctant to resist, at a time when the Second World War has largely receded from living memory, is an interesting historical and sociological question. Is it a pathetic attempt at national self-justification by a former imperial power in decline, looking back to the Second World War both nostalgically and assertively as our last independent heroic moment? As a blogger from Norway (a country which, after all, actually experienced Nazi occupation) who had lived in England for three years has commented, 'one of the things that struck me is your obsession with the war… get over it!' Whatever the reason, this national mania has yet to subside as we are now faced with a proposal to place a large memorial to the dead of RAF Bomber Command in Green Park. It is a project which has been vigorously opposed by, amongst others, the Thorney Island Society as an inappropriate intrusion into a precious green open space.

Now one must express reservations about this proposal with some diffidence as the sacrifice of the crews of Bomber Command has been shamefully ignored in the past. Not only did some 55,000 of them not return but the casualty rates approached those of the bloodiest (and most futile) campaigns of the First World War, with those young men having only a small chance of surviving a tour of duty of thirty missions. With the war in Europe over, however, Winston Churchill began to feel embarrassed about the campaign of indiscriminate area bombing of German cities which he had supported and which had resulted in huge civilian casualties. The result was that Bomber Command was denied its own campaign medal. And since then, of course, there has been much and heated controversy over both the morality and the economic and social effectiveness of the systematic destruction of German cities – many of them historic and beautiful, like Lübeck, Würzburg and, above all, Dresden.

But the rights and wrongs of the campaign waged by Bomber Command should have absolutely no bearing on a proposal to commemorate the young men who were so prodigally sacrificed to achieve the goals set by its single-minded, ruthless leader, the repellent Arthur 'Bomber' Harris. On the other hand, given the controversial nature of Britain's bombing policy during the Second World War, is it really desirable to make the proposed memorial quite so conspicuous, and so *big*? After all, there is already the Royal Air Force memorial on the Victoria Embankment erected after the First World War, now accompanied by the recent Battle of Britain memorial with its excruciatingly vulgar sculptures by Paul Day (the man who gave us the 'Meeting Place' at St Pancras Station), in addition to the Runnymede Memorial to airmen with no known grave and St Clement Danes restored after bombing as the RAF memorial church. Furthermore, most of the survivors of those who flew over Germany in Wellingtons, Stirlings and Lancasters have, sadly, now passed on.

And then there is the design of the proposed memorial. Now there is nothing wrong with designing in the Classical tradition, even if, today, it may have associations of pomposity and triumphalism which it did not in the past. Wisely, its architect, Liam O'Connor, looked closely at the original work of the Imperial War Graves Commission when he designed the Commonwealth Gates in Constitution Hill and the Armed Forces Memorial at the National Memorial Arboretum in Staffordshire, for the work of the 1920s by Lutyens, Baker, Holden and the Commission's other (great) architects showed how the Classical language could be spoken with originality and brilliance for a terrible contemporary purpose. But is the proposed Bomber Command design up to that high standard?

An open rectangular central pavilion is to be flanked by colonnades running along Piccadilly. Although both use the Doric order, these elements are not integrated as they are, say, with Decimus Burton's nearby (Ionic) screen at Hyde Park Corner; instead, the entablature of the lower colonnades springs arbitrarily from the side walls of the pavilion. And then there is the curious and awkward feature of the colonnades being terminated by freestanding bunches of four columns with the intervening gaps serving as entrances to the park – an awkward attempt at mannerism which seems entirely unnecessary as the very essence of a colonnade is its permeability. As for the central pavilion, it is a stiff and mechanical design, while an outline on the drawings reveals that it is intended to enclose a sculpture of a bomber crew. Knowing the low quality of most modern figurative sculpture, one can only regard this element with dread, for there is little chance of securing works in any way approaching the unsentimental idealism of the heroically brutal figures on the nearby Artillery Memorial at Hyde Park Corner by that greatest of British 20th century sculptors, Charles Sergeant Jagger.

The painful pedantry of the Bomber Command design seems to provide further melancholy evidence of the fact that, because Classicism is no longer mainstream or properly taught, its modern expression usually lacks sophistication and wit, let alone any true originality of expression. We have instead a sort of Classicism by numbers. But it is still possible to learn from the past, and what a modern Classical war memorial on this scale might be like is suggested, for instance, by that in Southport in Lancashire. For here, in the town centre, are colonnaded pavilions analogous to that proposed by O'Connor in Green Park. But those in Southport, as designed in the sophisticated 'Neo-Grèc' manner by Grayson & Barnish in the early 1920s, with sculpture by H. Tyson Smith, are delicate and subtle – as well as having the great virtue of making and defining a *place*. What is proposed in Piccadilly is, in contrast, a crude and alien intrusion into the park.

I do hope it is possible to suggest, without in any way denigrating the memory of those ill-used young men of Bomber

Command in the Second World War, that their proposed memorial is too big, too pompous, and in the wrong place.

June 2010

[Unfortunately, the Bomber Command Memorial went ahead, and this embarrassingly triumphalist and mediocre structure was unveiled in 2012. As executed, the free-standing clusters of columns serve as Doric lamp posts as they support small Neo-Victorian lamps, thus making them ridiculous as well as illiterate. The central pavilion contains a sculpture of a bomber crew by Philip Jackson. The discreet inscription on the inner frieze above, claiming that the memorial 'also commemorates those of all nations who lost their lives in the bombing of 1939-1945', was clearly an afterthought in response to the criti-cism of those who dared question the suitability of this belated tribute to the ill-used casualties of Bomber Command.]

Tragic Triumph

On 1 July we commemorate the 90th anniversary of the first day of the Battle of the Somme, perhaps the greatest tragedy in British military history. Many other terrible, bloody battles occurred all over Europe during that prolonged, suicidal exercise in industrialised slaughter between 1914 and 1918 which we used to call the Great War, but, for the British, 1 July 1916 is the defining event, by which we are still obsessed, still haunted. On that day, thanks to the naïve optimism and tactical stupidity of that very tarnished hero, Douglas Haig, the volunteers of Kitchener's New Army were flung against well-prepared German defences and machine guns. The result is all too well known: some 60,000 casualties by the end of that first day – 19,240 of them dead. By the time Haig called off the offensive the following November, the British casualties alone amounted to 420,000.

Paradoxically, the struggle that so damaged European civilisation generated great art. We now tend to try and understand the vast, melancholy tragedy of the Great War through the canvasses of Paul Nash, William Orpen, Stanley Spencer and other official war artists, as well as by reading Wilfred Owen, Siegfried Sassoon or Robert Graves. What is less well appreciated is that the First World War also generated some magnificent architecture, and sculpture, such as the Artillery Memorial at Hyde Park Corner with its searingly unsentimental sculpture by Charles Sargeant Jagger – surely the greatest British sculptor of the 20th century – or Robert Lorimer's Scottish National War Memorial in Edinburgh. It is often argued that the war created a clean break between traditional art forms and modernism but, in truth, the terrible exigencies of the conflict allowed a last creative flowing of Classicism.

This is evident, above all, in the work of the Imperial War Graves Commission, which had the task of burying or commemorating over a million British Empire casualties. It was perhaps the largest programme of public works every carried out by a British agency, and – for once – the government employed the best architects. Such men as Charles Holden, Lorimer, J.J. Burnet, Reginald Blomfield, Herbert Baker and, not least, Edwin Lutyens, together with a team of assistant architects, designed almost a thousand permanent war cemeteries along the line of the Western Front. And then there were the missing: the half-million men who simply had disappeared, their bodies never found or identified. Each of them has his name carved into stone on one of the several Memorials to the Missing. The most famous is probably Blomfield's Menin Gate at Ypres, but the greatest, the most haunting and extraordinary is the Memorial to the Missing of the Somme at Thiepval, near Albert.

This memorial has to be seen to be believed, and comprehended. On its axes, it appears as an open arch in the triumphal arch tradition, yet different; from a distance it seems more like a tower. From other angles, however, it resembles a pyramid or ziggurat, for it is a pile of complex, cubic forms, each of which is penetrated by arched tunnels arranged in a precise geometrical heirarchy. By this means, enough internal wall space was created on which to carve the names of over 73,000 men who were missing after the Battle of the Somme. This extraordinary structure was designed by Lutyens and is the summation of his 'Elemental Mode', that sublime abstraction of Classical forms that he earlier demonstrated so poignantly at the Cenotaph in Whitehall. What Lutyens achieved at Thiepval is difficult to convey in words; the best attempt was made by the late Roderick Gradidge, who argued unfashionably that the extraordinary grasp of three-dimensional form that he demonstrated here stemmed from his roots in the Gothic Revival, and that 'For the first time in two thousand years an architect has found something new to do with the triumphal arch.'

All this has been much on my mind recently as I have written a short book about the Memorial to the Missing of the Somme for Mary Beard's 'Wonders of the World' series (Profile Books). Surprisingly, although it is now recognised as one of Lutyens' finest creations (and one which suggests what his great unexecuted design for the Catholic cathedral at Liverpool would have been like), no detailed study of the genesis of the design for the Thiepval Arch has been made before. I was therefore delighted when the editors agreed that it could enjoy equal stature with the Parthenon, Westminster Abbey and Stonehenge. If any reader doubts that, I can only urge him or her both to contemplate the awesome gravity of the significance of Lutyens's creation and to go and see it – to experience the deep intellectual sophistication of its design and then to stand in the centre, where the complexity of its mass is dissolved and the visitor looks out through vast open arches in all four directions to see the sky over the pastoral landscape which is soaked in the blood of a lost generation. (And a visit is now much more comfortable and rewarding since an excellent new visitor centre, designed by Nicolas Ziesel and Dominique Vity of KOZ architectes of Paris, opened at Thiepval in 2004.)

Two unexpected themes emerged from my research. The first was the great difficulties the War Graves Commission had to surmount before the memorial was built. Lutyens had to alter and scale down his design twice as well as move its site. The original conception – so well conveyed in the sketch drawn on his office writing paper – was first worked out in 1923 for a proposed memorial at St Quentin. By the mid-1920s, however, the French were becoming 'disquieted' by the scale and number not only of the memorials the British wanted to raise on French soil but also of those proposed by the Canadians, South Africans, Australians and – largest in size in relation to the number of casualties commemorated – the Americans. So the St Quentin design was rejected.

Sir Fabian Ware, that fine man who founded the War Graves Commission, sympathised with the French, who were then undergoing severe economic and political difficulties. A compromise had to be reached, and the number of memorials the Commission proposed to erect in France was reduced – with the largest proposed for Thiepval, the site of an obliterated village overlooking the valley of the Ancre where some of the most prolonged and vicious fighting of the Somme campaign had taken place. The French were further mollified by the fact that Lutyens's design was reduced in scale to make it slightly lower than the Arc de Triomphe in Paris, that Napoleonic monument by Chalgrin which seems a rather crude conception – essentially a slab with a hole in it – when compared with the structural dynamism of the Thiepval Arch. They were also pleased that Thiepval was to be a joint Anglo-French memorial, for it is too often forgotten that the Somme campaign was not an exclusively British affair.

The second surprise was the critical reception, or, rather, the lack of one, which greeted the Memorial to the Missing of the Somme when it was finally inaugurated. The formal unveiling of the Menin Gate in 1927 had been widely publicised, but although the opening ceremony at Thiepval in 1932 was reported in the daily papers, the completion of a huge and magnificent creation by England's most famous architect met with a resounding silence in the architectural press. It was as if everyone had by now had enough of the war. Indeed, during those intervening years, 1927-32, *Journey's End* had been performed, *All Quite on the Western Front* and the memoirs of Graves, Edmund Blunden and many others had been published, so that, at last, the reality of the Great War as a monstrous, murderous tragedy was penetrating the public consciousness.

It is only since the Second World War that the greatness of Lutyens's memorial at Thiepval has been fully acknowledged. In 1981, Sir John Summerson wrote that it is 'the greatest of all Lutyens's memorials in size and the most liberated in form'. Today, it seems the most significant British monument of the last century, a memorial to official stupidity and cynicism but also life-affirming. As Geoff Dyer wrote in 1994 in his book, *The Missing of the Somme*, 'so much of the meaning of our century is concentrated here'. Somehow, that strange man, Edwin Lutyens, had been able to reinterpret tradition with true originality and create a monument which, without bombast or sentimentality, still conveys a sense of tragedy. As far as I am concerned, at once Classical and modern, it is the greatest British work of architecture of the last century and, yes, a wonder of the world. The irony is that such a superlative should stand not in Britain itself but on the opposite side of the English Channel, in rural Picardy, not far from Crécy and Agincourt.

July 2006

Steam Ahead

There are some crimes which cannot be forgiven, or forgotten. One such is the demolition of the so-called Euston 'Arch' in 1961 which meant that London lost the greatest monument of the Railway Age. When Euston Station was built as the terminus of the London & Birmingham Railway – the first great trunk railway line linking the capital with the provinces, engineered by Robert Stephenson – the directors decided to celebrate this triumph of Man over Nature by announcing it with a Doric *propylaeum* or gateway (*not* a triumphal arch). Designed by Philip Hardwick, it was huge – the columns were 44 feet high – and hugely expensive, but it was a gesture worth making and ancient Greek architecture, strangely perhaps, was associated with modernity. This noble structure commemorated, as Sir John Summerson put it, 'as no other structure in the world the moment of supreme optimism in the marriage of steam and progress'.

When Euston was opened in 1837, nobody really knew how a railway terminus might evolve into a new architectural form. In consequence, the station grew in a piecemeal way and was never really satisfactory. So it was not surprising that in the late 1950s British Railways proposed the complete rebuilding of Euston as part of its modernisation and electrification of the main line to the North-West and Scotland. Not only the early surviving cast-iron train sheds but the grand but inconveniently sited and impractical Great Hall – designed a little later by Hardwick's son – inevitably had to go. The Arch was also in the way, but what made its demolition such a crime – the 'Euston Murder' the *Architectural Review* called it – was that it could have been saved. Earlier, just before the Second World War, the London Midland & Scottish Railway had also proposed the rebuilding of Euston, to an American-inspired design by Percy Thomas, but the newly founded Georgian Group successfully demonstrated to the directors that Hardwick's propylaeum could perfectly well be re-erected further south, on the Euston Road. And the LMS agreed.

No such arguments swayed the British Transport Commission, which claimed to be unable to afford to save and rebuild the Arch. Ultimately, however, the murderer was the Prime Minister, that cynical Whig politician Harold Macmillan. In October 1961, a distinguished deputation went to see him to plead that, if all else failed, the structure should be carefully dismantled and the stones numbered for possible re-erection elsewhere. 'Macmillan listened – or I suppose he listened', recalled J.M. Richards; 'he sat without moving with his eyes apparently closed. He asked no questions; in fact he said nothing except that he would consider the matter. A statement was issued later to the effect that the Government had decided not to intervene.' Demolition began soon after. The whole affair was an example of the conventional, blinkered prejudice against 19th century architecture still prevalent among the ostensibly educated establishment in Britain.

The gratuitous destruction of the Euston Arch was a serious defeat for the newly founded Victorian Society in particular, although its loss – along with that of the Coal Exchange in the City of London the following year – was never forgotten and it encouraged a change in the climate of opinion which prevented British Railways from doing away with both St Pancras and King's Cross Stations just a few years later. But in 1961, the image of the railways represented by the Doric propylaeum, that relic of the steam age, was simply unacceptable at a time when Britain was desperate to appear modern, and was consumed by the Gadarene desire to worship the motor car. Public money was being poured into motorway building and railways seemed to belong to the past. Soon after, that repellent fat-cat executive, Dr Beeching, would be invited to wield his axe and truncate the country's railway system. We continue to suffer from the consequences of those blinkered decisions.

Opened in 1968, the new Euston that eventually emerged from the rubble of the old certainly reflected the tawdry glamour of its time. The only architectural gesture was the large concourse or booking hall – then uncomfortably empty but today cluttered up with kiosks and shops. Elsewhere, passengers were obliged to board their trains between raw concrete columns and under a low concrete roof. The sense of occasion, of adventure, which the great Victorian termini gave to the traveller was entirely – deliberately – absent. Euston did not want to be a railway station but to look like an airport, just as the interiors of trains were now designed like airliners. 'What masterpiece arose on the site of the old station? No masterpiece,' wrote John Betjeman, who had fought so hard for the Euston Arch. 'Instead there is a place where nobody can sit; an underground taxi-entrance so full of fumes that drivers, passengers and porters alike hate it. A great hall of glass looks like a mini-version of London Airport… I have heard the excuse for this disastrous and inhuman structure, which seems to ignore passengers, that British Railways originally intended to make it pay by adding multi-storey hotels and office blocks to the flat roof. This seems a lame excuse for so inhospitable a building.'

Betjeman was right. BR's plans had fallen foul of the Labour government's ban on office building in central London. Eventually, in 1974-78, three squat black office towers designed by Colonel Seifert's firm were built in front of the station – on the land where the Arch could have been re-erected. Nobody – surely? – can really love the new Euston, and now it is proposed for replacement having lasted far less long than Old Euston. Not that rebuilding is proposed for the benefit of railway travellers: it is only because of the immense value of the site. A development of office, residential and, of course, 'retail and leisure' space which involves building on top of the railway platforms as well as replacing the Seifert towers is now envisaged in a deal between the developers British Land and Network Rail. The only loss is likely to be the concourse which, although architecturally vapid, is at least a grand space worthy of a public building. But, in compensation, the redevelopment offers an opportunity which ought to be seized – the opportunity of re-creating the Euston Arch.

Why not? A decade ago, in 1996, the historian Dan Cruickshank attempted to launch the Euston Arch Trust dedicated to rebuilding the propylaeum. The estimated cost then was £5 million. Even if that figure would need to be doubled, or even tripled, today, it would still be comparative peanuts compared with British Land's proposed budget of £1 billion – of which a quarter (£250 million) is to be spent on improving the station. The Arch can be placed where the Georgian Group suggested seventy years ago: on the Euston Road between the old station entrance lodges. It would, of course, have to be a replica. Cruickshank discovered that over 60% of the original 4,420 tons of Bramley Fall stone used for the Arch survives – some dumped in the River Lea, some in the garden of Mr Valori, the demolition contractor, in Bromley. But even if salvaged, these stones would be too damaged to be re-used, for after permission to number them was refused, the demolition was rapid and brutal.

A replica is surely justified. Recreation from scratch is both possible and necessary when important buildings are destroyed in war – as with the Frauenkirche in Dresden – so why not with a victim of vandalism? Hardwick's working drawings survive, so rebuilding is a practical possibility. Despite the impression given in J.C. Bourne's evocative watercolour of the Arch under construction (one of the many beautiful drawings he made of building the London & Birmingham Railway), the propylaeum was not built as the Greeks would have built it. The columns were in fact hollow, with each drum consisting of four pieces of stone, while wrought iron as well as brick arches were used in the construction of the entablature and pediment. The Arch could therefore be built again, using modern methods of construction.

A new Euston Arch would be a powerful symbol. Just as Greek Revival architecture represented modernity in the 1830s, so today it would symbolise the revival of Britain's railways after the disastrous century of the motor car – a revival tangibly represented by the re-opening of St Pancras next door as the terminal for the Eurostar. All that is required is for English Heritage and the London Borough of Camden to insist that re-creating the propylaeum is a condition for granting planning permission for rebuilding Euston. It would be a fine way of atoning for a great crime.

October 2007

[It is not yet clear if the questionable and controversial decision to bring the new high-speed line to the North – HS2 – into a rebuilt (yet again) Euston will facilitate or impede the project to re-create the 'Arch'.]

Long Journey's End

Sometimes to say, 'I told you so', is not so much a pleasure as a duty. The Victorian Society must feel this about the recent reopening of St Pancras Station as the London terminus for Eurostar trains to the Continental Europe. Just over forty years ago, in 1966, British Railways announced plans to demolish both St Pancras and King's Cross Stations – two of the greatest monuments of the Railway Age – and replace them by a single joint new station. St Pancras, it was claimed, with its High Victorian Gothic Revival former hotel, was not only out of fashion but utterly out of date. Today, not only is Gilbert Scott's Midland Grand Hotel being restored – as an hotel – but the stupendous train shed by W.H. Barlow, chief engineer to the Midland Railway – once the largest unsupported span in the world – has been magnificently revamped as a railway station for the 21st century.

In addition to boasting the longest champagne bar in

Europe, the restored and rearranged concourse is the setting for two works of sculpture commissioned as a dubious enhancement to the success of the whole enterprise. Of the larger, the monstrous 30-foot high representation of a canoodling couple by Paul Day, called *The Meeting Place*, it would be perhaps kinder to say little as it is simply beyond criticism in its coarse vulgarity. The rather smaller and less objectionable bronze piece is a representation of the late Sir John Betjeman by Martin Jennings. The implication of the accompanying inscriptions is that it was he who saved St Pancras from destruction. The truth, however, is sometimes inconvenient. Although Betjeman, whose memory I revere, certainly did his best, if there was any one saviour of St Pancras it was his rival, Sir Nikolaus Pevsner, then chairman of the Victorian Society. The society – which celebrates its 50th birthday this year – did all it could to thwart British Railways' blinkered plans by proposing intelligent alternatives. In the event, the listing of St Pancras – both station and hotel – at Grade I in 1967 saved both stations. That was not the end of the battle, however, as over the years the society had to campaign against the neglect of Scott's hotel and to prevent the old ticket hall from being mutilated. Yet no representative from the 'Vic Soc' was invited by London & Continental Railways to attend the grand ceremony when St Pancras was re-opened by the Queen.

The Victorian Society was founded in 1958 by Betjeman, Pevsner and others; it was a response both to the growing appreciation of 19th century architecture among the aesthetically and historically literate and to the recognition that some of the finest examples would soon be under threat. Old, blinkered prejudices prevailed, however, and the new society's career began with two unforgivable defeats. The first was the wickedly unnecessary demolition of the Doric propylaeum at Euston Station (see page 178), closely followed by that of the Coal Exchange in the City of London, that extraordinary structure of both masonry and cast-iron which Henry-Russell

Hitchcock, in a telegram sent from the U.S., described as the 'Prime mid-century monument of iron and glass construction, not alone of Britain, but of World' [sic]. The saving of St Pancras came as the society's first major victory, one that would be closely followed by the rescue of the Foreign Office, New Scotland Yard and other fine buildings from the megalomaniac plan for rebuilding all Whitehall by Sir Leslie Martin.

What is peculiarly gratifying to those of us who admire Victorian architecture is how the revival of St Pancras has caught the public imagination. There has been an enthusiastic response to the way a great 19th century structure of brick and wrought iron rather than a modern steel and glass 'masterpiece' by, say, Norman Foster now represents the future. Many journalists have written about the reopening of St Pancras as if the railway service to the Continent is entirely new when, in fact, it has been operating since 1994. Perhaps this celebration of St Pancras is a tribute to the fact that not only did the Victorians build solidly and to last, but that they did so with imagination and a sense of occasion. Not for nothing did contemporaries describe the great urban railway termini as the 'cathedrals of the 19th century'.

St Pancras is still astonishing today; it must have been breathtaking when it opened in 1868. The upstart Midland Railway company wanted its own main line to London and intended to make a spectacular impression when it arrived, so the scale and grandeur of its terminus was the ultimate in advertising. The new station was designed to outshine both nearby Euston and its immediate neighbour, King's Cross, that cheap but elegantly utilitarian structure which was once extravagantly admired by modernist critics in comparison to the expensive Gothic of St Pancras. So a famous architect was secured, via a rigged competition, to design the railway hotel while the company's engineer was given a generous budget to construct a huge train shed with wrought-iron arches 240 feet wide. And, *pace* those blinkered critics who affected to see a dichotomy between the forward-looking engineering and the backward-looking Gothic Revival architecture, masonry and metal were intelligently integrated. Gilbert Scott had no problem with Barlow's shed: 'as if by anticipation', he happily recorded in his *Recollections*, 'its section was a pointed arch'.

The Midland Railway was a proud and ambitious concern. As it was building its huge London terminus, it had just begun to build the spectacular railway high across the Pennines to take its express trains to Scotland. And those expresses were the first in Britain to include luxurious new Pullman carriages – an American import. Later, it was all downhill. The Midland was 'grouped' with other companies in 1923 to create the London, Midland & Scottish Railway, within which St Pancras and its line were downgraded. And in 1935, Gilbert Scott's hotel, by now dowdy and critically risible, was closed and the building used as offices. But, as Simon Bradley points out in his excellent new book on St Pancras, this probably saved it from destructive modernisation, enabling it to reopen as an hotel in 2009.

Meanwhile, Barlow's great iron cathedral continued to shelter trains to Nottingham, Derby, Sheffield and beyond. In my youth, there was still the glamour of the Thames Clyde Express travelling over the Settle & Carlisle from St Pancras to St Enoch in Glasgow (can there ever have been a more bizarre connection between two more obscure saints?). Today St Enoch has gone, both hotel and magnificent double-arched train shed foolishly replaced by a tawdry shopping centre, while the Midland's St Pancras look-alike in Manchester is now a conference centre. St Pancras, however, happily survived as a station. One excuse for the huge outlay on the vast train shed was that it would allow internal flexibility although, in fact, the position of the tracks and platforms remained unchanged until it closed in the 1990s. But now Barlow's concept has been fully justified as the single span has allowed the internal space to be rearranged and the iron-columned basement – designed on a module of Burton beer barrels – partly hollowed out for the Eurostar facilities, while an additional flat-roofed shed designed by Andrew Lansley has been tactfully tacked on for English destinations. But it is the 1868 shed that thrills.

For a citizen of the nation that created that great boon to civilisation, the railway, the last half-century of decline and closure was utterly dispiriting. Even with the advent of the Channel Tunnel, how typical and humiliating it was that while the French were content to let the Eurostar trains stick out the back of the Gare du Nord in Paris (a mid-19th century station with iron columns cast in Glasgow) so as to concentrate on building a new high-speed line to Calais, we British built an over-elaborate 'high-tech' terminal at Waterloo by Nicholas Grimshaw from which the trains trundled slowly over old lines through Kent. But now, at last, all is redeemed: a new railway to the Channel is completed while a great Victorian station has come into its own again. The trains no longer go to Glasgow but to Brussels, Paris and soon, I hope, far beyond. Somehow, I don't think W.H. Barlow would be surprised.

January 2008

[This article inevitably repeats much that I wrote on the threatened demolition and restoration of Gilbert Scott's hotel in the earlier article on page 79.]

Battlebridge

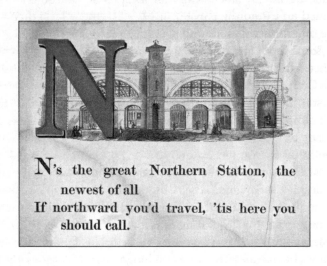

N's the great Northern Station, the newest of all
If northward you'd travel, 'tis here you should call.

Travellers to York, Durham and Edinburgh might today leave from London Battlebridge if it were not for the memory of a free-standing police station at a major road junction on which stood a statue of King George IV. Long regarded as ridiculous and satirised by Pugin, the remains of this structure were cleared away six years before King's Cross Station was opened in 1852. Built on the cheap and long thought of as shabby and inconvenient, this London railway terminus has no regal associations (although both George V and George VI made their last journeys to it from Sandringham). But now, after the triumphant restoration of its neighbour, St Pancras, which has demonstrated that railways are of both the past and the future, King's Cross has also been given a new lease of life by a brilliant £550 million modernisation scheme that shows how – sometimes – historic architecture can be enhanced by a new architectural vision.

For almost a century and a half, the two great termini standing side by side at the end of the Euston Road have presented an extraordinary and instructive contrast: one Gothic, the other Classical; one expensive, the other economical; one, so some thought, harking back to the Middle Ages while the other anticipated Modernism. In 1872, that ferocious critic of the Gothic Revival, J.T. Emmett, described Kings Cross in contrast to 'showy and expensive' St Pancras as 'not graceful, but it is simple, characteristic, and true. No one would mistake its nature or its use.' A century later, John Betjeman recalled how 'In the 1930's we were all told to admire King's Cross for its functional simplicity, an earnest of the new dawn. We were told to despise St Pancras for its fussiness though we were allowed to admire the engineer's roof.' But comparison between the honest expression of the one with the elaborate front of the other was unfair, for whereas at King's Cross the railway company's hotel was a detached building on one side, at St Pancras the hotel – Gilbert Scott's Gothic masterpiece – was sited in the obvious place, right in front of Barlow's great train shed. And now there is a new architectural contrast. St Pancras was made suitable for both national and international trains by adding a utilitarian steel and glass box at the rear. King's Cross, on the other hand, has been expanded with a new concourse which is covered by a most spectacular and elaborate new domed roof.

In celebrating the present, it is well to be reminded of what might have been – that is, of the blundering and prejudiced ineptitude which nearly did away with both buildings and could have wrecked the area around. Notoriously, both stations were threatened with demolition in the 1960s to create a new joint station. After that was defeated, a new threat emerged in the plans to develop the King's Cross Railway Lands, the area north of the termini consisting of gasometers, canals, railway tunnels and the buildings on the old goods yard site. This was the hard but enthralling Victorian industrial landscape which can be enjoyed in that great Ealing film of the

1950s, *The Ladykillers*. Almost everything – including the Great Northern Hotel – would have given way to a dense commercial development. Then came the Channel Tunnel and British Rail's crass scheme to burrow under half London and build an international terminal underneath King's Cross – destroying much of the shabby but rewarding buildings to the east. In the end, local opposition and common sense prevailed – but it was a close run thing. St Pancras was used for the Eurostar trains and most (alas, not all) of the historic structures on the site have survived: the huge Granary in the goods' yard has become the University of the Arts; the German Gymnasium survives (if truncated) and the Great Northern Hotel not only still stands but is the key to the success of the King's Cross scheme.

The Great Northern Railway was open just in time to help transport the millions who visited the Great Exhibition, but the permanent terminus was not ready for another year. Built on the site of a smallpox hospital, it was designed by Lewis Cubitt, of the famous family of builders. The plan was simple: two parallel arched train sheds, one for departures, the other for arrivals. Offices and the booking hall were placed along the western side. The front was but an arcaded screen wall, with two giant semi-circular windows indicating the train sheds behind. A similar form of expression was adopted by Hittorff for the Gare du Nord, but whereas the Paris facade is richly treated, King's Cross is simply of yellow London stock brick: the only ornament is the central Italianate clock tower between the arches. The chairman of the GNR, Edmund Denison, was able to reassure shareholders that 'it is the cheapest building for what it contains and will contain that can be pointed out in London'.

The Great Northern Hotel followed two years later. A detached and more elaborate Italianate building to the west, six storeys high and also designed by Cubitt, it was gently curved in plan. This has puzzled subsequent generations, but the curve was not arbitrary for it followed the old irregular line of Pancras Road. But when the Midland Railway's terminus was built the following decade, the street plan was rationalised and the little houses in front cleared away to leave King's Cross facing a triangular open space. At first this was occupied by a vendor of garden furniture; subsequently it was filled by a cast iron canopy and an unsightly collection of various wooden shacks and cab shelters and an entrance to the tube railways below, all of which hid the original open arcade of segmental arches. In the 1960s all this was cleared away only to be replaced by a new unsightly extension to the station.

This structure was required because King's Cross was long lacking in circulation space and other facilities, but the problems remained – hence the new concourse. Designed by John McAslan & Partners, this lies beside the station where once there was the hotel's garden. It is a most happy solution, for it not only restores the original logic of the station's plan but retains the hotel and exploits its geometry, for by extending the curve a large semi-circular space has been enclosed, centred on the original 1852 entrance and ticket office. This might have been covered by a utilitarian roof; instead, something in the best Victorian railway tradition has been created: a soaring diagrid shell structure of complex geometry designed by Arup which is high enough to enclose a long and pleasingly sinuous first-floor balcony to contain more of the facilities a modern station needs: cafés and shops. With light coming down from the centre, this dramatic semi-dome is reminiscent of the oval roof of Cuthbert Brodrick's Corn Exchange in Leeds – another spectacular Victorian structure – except that, in the centre, the ribs rise from the floor to spread out like a tree.

Meanwhile the handsome brick arcades and the arched roof of the original station have been cleaned and restored, and look magnificent. All that remains to do is to clear away the 1960s rubbish in front of King's Cross to expose Cubitt's original, elegant facade as it was intended to be seen.

October 2012

Tent for a Prince

Placed over the balconies that flank the high altar in the Peterskirche in Vienna, that masterpiece by Lukas von Hildebrandt's, are exotic onion-shaped semi-domes. These are tangible reminders of the distinctive military tents that the Viennese could see outside the city walls when the Habsburg capital was besieged by the Turks in 1683 – the high water mark of the Ottoman Empire. Fortunately, this final assault on Christendom was defeated and the Turks retreated, leaving behind them a taste for coffee and a memory of exotic architectural forms.

The Ottomans and their efficient, ruthless armies both frightened and fascinated Western Europe. In particular, the colourful, decorative tents which the Turkish forces raised in their military camps caught the imagination of monarchs and wealthy patrons who were already developing a taste for Chinese pavilions and other exotic conceits to ornament parks and gardens. Louis XIV had tents made à la *Turque* for processions and ceremonies. These, like the Ottoman originals, were temporary, movable structures but some made their Turkish tents more permanent. In the Vauxhall Gardens in London, one was built in 1744 as a dining room. Henry Colt Hoare had his Picturesque landscape at Stourhead enhanced with a similarly exotic feature to compliment the Classical temples (originally a mosque with a minaret had been intended). And in the gardens at Painshill Charles Hamilton erected a domed open tent designed in about 1760 by Henry Keene which was partially constructed of brick. It has been recreated, but all the other structures have disappeared.

What survive, however, are the Turkish tents erected by Gustavus III in 1787 at Haga, the royal park outside Stockholm. The designer was the French architect and stage designer, Jean-Louis Desprez, who made these guard houses for the royal *corps-de-garde* permanent by facing the timber structures with copper, painted to look like fabric. Although so very far from Constantinople, three of these copper tents still stand together as a strange reminiscence of Ottoman prowess. The outer ones are more like conventional marquees, if with walls curving outwards, but the central tent, clearly Turkish in inspiration, has an elaborate entrance, as if the cloth walls were drawn open, over which rises a conical roof culminating in a finial topped by the crescent moon. Lovingly restored, all are gaily painted in the Swedish national colours of blue and yellow.

Such permanent 'temporary' structures were not necessarily à la *Turque*, as is the case with the one extraordinary example which survives in England. This was also in origin a royal building. As King George III, became increasingly incapacitated, Carlton House, the residence of his extravagant son, the Prince Regent, became a royal palace and the focus of social life in London. Banquets, fêtes and grand receptions were staged there, but as the house was not really large enough for such events, the Prince Regent had marquees set up in the gardens overlooking St James's Park. And as the entertainments became more elaborate, and the cost of hiring and erecting tents increased, it was decided to erect temporary buildings in the gardens of Carlton House. These became the responsibility of John Nash as one of the architects to the Office of Works.

These structures were needed for the festivities held in the summer of 1814 when the abdication of the Emperor Napoleon was celebrated (prematurely, as it turned out) and the victorious Allied Sovereigns – the King of Prussia and the Emperor of Russia – were in London, an occasion which happily coincided with the centenary of the Hanoverian monarchy. The culmination was the ball held by the Prince Regent on 21 July 1814 in honour of the Duke of Wellington, and for this the new temporary buildings by Nash, assisted by William Nixon, were used for the first time. The centrepiece was the Polygon Room or Rotunda, 120 feet in diameter, designed in the form of a large tent. No depictions of this appear to exist, but we have a contemporary description. 'Each side of this spacious room was groined and supported by fasces, ornamented with flowers: from these arose an elegant umbrella roof, terminating in a ventilator, decorated with large gilt cords, and painted to imitate white muslin... The walls within the groins were decorated with muslin draperies and eight large plate glasses... In the centre was a garland of artificial flowers in the shape of a temple, connected by a very large gilt rope from the roof; this was used as an orchestra for two bands.'

The structures at Carlton House did not last long, although they had a longer life than the Pagoda Bridge in St James's Park, one of several temporary structures by Nash erected for the Grand National Jubilee, which was largely destroyed by fireworks on the opening night. These festivities and pyrotechnics had been planned by Sir William Congreve, M.P., a favourite of the Prince Regent and an enthusiast for military projectiles who (inspired by similar Mughal weapons) invented the Congreve rocket. Congreve may possibly have collaborated with Nash on designing the prefabricated timber structure of the polygonal ballroom, and he seems to have had in mind from the start its eventual re-erection at Woolwich, for he also happened to be Comptroller of the Royal Laboratory and Superintendent of the Military Repository there. And so it came to pass. In 1818, the Surveyor General was informed that 'It is H.R.H.'s desire that it should be transferred to Woolwich, there to be appropriated to the conservation of the trophies obtained in the last war, the Artillery models, and other military curiosities usually preserved in the Repository of the Royal Artillery.'

Nash supervised the re-erection of the Rotunda on an open site west of the Royal Artillery Barracks. To make it permanent, its exterior was encased in a circular brick wall, penetrated by windows. Above, the curved roof trusses supported a tent roof faced in lead, reaching up to the tall ventilator finial. Inside, the timber was concealed by a canvas ceiling, with ornamental ropes reaching out to the 24 fluted timber columns standing within the walls while a tall Roman Doric column was substituted for the central tent pole. The Rotunda was opened to the public in 1820, and there it has stood since, its collection of trophies being augmented over the following century and a half by cannon and other relics resulting from Britain's colonial and other wars. But no longer.

Under a plan to unite the several historic artillery and other military collections in a much larger new museum in the historic Woolwich Arsenal site, the Royal Artillery Museum closed in 1999. It re-opened in 2001 in its new premises under the new name of 'Firepower'. Although it has much to recommend it, the move has meant that Nash's remarkable Rotunda is no longer accessible. For the last decade, it has been used as a store for some of the museum's large collection but the remaining pieces must be removed by early next year. After that, it will be redundant. What to do with it? There have been various proposals, such as a museum of small arms and, surprisingly, a museum of chocolate, but all have come to nothing.

The adjacent site is to become the home of the King's Troop, but they have no use for the Rotunda, not even as an offic-ers' mess. Meanwhile, the fabric is deteriorating and water is coming through the (rather impractical) tall lead roof.

It really is a scandal that this remarkable historic structure, listed at Grade II* – the only surviving relic of that long-lost wonder, Prinny's Carlton House – should be redundant and neglected in government ownership. If no suitable use can be found for it where it stands, perhaps it should be re-erected elsewhere – it has been moved once before, after all. Perhaps it should return to St James's Park, close to Carlton House Terrace, where this festive tent could make a fine and histori-cally resonant café and restaurant. Why not?

May 2009

[The Rotunda remains closed, and unused.]

An Artist's Villa

J.M.W. Turner once told a friend that, 'if he could begin life again, he would rather be an architect than a painter'. England's greatest landscape artist often depicted architectural subjects, of course, particularly in his earlier watercolours. He had also worked as a draughtsman for several architects, such as Thomas Hardwick, who apparently advised the young artist to abandon architecture for painting. Later, Turner made perspectives drawings – and paintings – of James Wyatt's designs for William Beckford's astonishing Gothic folly, Fonthill Abbey, and in 1807 he was appointed Professor of Perspective at the Royal Academy – a year after his friend John Soane had been made Professor of Architecture.

It is, perhaps, not surprising therefore that Turner not only added a gallery to his house in Queen Anne Street in Marylebone but also designed his own house, a country retreat near the Thames at Twickenham. Many artists, of course, built their own studio houses, often working closely with their architect: Frederick Leighton with George Aitchison, James Whistler with E.W. Godwin, George Boyce with Philip Webb, for instance. Earlier, another fine topographical artist, Paul Sandby, had built a studio in the garden of his house in Bayswater which was probably designed by his brother Thomas. But Sandycombe Lodge is unique. Not only was it intended purely as a residence, without a studio, but Turner was his own architect – even if he may have enjoyed a little help from his friend Soane.

Turner needed a retreat from London and, like many before and since, enjoyed the semi-rural Thames valley upstream from the city. As a child, he had stayed in Brentford where he had been at school, and at first he rented a house in Isleworth, and then one in Hammersmith. In 1807 he bought land in Twickenham, not far from Marble Hill. A particular attraction was the nearby villa built by Alexander Pope and Turner was outraged when, shortly afterwards, its new owner, Baroness Howe, demolished the celebrated building because it continued to attract curious visitors (an example of selfish vandalism justified by property rights which, unfortunately, is not unique in England: New Place, Shakespeare's house in Stratford, had been destroyed for similar reasons half a century earlier). Turner achieved a sort of revenge when he painted *Pope's Villa at Twickenham, during its Dilapidation* the following year.

Turner's surviving sketchbooks show various alternative schemes for his house. Building commenced at the beginning of 1812 and it was completed almost exactly two centuries ago. The villa was built close to an existing lane on a sloping site and the garden front looks east towards Richmond and the river. It was small and symmetrical, originally consisting of a two-storey central block flanked by single-storey wings. In style, it might be described as Italianate, for it had broad eaves in the simple Tuscan manner used by Inigo Jones for his church in Covent Garden (where Turner was born). The wings were more elaborately treated, however. And here the name of Soane must be mentioned, for they have rounded corners like some of his early rustic buildings and there were Soanian recessed blank panels flanking the windows. There was also a band of Doric triglyphs made of simple bricks running below the pediment on the central block, a detail which can be found on Soane's buildings at the Chelsea Hospital. But what is most intriguing is that these triglyphs also appear on the recessed rounded corners of the wings as if a Doric order is buried in the wall and exposed at these points – an essay in Mannerism which might be Turner's own invention.

Inside, the debt to Soane is even more evident. The front porch leads to a transverse corridor or hall. This space is articulated by tall round arches with a simple thin moulding not unlike those in the Dulwich Picture Gallery while the simple and elegant semi-circular staircase under a skylight which opens off the corridor is irresistibly reminiscent of that in Soane's own house in Lincoln's Inn Fields. Other details also suggest that the amateur architect looked closely at Soane's buildings even if his friend did not actually oblige with some sketches. Nevertheless, this simple and truly Picturesque building – which also recalls the ideal villa designs made by J.M. Gandy – does not resemble any one of Soane's works: it is the artist's own creation.

Turner originally called his retreat Solus Lodge, but as he shared the house with his widowed father and entertained there, he soon changed the name. He sold it in 1826, by which time his father had become too frail to live so far from London while Margate had also by then come to seem more attractive than Twickenham. Subsequent owners altered the building by heightening the single-storey wings. The railway came in the 1840s, stimulating the suburban development which would eventually overwhelm the villa. In fact, its survival today seems almost miraculous, especially as it was requisitioned and used for manufacturing airmen's goggles during the Second World War.

Sandycombe Lodge was saved by Professor Harold Livermore, a specialist in Iberian studies, and his wife Ann, who bought the dilapidated house in 1947. Long anxious to see his home become 'a monument to Turner in Twickenham', Livermore set up what has become Turner's House Trust which became its owner following his death two years ago. This trust now opens the house to the public on certain days and hopes to restore the building to its original condition and appearance – for the wings must be lowered to their original height and lost detail restored. To this end, an application has been made to the Heritage Lottery Fund.

To restore and make available to the public a peculiarly fascinating building designed by one of the nation's greatest artists is obviously a worthy aim, but the problem remains of what eventually to do with it. The contents and furniture are long dispersed and as there is no evidence of the original appearance of the interiors it cannot really become a Turner museum, even though Professor Livermore assembled a collection of the artist's prints. Nor can it be made into a centre for Turner studies when the Turner Bequest is housed at the Tate on Millbank. Sandycombe Lodge is not to be compared with Leighton House which, mercifully, survived as a museum despite the sale of Leighton's collection soon after his death, for the rooms in that intriguing building were fully documented allowing many of the contents to be retrieved or replicated in recent years.

One solution has been suggested by Andrew Wilton, the former curator of the Turner Collection at the Tate who is a trustee of the Turner House Trust. Turner had bought other plots of land in Twickenham and in his will he indicated his wish to build there a 'College or Charity for decayed English artists (Landscape Painters only) and single men' (both Turner and Soane were founder members of the Artists' General Benevolent Institution). Notoriously, after Turner's death in 1851, his relatives challenged his will and betrayed his intentions. Recompense would surely be made if, after its restoration, his Twickenham villa was let to an artist (decayed or otherwise), perhaps under the auspices of the Royal Academy of Arts (to which Turner was devoted), with public access allowed for a specified period each year.

This would surely be an eminently practicable solution, especially in these increasingly straitened times when all museums seem to be struggling. What is clear is that Sandycombe Lodge is extraordinarily interesting and needs, and deserves, help.

December 2012

[The Turner's House Trust has since been awarded grants from the Pilgrim Trust and the Heritage Lottery fund towards the restoration of the villa.]

Villa Frankenstein

In 1872, John Ruskin decided to leave his home in Denmark Hill in South London and up sticks for the Lake District. The reason, as he explained in a much quoted letter, was that 'I have had indirect influence on nearly every cheap villa-builder between this and Bromley; and there is scarcely a public-house near the Crystal Palace but sells its gin and bitters under pseudo-Venetian capitals copied from the Church of Madonna of Health or of Miracles. And one of my principal notions for leaving my present home is that it is surrounded everywhere by the accursed Frankenstein monsters of, indirectly, my own making.' The problem was that architectural details had been cribbed from *The Stones of Venice* and applied to the detached and semi-detached middle class villas that were springing up near the new railway lines all around London.

Worse was to come. By the 1870s, the word 'villa' was being applied to the brick terraced houses built with the help of building societies for the 'superior artisan'. No longer could it be applied to any detached house with any pretensions to aesthetic merit, like those in the new 'Queen Anne' suburb of Bedford Park with its houses by Norman Shaw. As Sir John Summerson put it, 'These villas, so familiar to all of us and so terrible in their familiarity, bring the ancient word 'Villa' down to a level inconceivable when Lord Burlington built the first and loveliest of villas at Chiswick a century and a half before. At last this ancient and Romantic word, Roman in ancestry, lordly in association, was brought down to the mud of Walham Green and trodden into the marshes of Leytonstone.'

The debasement of this word has been on my mind having contributed to what, sadly, was the last of the conferences on British domestic architecture organised by Malcolm Airs at Rewley House in Oxford. These conferences began by looking at country houses and then turned to the smaller villa, ending with its strange history in the 19th century. What had begun as an aristocratic architectural statement in the country, inspired by Palladio, evolved into those elegant Regency semi-detached houses on the edge of London designed by Nash and others, or the Picturesque asymmetrical Gothic cottage in outer suburbs. 'A villa,' insisted James Elmes in 1827, 'is a rural mansion or retreat, for wealthy men.' And then it turned into the middle-class detached house in its garden in the new suburbs so abominated by Ruskin and others, designed by minor obscure architects or run up by builders with the help of pattern books. Soon William Morris would be sneering at 'the hideous vulgarity of the cockney villas of the well-to-do, stockbrokers and other such', although his own famous Red House, out in Kent near a railway line, was, in truth, a villa.

But there is no reason why we should be influenced by the anti-industrial and social snobberies of the Arts and Crafts movement. Suburbs remain desirable places to live and the best Victorian suburban houses are creations of considerable imagination and charm. They deserve serious study. Besides, as the artist Barbara Jones wrote, 'They are the children of the railway and the buses and the tubes; they are one of the main contributions of the last hundred years to our architecture.' That was written in 1947, and it seems to me that there was far more interest in the suburbs and in ordinary houses, or villas, sixty years ago than there is today, when historians tend to concentrate on the grand country house, or public buildings or churches.

The above quotation from Summerson comes from his perceptive article on 'The London Suburban Villa' which appeared in 1948. And two years before that, J.M. Richards had published his remarkable book (illustrated by John Piper) called *The Castles on the Ground* which explored the social and emotional reasons why the English liked living in their villas, nostalgic and romantic in style, in leafy suburbs. He recognised that 'The suburban style – that style which is, we are told, the very citadel of debased and vulgar taste – is, in fact, part of the background of England we have all grown up in' and also that it was the architecture of true democracy, of a society in which people could choose where they live. All this outraged all Richard's modernist colleagues, who thought the future must consist of New Towns, planning and high-rise flats.

It must be admitted that, by the 1940s, few wanted to live in the surviving big Ruskinian villas that Ruskin disavowed, and many would be replaced by flats. This has happened in Sydenham, so close to Ruskin's home where houses grew up around both railways and Paxton's iron and glass structure for the great Exhibition which he re-erected (even bigger) on the top of Sydenham Hill in 1854. Even so, it remains a rewarding place to study the mid-Victorian villa, and Barbara Jones thought it 'one of the best early suburbs to see', where, 'clustered around the beauty of the stark and shining Crystal Palace, there arose a wealthy suburb of the highest fantasy. The gardens are shady and so large that they are almost grounds, the winding roads are lined with trees, and everywhere still hangs the atmosphere of the vanished Palace.' It perished by fire, of course, in 1936 and the following year Henry-Russell Hitchcock used a photograph of its ruins as the frontispiece of his exhibition on *Modern Architecture in England* held at the Museum of Modern Art in New York.

Modernists admired the Crystal Palace as a straightforward functional structure but had no time for the surrounding villas, whether Gothic, Italianate or in other eclectic historical styles. Nor did the architects of the next generation like Norman Shaw, who evolved a more sophisticated domestic style based on the rural vernacular of half-timbering and tile-hanging. The word 'villa' soon became so debased that it was anathema; 'house', 'home' or 'cottage' were now the acceptable names. In the appendix added by E.M. Forster to his novel *Howard's End*, described how the model for it was an old house to which he had moved as a child in 1883 and how 'Mother when she came heard that the house was to be called "Chisfield Villa" and nearly had a fit.' Yet, in fact, the villa, as the detached outer-suburban or semi-rural middle class family house in its garden, carried on regardless. Indeed, it was the basis of the great flowering of British architecture around 1900 which excited international respect, and most of the dwellings illustrated by Hermann Muthesius in his great study of *Das Englische Haus* could, in truth, be described as villas.

And then the villa, in its original conception, made an unexpected re-emergence – if under another name. Those pioneering flat-roofed white-walled Modern Movement houses of the 1930s extolled by Hitchcock were usually built in semi-rural settings and, like the 18th century villa, were conceived as ideal architectural statements, governed by a strict geometry. Part of James Ackerman's useful definition of a villa is that it 'is typically the product of an architect's imagination and asserts its modernity… The villa accommodates a fantasy that is impervious to reality.' Such, surely, was the Modern Movement house. But there is a delicious paradox, or irony in interpreting these buildings as villas. These houses were regarded by partisans as being in stark and virtuous contrast to what was generally regarded as a scourge: the suburban estates of detached and semi-detached Neo-Tudor houses which so proliferated between the two world wars. Yet, if the Modern Movement house can be interpreted as the modern successor to the Palladian villa, so, too, the lineage of the Tudor semi can be traced back to the *cottage orné* of the early 19th century via the Gothic villa and the vernacular revival of the later 19th century. Both – different as they are – can be regarded as the culmination of the story of the British villa since the Georgian period; both had grown out of the same tradition.

No wonder many of the historians at the Rewley House conference seemed a little vague about what a *villa* really is.

February 2007

Post-Haste to Closure

Visit most British towns and cities and you are likely to find, somewhere central, a handsome Neo-Georgian building, probably but not necessarily of red brick, which is elegant but restrained, having an air of authority and yet politely fitting in with the surrounding architecture. These days it is likely to be a shop or a bar or a restaurant, but once its purpose was proclaimed in noble bronze Trajan capitals placed carefully on its symmetrical façade: POST OFFICE. The closing and selling off of these official buildings is both a social and an architectural tragedy, for they once proclaimed the dignity and importance of the public realm in Britain.

Giving a dignified architectural expression to an important but popular public service was not, of course, peculiar to these islands. I was deeply impressed, on my first visit to New York, to discover the great Classical U.S. post office in Eighth Avenue bearing the noble inscription, chosen by the architects in Roman capitals carved into the frieze above the Corinthian colonnade: NEITHER SNOW NOR RAIN NOR HEAT NOR GLOOM OF NIGHT STAYS THESE COURIERS FROM THE SWIFT COMPLETION OF THEIR APPOINTED ROUNDS (and how cheering to learn that this noble building may become the entrance to a new Penn Station, somewhat atoning for the crime of destroying the great masterpiece of the same architects, McKim, Mead & White). In Britain, similarly, the first purpose-built Post Offices in the 19th century were Classical buildings, often designed by the obscure but talented Office of Works architect John Williams (I cannot think of any Gothic examples).

It was in the early 20th century, however, between the two world wars, that the General Post Office stamped its image on the country through design. First there was the selection of the design by Giles Gilbert Scott, in a competition organised by the late, lamented Royal Fine Art Commission, for a standard cast-iron telephone kiosk: that elegant red Neo-Georgian-cum-Soanian kiosk that was once almost the trademark of Great Britain. At the same time there was a campaign to build new district post offices all over the country. Designed by a talented team of architects in the Office of Works, these responded to the general architectural culture of the 1920s by being Neo-Georgian in style. It might be argued that this restrained, gentlemanly style became the national modern vernacular in the first half of the 20th century, for it was widely used not only for houses and public housing but also for schools, university buildings, town halls and for Royal Air Force bases (the authentic stylistic backdrop for Spitfires and Hurricanes is not Modern or Deco but Neo-Georgian) as well as for post offices.

Now Neo-Georgian has had a very bad press, when it has had a press at all. It has often been assumed to be a conservative, unadventurous, reactionary style, although in the hands of, say, Lutyens it could be subtly inventive. In his *Buildings of England* volumes, Nikolaus Pevsner would often pejoratively dismiss buildings as 'Neo-Georgian' when he felt they should have been Modern with a capital 'M'. The problem is partly the naïve association between modern Classical architecture and authoritarian regimes. Notoriously, Herbert Read once observed that, 'In the back of every dying civilization sticks a bloody Doric column', although these days we can see that, in the terrible history of the 20th century, a steel or concrete *piloti* could equally well prop up a tyranny. Besides, one of the merits of Neo-Georgian was that it did without an expressed order; it was an abstracted style, relying on Classical proportions as well on association, in the reign of King George V, with the civilised and admired architecture of the century of the first four Georges.

Soon after the turn of the 20th century, architects of the Arts & Crafts movement realised that the unpretentious Georgian rectory could be as good a model for a national vernacular manner of building as the rustic barn or cottage. The Georgian had the merit of simplicity as well as of making a virtue of good brickwork, so by the 1920s, with the growing taste for the austere, it could seem modern as well. And real Georgian architecture, so despised by the Victorians for its repetitiveness and dullness, had come back into fashion. Foreign observers could appreciate its qualities, and that it could be the basis of a good modern architecture. 'One hardly knows whether to laugh or to cry on seeing a modernistic architecture imported into London, which is far less suitable to the spirit of the age than the Georgian houses of about 1800,' wrote Steen Eiler Rasmussen, the Danish author of that classic, *London: The Unique City*.

Perhaps the most eloquent defence of ordinary Georgian architecture came from Robert Byron when he argued that 'it corresponds, almost to the point of dinginess, with our national character. Its reserve and dislike of outward show, its reliance on the virtue and dignity of proportions only, and its rare bursts of exquisite detail, all express as no other style has ever done that indifference to self-advertisement, that quiet assumption of our own worth, and that sudden vein of lyric affection, which have given us our part in civilisation.' Intelligent English architects, who sought a modern reticence and standardisation but who eschewed any vulgar parade of novelty, agreed. 'The period of domestic architecture from which of all others we have most to learn is the Georgian,' argued Trystan Edwards, the doughty defender of Regent Street, in 1924. 'The essential modernity of the "Georgian" style should be widely recognised. If we do not derive full benefit from this tradition, the failure will certainly not be justified by the extremely disputable suggestion that such a manner of building is unsuitable to our present social circumstances.'

So Neo-Georgian was widely adopted, a style which was English, gentlemanly and polite, which was reticent and standardised while achieving elegance and refinement through careful detailing. The more daring and sophisticated, meanwhile, took up the stuccoed, inventive Classicism of the Regency. No wonder that the Office of Works architects developed the Georgian manner when they were asked to design Post Offices. The results achieved by these official architects were sufficiently impressive to elicit the admiration of a proto-modernist like P. Morton Shand. In surveying recent Post Offices and telephone exchanges in the *Architectural Review* in 1930, he observed that, 'The governments of foreign countries avail themselves of every architectural opportunity to remind their citizens that, as the local headquarters of a department of state, enjoying all the authority and prerogatives pertaining thereto, a post office is a monumental symbol of the fact that they are governed. In Great Britain, on the other hand, our aversion to bureaucracy is such that its appearance is made as deliberately domestic as possible.'

It is that domesticity, combined with the achievement of variety within apparent uniformity, that makes these Post Offices so impressive. They manage to express an authority which is benign – for the Postman's uniform can surely never provoke hostility or fear – as well as fitting into the streetscape of English towns. Many are of brick: usually red but sometimes yellow when that is the local brick. Good manners was important: the dignified post office in Kendal in the Lake District, for instance, is built of stone while that at Cranbrook is faced in white-painted Kentish weatherboarding. And it is interesting to see the variations on the Neo-Georgian theme achieved by these unsung and now obscure Office of Works designers, like D.N. Dyke, J.H. Markham and E. Cropper. The one in Bath, of stone, of course, sports a Palladian window, and was later singled out for praise by the Architecture Club as it 'worthily maintains the architectural tradition of its setting'.

When I last saw that post office, it was being converted into a shopping mall. No longer does quiet Classical authority seem the right image for a Post Office which as een its important social role reduced by successive governments and is strapped for cash. So tawdry logos replace Trajan capitals as countless post offices are closed and the surviving counters moved into shops or supermarkets. It is a state of affairs which proclaims for all to see the collapse of the public realm, of the national civic sense. Post offices, like public libraries, built and designed with a philanthropic concern and with great care, are now dispensable. At least the buildings themselves survive, if in less dignified use, to proclaim the merits of the true modern national style of the 20th century: Neo-Georgian.

May 2008

[The architecture of Post Offices – in all styles – is explored by Julian Osley's book, Built for Service, published by The British Postal Museum & Archive in 2010. And now police stations are threatened, as discussed in Apollo for January 2013, owing to the present government's ferocious ideological assault on the public realm.]

In Carceri

THE NEW CITY PRISON HOLLOWAY

L ook at early-19th-century maps of London or of any British
city and the most conspicuous buildings depicted are
not great churches or monuments but large institutions with
precise geometrical plans. Often placed in isolation outside
built-up areas and designed to conform to ideal utilitarian
Benthamite or 'Panopticon' plans to facilitate the efficient
supervision of their occupants, these polygonal, walled
structures are, of course, prisons. Millbank Prison by the
Thames was a representative example: built in 1812-28 on a
huge octagonal plan originally drawn out by Jeremy Bentham
himself, it housed 860 prisoners in single cells. The prominence
and scale of such buildings, together with the similar presence
of large barracks, reflected both the cruel penal laws of the time
and also the fear of revolution in Britain during the turbulent
decades after the Battle of Waterloo.

Prisons are less conspicuous today – at least on maps. With

that obsession with secrecy which appeals to the official mind if not to common sense, prisons – like military establishments – are indicated as if they do not exist. On the *London A to Z*, for instance, the Hammersmith Hospital in Du Cane Road is marked with all its buildings carefully outlined but its immediate institutional neighbour is a large empty space simply labelled 'H.M. Prison'. This in fact is the celebrated – or notorious – Wormwood Scrubs and cartographic censorship seems rather superfluous when the massive yellow-brick buildings can be easily studied from the street or from the Central Line embankment immediately to the south.

In the centre is a massive castellated gatehouse bearing Hampton Court-style portrait roundels on its two towers of two of those great prison reformers whose work helps redeem Britain's enthusiasm for incarceration: Elizabeth Fry and John Howard. Behind can be seen the four dominating multi-storey cell blocks, whose end elevations are enlivened by large Lombardic-traceried windows and which are each aligned north-south so that all cells would receive either morning or afternoon daylight. The whole complex was built in 1874-91 to replace Millbank (so freeing that site in Pimlico for building the Tate Gallery). And it was all designed by a former Royal Engineer, Major-General Sir Edmund Du Cane (1830-1903), the then Surveyor-General of Prisons, who became the chairman of the Prison Commission in 1878 and assured the public that those judicially confined would enjoy 'Hard Labour, Hard Fare and Hard Board'.

I went to prison for the first time recently. The reason was to see the remarkable but little-known chapel built by Du Cane at Wormwood Scrubs, as it is to be the venue in October for an exhibition and arts auction organised by the Koestler Awards Trust (an opportunity for the public to visit the building as well as to support the Trust's enlightened and necessary work with prisoners). Sited in the centre of the prison and consecrated in 1894, this large structure was built not of brick but of smart

Portland stone in a French Romanesque style which looks as if it were taken straight from the engravings in Viollet-le-Duc's *Dictionnaire*. Outside it is a repetitive composition of round-arched windows; inside it is a broad-aisled space under a timber roof, culminating in a great wide apse. This chapel is at once grand and poignant, and the necessarily institutional character of the building is redeemed by the images of saints and religious scenes in the arches and lunettes of the apse painted on mail-bag canvas by prisoners who used fellow prisoners as models.

The most sophisticated work, however, is the mosaic floor in the narthex (now, alas, partially hidden by crude partitioning) which must be an example of so called *'opus criminale'*: mosaic floors made by female convicts in Woking and Parkhurst prisons. One of them was Constance Kent, a young woman who confessed to the murder of her half-brother in 1865 and whose death sentence was commuted to life imprisonment after a sensational trial which involved Fr Arthur Wagner, the great Brighton church-builder, refusing to reveal the secrets of the confessional. It is known that Miss Kent made a mosaic floor for the crypt of St Paul's Cathedral and another for St Peter's, The Grove, on the Isle of Portland, opened in 1872. As this was another church built for and by convicts and was designed by Du Cane in the same Romanesque style, I should like to think the wretched Constance worked at Wormwood Scrubs as well.

All this raises a question: is it legitimate to be concerned with the preservation of such things on aesthetic grounds when they are associated with so much suffering? Prisons can certainly make magnificent architecture. Piranesi knew that when he made his etchings of *Carceri*: those sinister, dark vaulted interiors filled with menace which remain the ultimate in Sublime fantasy architecture. Such images certainly inspired George Dance junior – Soane's master – when he designed Newgate Prison. This was a terrible place where unspeakable things were done, but the facade was magnificent: a truly Sublime monumental rusticated Classical composition which powerfully symbolised its intimidating function. An 1854 guide to London described it as 'the most grim of all the mis-built London prisons... Its exterior architecture, however, has been much admired by foreigners'.

It was admired again by London architects by the time it was demolished in 1902 to make way for the Old Bailey, so that its memory is perpetuated by the blank aedicules on the former L.C.C. sub-station – now an antiques mall – in Upper Street, Islington. When William Nicholson was about to start on his lithographs of Oxford colleges, his friend Edwin Lutyens took him there by night as 'I wanted him to see Newgate before it goes. It would be splendid for his woodblock-cutting methods – the stone upon stone, its grim severity and grace withal.'

As the functional problem of keeping people in is not so very different from that of keeping them out, the Gothic castle-style was preferred to the Classical for most of the many, many new prisons built in the 19th century (my 1854 guide notes how prisons 'have frightfully increased in recent years, and continue to do so with an advancing rate of increase' and ninety were built between the opening of Pentonville in 1842 and the Prison Act of 1877, which, on Du Cane's advice, put all prisons under central government control).

Reading Gaol – where poor Oscar was sent – was designed in a castellated manner by the young Gilbert Scott (whose sometime partner, W.B. Moffatt, ended up in debtors' prison) but the ultimate penal castle was surely Holloway. Originally the City of London's House of Correction and built in 1849-52, it was designed by the City Architect, J.B. Bunning and given a massive fortified gatehouse flanked by polygonal Tudor-Gothic wings. All this has now gone, replaced by a 'secure hospital' for 500 women built between 1970 and 1983.

When Bunning's scenic penal masterpiece was proposed for demolition, I recall Sir Nikolaus Pevsner persuading the committee of the Victorian Society that it would be morally wrong to defend it, as social purpose transcended architectural importance and the new prison promised to be more humane. Travelling past the site in Parkhurst Road the other day, I doubted whether Pevsner had been right. Instead of a grand, symmetrical pile symbolising power and authority, the new Holloway looks informal and unpretentious – but this is cruel deception, an exercise in public relations. The language of modernity may avoid historical references and affect the demotic, but there are still bars on the windows, still walls around it outside. Bunning's castle was at least honest about its purpose but the new prison is a lie: the mailed fist is concealed in a progressive velvet glove. And, as architecture, it is mediocre, inept and depressing.

Victorian prisons have a bad press, but this is often unfair. They may reflect unfashionable social attitudes, but they were enlightened and progressive institutions in their day and their architects did not forget their duty to the wider public. Today we try to deceive ourselves that we are less smugly authoritarian, for we still seem to need prisons and – thanks to several recent Home Secretaries – Britain now puts far too many people in them. Desperate unsanitary overcrowding was the principal explanation for the 25-day revolt at Strangeways Prison in 1990.

When Strangeways opened in 1869, what is now called 'H.M. Prison Manchester' was a model institution, very well built on a polygonal plan, in which every prisoner had his own cell. Designed by the accomplished architect of Manchester Town Hall, Alfred Waterhouse, in collaboration with Joshua Jebb, the Surveyor-General of Prisons, it was really rather handsome and a great local landmark. In 1990, it housed 1,647 prisoners yet it was designed to accommodate only 970: no wonder there was a riot. At that time, Britain's prison population was 44,000; today – despite Lord Woolf's report – it is approaching double that figure. To its shame, Britain bangs up more people than any other European country. Mere architects should not be blamed for everything.

August 2004

[Clearly I had yet to exploit Google Earth when this article was written, for aerial views of Wormwood Scrubs and other prisons can now clearly be seen on the computer screen. The sad, intriguing case of Constance Kent was celebrated in Kate Summerscale's book, published in 2008, The Suspicions of Mr Whicher.*]*

Taking the Plunge

Isuppose I can take a little credit because I was a member of English Heritage's Historic Areas & Buildings Advisory Committee when the proposal came up to fit a new spa building designed by Sir Nicholas Grimshaw into the delicate, historic Georgian fabric of Bath – stuffed with listed buildings, a World Heritage Site, etc. What won us over was, I think, the thrilling concept of an open-air rooftop pool in which swimmers in spa water could gaze over the roofs and chimneypots towards the great central tower of Bath Abbey. And so it has come to pass. The new Royal Bath building may be way over budget and three years late and still dogged by litigation, but the result is a triumphant success. The visitor can now be steamed, pummelled, coated in Bath mud and enjoy all sorts of (expensive) treatments in what is now called Thermae Bath Spa but, above all, can splash about in the warm, mineral-rich water high up under the open sky in the centre of England's oldest and most celebrated spa.

Bath is back in business, and Grimshaw's building already looks set to revive its fortunes. Conspicuously modern it may be, with its relentless glass walls, but it also represents a welcome return to tradition. 'One would think the English were ducks; they are for ever waddling to the waters,' complained Horace Walpole in 1790. But, as the late E.S. Turner continued in his *Taking the Cure* published in 1967, 'the English are much less spa-minded than they used to be. They are tourists, not *curistes*. They tend to look askance at those dank, if not dubious, wells capped by flanking pavilions, those dingles haunted by arthritic semi-ambulants...' This is reflected in the wretched recent history of Bath. Such is our subservience to mechanistic medicine and the drug companies that the National Health Service withdrew support for water treatments in 1976 and two years later a suspected fatal bug in the water resulted in the closure of all the baths. Scandalously, the people of Bath, and Britain, were denied access to the sacred hot waters which bubble up from deep below ground and which had been used and enjoyed for millennia – since Roman times and beyond.

All that now remains to redeem Bath is for the Roman Bath and King's Bath by the Pump Room to be reopened for swimmers and not just to be treated as archaeology to be gazed at by tourists. But, for the moment, we have Thomas Baldwin's Late Georgian enclosure of the Cross Bath, restored and rebuilt by Donald Insall Associates (unfortunately in a manner which makes nonsense of the historic fabric); John Wood's Hot Bath, now roofed over with glass; and Grimshaw's New Royal Bath tucked behind. This is a multi-storey structure: a stone-faced cube within glass walls that follow the street lines on two sides. At the bottom is the Minerva Bath (the Romans dedicated their spa here to that fierce goddess), surprisingly curvaceous in plan (for a minimalist, high-tech architect, that is) in which swimmers can negotiate around four reinforced-concrete 'dendriform' columns. These spreading supports – reminiscent of Frank Lloyd Wright's at the Johnson Wax Factory – rise up through the building – through the changing and treatment rooms, and through the circular glass enclosures in the science-fiction steam rooms – to support the immense weight of the rooftop pool.

All this is a triumph of engineering, but is it great architecture, worthy to be compared with the Pump Room, the Assembly Rooms and the creations of John Wood and others that make Bath so distinguished as a Classical city? The problem is that architects of Grimshaw's generation and outlook cannot engage with other architectural styles and have a Puritanical horror of colour and decoration. The size and confinement of the site required that the new building be properly urban, following the street lines, but why does the exterior have to be almost all of a pale green glass (opaque at low level as a requirement of the brief was that bathers should be invisible from outside)? When in doubt, a modern architect will always reach for the glazing catalogue; as Ellis Woodman has written in *Building Design*, the new approaches the older, stone buildings 'as if history were a contactable disease'. As for the interiors, all surfaces are relentlessly, tediously white. The underwater lighting around the columns in the Minerva Pool create interesting effects (especially at night), but the possibilities of colour and pattern are ignored. The aesthetic is clinical rather than enjoyable – but that was always true of the Modern Movement.

I am not proposing that the new building should have been Classical (although why not?), but that spa architecture could be richer and more decorative. This is suggested by examples in Continental Europe where, in recent times, the medicinal and social value of spas has been taken far more seriously. Above all there is the most enjoyable swimming pool I know, that at the centre of the Gellért Medicinal Baths in Budapest – a city with a bathing culture which, as in Somerset, goes back to the Romans but was here sustained by the Ottomans. These baths are on the site of thermal springs at the foot of a hill on the west side of the Danube. The present buildings, a complex of baths both enclosed and open air, treatment rooms and an hotel, were built by the municipality and begun in 1911 to the designs of Artúr Sebestyén, Ármin Hegedüs and Izidor Sterk. The style is a sort of late *Jugendstil* Classical, heavy and richly decorative. There is a long central hall with a vaulted and glazed roof, worthy of a law court, off which the various baths open. The main swimming pool is a double-height space where the pool is surrounded by columns faced in textured ceramic. Warm spa water gushes not from stainless steel pipes (as in Bath) but from grotesque ceramic heads. Most enjoyable, perhaps, are the hot baths where the walls of the vaulted space are lined with tiles of deep turquoise-blue and decorative mosaic, enhanced by ceramic sculpture.

Everything about the Gellért Baths is richly sensual, not least visually. They seem to reinterpret the form of ancient Roman baths, with their vaulted communal spaces, in an expressive contemporary style. Of course, not only are the baths in Budapest much larger than those in Bath but they reflect the aesthetic ideals of the beginning of the 20th century rather than those of its end: the contrast is extreme. But it surely would be possible to design a modern bath complex today which is nevertheless colourful and sensual in its architectural treatment. Indeed, it has been done: at Vals in Switzerland. The new thermal baths here, built in 1990-96, are the work of Peter Zumthor, who has become a cult-figure among architects. He is a sort of modern Philip Webb who has produced a limited number of carefully crafted buildings.

There is nothing clinical about the baths at Vals as Zumthor is a thoughtful designer who believes that architecture should be a balance of emotion and reason. The architectural forms are rectilinear and austere, but the walls are built of the local Valser quartzite and brick as well as of exposed concrete.

Colour and texture are therefore introduced while the interior spaces are given drama by the handling of natural light. Some are dark and grotto-like while in others windows allow views of the surrounding mountains. Furthermore, there are both indoor and outdoor pools (as at the Gellért). What Zumthor has done is draw on the tradition of Roman and Turkish Baths not by copying their forms but by recreating their atmospheres through the handling of space, light and the colours of natural materials. 'In order to design buildings with a sensuous connection to life,' he writes, 'one must think in a way that goes far beyond form and construction.'

So successful were the new thermal baths at Vals that the building was given legal protection only two years after it opened. I have not seen it myself, and long to go off to Switzerland to enjoy those steamy spaces. But I also look forward to returning to Bath and splashing about on the roof of the new Royal Bath. In his own terms, Grimshaw has also created a remarkable spa building which combines structural logic with sensual experience. As the Georgians well understood, fine architecture enhances the experience of taking the waters.

October 2006

Aerial Travellers

A few miles to the south of Bedford, the flat, rather dreary landscape is dominated by two colossal structures standing side by side which stand out against the sky. Measuring over 800 feet long and some 150 high, consisting of steel skeletons covered in corrugated metal with gigantic buttressed doors which move on rollers, these are the Cardington airship sheds and they are astonishingly impressive. Shed No.1 was erected in 1917 by Short Brothers to build airships to vie with the Zeppelins which were then bombing London. The firm also constructed Shortstown, a small garden village to house its workforce. After the war, Cardington became the Royal Airship Works and Shed No.2, first made elsewhere in 1916, was re-erected here in 1928. Rare survivors of this once internationally ubiquitous building type, these steel 'cathedrals' are now listed buildings.

That inspiring architectural writer Ian Nairn was born in Bedford in 1930 (describing it as 'the most characterless town in

England'). His father was an 'airship draughtsman' and lived in Shortstown. Soon afterwards, however, Nairn senior had to become a civil servant and move to West Surrey (another place that engendered in his son 'a deep hatred of characterless buildings and places'). This was because of the disaster that occurred two months after Nairn's birth. Shed No.1 had been enlarged in 1926-27 to construct the R.101, a government sponsored giant airship that proved to be plagued by design faults – unlike the contemporary R.100 designed by Barnes Wallis (he of the Dam Busting 'bouncing bomb') built at Howden in Yorkshire. Overloaded and not properly tested, R.101 left Cardington on 5 October 1930 for its inaugural flight, with several dignitaries on board. Its destination was India but the ship came down at Beauvais that night in a storm and burst into flames, killing 46 people including the Secretary of State for Air. This brought a sudden end to the British airship industry, and R.100 was broken up in Shed No.2 not long afterwards.

It was a sad conclusion to the story of lighter-than-air flight in England which had begun a century and a half earlier when, on 15 September 1784, a glamorous Italian adventurer, Vincenzo Lunardi, ascended from the grounds of the Hon. Artillery Company in the basket of a hydrogen balloon in front of the Prince of Wales, the Prime Minister William Pitt, and the largest crowd London had ever seen. He thus became the first man to rise into the air from English soil (not *British*, for James Tytler had made a brief ascent in a hot-air balloon a few weeks earlier in Edinburgh). Born in Lucca, Lunardi was secretary to the Neapolitan Ambassador in London and, inspired by the first balloon ascents in France the previous year, decided that this was the way to find fame and fortune. His successful pioneering flight made him a sensation. Lunardi's balloon was exhibited in James Wyatt's Pantheon in Oxford Street, that remarkable hall modelled on the interior of Haghia Sophia, where the young and handsome aeronaut was feted by his many female admirers.

Lunardi's second ascent, in a new balloon decorated with the

Union Jack, was less remarkable. His third – from St George's
Fields in Southwark on 29 June 1785 – was more interesting as he
intended to take with him both his friend George Biggin and also,
as a publicity stunt, an actress friend, Letitia Sage, who had once
been understudy to the celebrated Sarah Siddons. Unfortunately,
there were the usual problems in producing enough hydrogen,
causing delays that tended to make the crowds dangerously rest-
less. The result was that the balloon proved unequal to the task,
especially as Mrs Sage, on her own admission, weighed over 200
lbs. Lunardi therefore gallantly stepped aside to permit the other
two to take off – and allow Mrs Sage proudly to become 'the first
English Female Aerial Traveller'. The pair enjoyed a lunch of
chicken and ham as they drifted over St James's Park, tossing
empty wine bottles over the side, before coming down in Harrow.

Lunardi made other balloon ascents in England and
Scotland, but fashion is fickle and his star waned. He returned
to Italy in 1786 and died, ill and impoverished, in Lisbon twenty
years later. But there was no stopping the craze for ballooning.
China and furniture was designed ornamented with the happy
geometrical form of the balloon, although, sadly, as far as I am
aware no building was ever erected in that shape. No fete or
celebration was complete without a balloon ascent. The new
Hungerford Market, that magnificent complex of shops and
arcades later replaced by Charing Cross Station, was opened
in 1833 with George Graham rising into the sky from the lower
courtyard. Graham, together with his wife Margaret, were
two of a number of aeronauts who became famous. They were
astonishingly accident-prone however, and the tiled roofs and
brick parapets of London houses repeatedly suffered from their
exploits. 'The really amazing thing,' as L.T.C. Rolt remarked, 'is
that Margaret Graham should have soldiered on in this way for
no less than thirty years without… becoming any more skilled
in the art of balloon management, and yet have survived to die
in her bed.' Rather more competent was Charles Green, who
made over five hundred ascents and set a distance record in

1836 by flying 480 miles from London to the Duchy of Nassau in Germany.

The problem with such balloons was, of course, that they were at the mercy of the wind. The dirigible, a lighter-than-air craft that was powered and could be steered, was developed later in the 19th century, but in France rather than Britain. As with heavier-than-air flight, what was needed was a light-weight source of power and that arrived with the internal combustion engine. And it was a German, Count Ferdinand von Zeppelin, who perfected the rigid powered airship in the early 20th century. This was a line of development that came to a dramatic end when the airship *Hindenburg* burst into flames when docking in New York in 1937. Lighter-than-air flight continues today, what with the vogue for hot-air balloon ascents, but its great and glamorous days have now long passed.

A stone in a field near Ware in Hertfordshire marks the spot where that first aerial voyage in England came finally to rest, but otherwise there is no memorial to the gallant Lunardi. No building in London associated with him now seems to survive on which English Heritage might place a Blue Plaque and, sadly, Mrs Sage's house in Covent Garden has also long been demolished. The Pantheon, too, has gone, as has the Lyceum in the Strand where Lunardi's balloon was also exhibited. The Hungerford Market has long disappeared, as have the Vauxhall Gardens, the Cremorne and the other pleasure grounds in London much used by balloonists, along with the Crystal Palace at Sydenham from whose grounds many later ascents were made. All that is now left to testify to the courage and enterprise of all those British aeronauts and to the many, many balloons and airships that were constructed and flown (apart from the memorial to the victims of the R.101 in Cardington churchyard designed by Albert Richardson) are those two colossal steel sheds that still stand so proudly in Bedfordshire.

April 2011

Streamlined

A sad farewell ceremony took place in Oxford Street just before Christmas when the last red double-decker Routemaster bus on a regular route left on its final journey across London. A huge crowd had gathered, and the event had been preceded by massive coverage in the press. So did the (premature) extinction of a familiar London mobile landmark deserve so much fuss? Surely yes. The first Routemaster may have appeared exactly sixty years ago, but there was life in the vehicle yet. It does more miles to the gallon than its replacements (so is more environmentally friendly), is more comfortable to ride, and is just better designed. What did for it was the Mayor of London's craven subservience to political correctness and that charter for vandalism, the Disability Act, for wheelchairs could not negotiate its popular feature of an open rear platform which allows passengers to board and alight where they chose rather than be trapped behind automatic doors.

Machines may have a shorter life than buildings as their parts wear out (although buildings of the 1960s were often designed – criminally – for a life of thirty years or less, and it shows), but there is no necessary reason why an efficient design should become obsolete. The excellence of the Routemaster was a consequence of both its technology and its design being the products of evolution. The bus was developed over many years by London Transport, and the design – by Douglas Scott – was the product of careful thought. The curves of both the exterior and interior, the ergonomic design of handles and rails, the avoidance of conflicting movement by placing the stairs at the rear, and the seeming inevitability of every detail, were all a joy to see and experience – especially in comparison with the newer, alien boxy buses, full of sharp projections and discordances inside. (The story is well told by Travis Elborough in *The Bus We Loved: London's Affair with the Routemaster*, recently published by Granta Books.)

In truth, however, the Routemaster was not the *most* beautiful of buses. There was something slightly stodgy about its unfashionable and ungimmicky appearance: hence its timelessness, perhaps. No, the most elegant public conveyance ever to grace the streets of London was its predecessor, the RT, which had evolved just before and after the Second World War. Slightly narrower than the Routemaster while having the same rounded corners and interior treatment, it was characterised by a more pronounced slope at the front, curving back from its vertical radiator, while the rear was proudly vertical. This, not the Routemaster, was the bus that starred in Cliff Richard's *Summer Holiday* and such vehicles were admired not least by Le Corbusier who, on a visit to London in 1936, wrote how 'The buses are splendid – red, covered with beautiful lettering; tall, strategic towers.'

Mention of Le Corbusier, the apparent apostle of a purely functional architecture, invites discussion of the strange formal relationship between buildings and technology. This works two ways. There are machines that are treated as architecture, like pumping stations with the engines supported on cast-iron Doric columns, or such conceits as Pope Pius IX's railway carriage, with its balcony and roof supported on twisted columns. And then there are buildings that try and look like machines, such as Mendelsohn's Einstein Tower at Potsdam which resembles the conning tower of a submarine, or the fantastic Russian Constructivist projects in the shape of giant cogwheels. Such ideas of an *architecture parlante* or literal symbolism can be traced back to Ledoux and his ideal city of Chaux in France, in which the house of the cooper is inspired by the circular form of a barrel, and the Oikéma, or House of Pleasure is given a phallic plan.

But is was Le Corbusier's book, *Vers une Architecture*, with its photographs of cars juxtaposed with Classical temples and such compelling slogans as 'A house is a machine for living in', which did most to encourage machine imagery in architecture. The message was clear; buildings need to work, to be efficient like machinery, ignoring the fact that buildings are obstinately static objects with, ideally, a much longer life than machines and which have emotional and psychological functions as well as purely physical ones. That old reactionary, Sir Reginald Blomfield, exploded this mechanical fallacy in his rant against *Modernismus* published in 1934: 'That some forms of mechanical construction have an accidental beauty of their own under certain conditions, one may readily admit; a great liner, for example, coming towards one on a sunlit sea, or the fine thin lines of steel construction, such as cranes or electric towers and the like; but change the mechanical object and the argument falls to pieces. Big Bertha, for example, could drop a shell into Paris from a range of thirty miles, undoubtedly efficient but unspeakably ugly.'

The machine aesthetic was particularly influential between the world wars, when so much new architecture was streamlined with rounded corners and horizontal banding even though, by their nature, buildings do not move and do not need to be aerodynamic in form. Two machines – forms of transport – particularly inspired architects: the aeroplane and the ocean liner. Corb's book, first published in France in 1923, had chapters about machines entitled 'Eyes which do not see'. One was devoted to 'Airplanes' and illustrated with photographs of early biplane and triplane airliners and bombers, with their wings connected by struts. Such images were powerful and the consequences soon manifest – for what are the 'pilotis' or thin columns on which Le Corbusier and his imitators raised up their creations but aeroplane struts?

Yet by the end of the 1930s the biplane had largely been replaced by sleek monoplanes, just as the 1921 Delage 'Grand-Sport' which Le Corbusier juxtaposed with the Parthenon soon looked much more old-fashioned than a Greek temple. Machines soon date, and become obsolete, but gullible architects did not mind. The desirability of pilotis, together with the moral necessity of a flat roof, soon became articles of faith among modernists. But perhaps raising structures on struts to free the ground floor is less absurd than giving buildings cantilevered reinforced concrete wings – like Norman & Dawbarn's airport at Birmingham. The best example of this sort of thing was the elegant Ramsgate Aerodrome terminal by David Pleydell-Bouverie, which had a thin projecting flat roof supported on metal piers which tapered towards the extremities; from the air it apparently looked like an aeroplane.

And then there were ships – those magnificent, glamorous liners which enabled passengers to cross the Atlantic at speed and in comfort. Le Corbusier naturally illustrated some of these modern wonders, and it is interesting how the white-painted upper decks and promenades of the *S.S. France* or *Aquitania*, sometimes curved and cantilevered outwards, resemble early Modern Movement houses. Indeed, what are the sun-roofs of such houses, often reached by metal ladders, but the First Class decks of ocean liners floating over the green hills of Surrey or Buckinghamshire? By the sea, of course, nautical imagery has more purpose. Marine Court at St Leonards on the Sussex coast is but a huge liner of brick and concrete, while at the Pleasure Beach at Blackpool Joseph Emberton played with funnel-like shapes and those modish porthole windows. Such examples are paralleled by countless examples in the United States, but few are quite as literal as the homage to the great French liner, the *Normandie*, which is to be found sailing among the sand dunes on the Belgian coast near La Panne: an hotel and restaurant of solid masonry complete with bow, stern and funnels.

Perhaps architecture has become a little more sophisticated since then in its attitude to technology, although streamlined Art Deco buildings of the 1930s remain models of glamour and stylishness. Even so, much architectural thought remains as essentially childish as ever, and it is undeniable that much of the imagery of the 'high-tech' architecture which emerged in the 1960s came from the Dan Dare comic strip in the *Eagle* and other science-fiction publications. In fact, high-tech can be engagingly old-fashioned, and the external glass lifts on, say, Richard Rogers's Lloyd's building hark back to those lifts whizzing up and down in glass tubes in Alexander Korda's futuristic nightmare, *The Shape of Things to Come* of 1936. And I recall once visiting the Norman Foster office when it was in Fitzroy Street in which the internal doors were all like bulk-head doors on a ship, that is, with rounded corners and a raised sill to trip over. So much for functionalism: architects seem to be peculiarly susceptible to the promises of technology so that machine-worship continues to triumph over common-sense and practicality.

Even so, I have yet to experience a high-tech building which is as efficient, as ergonomically sensitive and as elegant as the interior of that architectural masterpiece on wheels, the Routemaster bus.

February 2006

[A positive development is that the next Mayor of London commissioned a design for a new London bus from Thomas Heatherwick and the result, introduced first on the No. 38 route in 2012, is a triumph of intelligent, thoughtful design – not least in having, like true London buses, an open platform at the rear as well as two internal staircases.]

Bring Back the Railings

Where did it all go? One of our national myths concerns the drive for salvage during the Second World War, when metal was collected to aid the war effort. But, so the story goes, the cast-iron railings removed from parks and gardens proved to be useless for turning into guns and tanks, just as the aluminium saucepans sacrificed by so many housewives were never made into Spitfires. So what happened to it all? Official documentation is, curiously, silent on the mystery, but as 22,000 tons had already been collected by October 1940, these mountains of metal must have gone somewhere. The consensus today is that most of it was dumped in the Thames Estuary.

From an architectural point of view, this was a tragedy. Our towns and cities were denuded not only of iron railings but also of ornamental ironwork, lamp brackets, balcony fronts and much else of aesthetic as well as practical value – and all, it would seem, to little purpose. But it is clear that the salvage drive was really an exercise in creating a sense of solidarity at a time of national emergency, with the real threat of invasion by Nazi Germany. The appeal for old iron bedsteads and the like was launched at the beginning of 1940, but it was the removal of railings which caught the public imagination. This was generally held to be a Good Thing. Dislike of railings would seem to have been inspired both by a feeling that they were anti-democratic (a folk memory of the 1866 Reform demonstration when the railings of Hyde Park were uprooted by an angry crowd?) and anti-Victorian prejudice. 'Dare one hope that the exigencies of war will at last rid London and other places of one of their major disfigurements – iron railings?' was the typical attitude of correspondents to *The Times*.

The campaign was organised by the National Federation of Scrap Iron and Steel Merchants and a thousand tons a week of architectural ironwork was soon being collected by local authorities. Thirty tons came from the Royal Parks and Hyde Park lost its railings again – this time officially. To be opposed to this cull was to run the risk of being thought unpatriotic, and the campaign was conducted with an enthusiasm amounting to mania. Sometimes it was pursued with malice – as when the iron gates were deliberately taken from the Worcestershire seat of the former Prime Minister, Stanley Baldwin. A few dared to advise caution. In May 1940 Sir Giles Gilbert Scott opened an exhibition at the Building Centre about 'Railings for Scrap' which was 'designed to show not only what railings might be removed with advantage but also what railings ought to be retained on aesthetic grounds'. Shortly afterwards, Albert Richardson, as vice-chairman of the Georgian Group, deprecated 'the removal of any iron-work of historic or aesthetic interest' and suggested 'that railings and architectural features, both of wrought and cast iron, executed before 1850 are worth keeping, and that the greater part – but not all – of iron-work erected after 1850 could wisely be spared for scrap'. But it was surely brave of a group of artists to protest against the scrapping of 'the noble Georgian railings of Berkeley Square' while the Battle of Britain was being fought overhead.

What the railing-haters ignored was the simple fact that the things usually had a purpose. The gardens in London squares were maintained by the surrounding householders, who soon wanted protective railings put back, while parks without railings soon looked scruffy and unkempt while people got up to things in them at night of which both the police and the general public took a dim view. Hyde Park soon had railings back again. In August 1944 George Orwell noted that, 'I see that the railings are returning – only wooden ones, it is true, but still railings – in one London square after another. So the lawful denizens of the squares can make use of their treasured keys again, and the children of the poor can be kept out.' By the end of the war, most squares had their gardens enclosed by barriers of chicken wire on crude metal supports, with the low stone plinths, pitted with regular holes or punctuated by sawn-off iron studs, pathetically testifying to the former presence of proper railings.

Since then, the iron railings have usually returned. Some – like the fine contemporary railings around St Paul's Cathedral – had been temporarily removed but not destroyed. Although the removal of railings was, as Orwell put it, a 'democratic gesture', the replacement of rusting wire with proper cast-iron railings has generally been regarded as a civic improvement which enhances the appearance of London squares both rich and poor. A good example is what has happened in the centre of Birmingham, where the railings have recently been restored around the large churchyard of Thomas Archer's magnificent Baroque cathedral in the city centre. Before, the unprotected churchyard looked neglected and hostile, with the monuments subject to vandalism; now it looks smart and urban – and is much more enjoyable (and safe) for the public to use. And railings are often an integral part of great architecture. It was important, for instance, that the restoration of Hawksmoor's Christ Church, Spitalfields, was heralded by the restoration of the railings around the west end and steps. And the appearance of both the Manchester City Art Gallery and the National Gallery of Scotland has been much enhanced by the restoration of well-designed railings.

Which brings me to the case of the National Gallery in London. When the building designed by William Wilkins opened in 1837, iron railings maintained the street line defined by the projecting central portico flanked by steps. The spaces behind were subsequently laid with grass and dwarf fig trees grown around the perimeter next to the walls. At some point towards the end of the Second World War these railings disappeared. Today, the lawns have become victims of the 2003 pedestrianisation of the north side of Trafalgar Square, the chief result of which, as the director of the Gallery, Nicholas Penny, rightly complains, 'has been the trashing of a civic space'. The heart of the capital is now used for a succession of commercial events generating amplified noise which 'has an impact on the ability of the public to appreciate works of art'. As for the railingless lawns, these are now frankly squalid, especially in hot weather, with half-undressed people lying on the grass and others, not necessarily sober, committing nuisances, as they used to say, against the walls. And every morning the Gallery's staff has to clear away the mass of rubbish. This use of the lawns scarcely makes for a dignified setting for a great national institution. As Dr Penny puts it, 'A lot of people find it rather extraordinary that a temple of art should be surrounded by abandoned beer cans and litter.'

Can anything be done? A recent controversy over placing a café on one of the lawns has raised the question of putting back the missing railings. Those who like Trafalgar Square being a sort of permanent Glastonbury Festival naturally consider the idea as being elitist and anti-democratic. However, proper, dignified stone seats could be placed on the North Terrace in front of the Gallery as compensation. Besides, an interesting wartime propaganda film of 1942 shows office workers at lunchtime sitting on the lawns eating their sandwiches *with the railings still in place*. Evidently the gates were open during the day but closed – like those around Hyde Park – at night. It can be argued, therefore, that restoring the railings would not only enhance Wilkins' architecture but be socially as well as visually desirable. Bring back the railings!

September 2010

[Alas, at the time of writing, no railings have reappeared in front of the National Gallery, but one lives in hope…]

Out With the Old

Years ago I met the elderly aunt of a friend, who told us about a frightening experience in her childhood. Cycling along a country road near Newark, she was alarmed by a noise and a bright light overhead, which made her ride into a ditch: 'It was a Zep – looking for Nottingham!' I do not know if that Zeppelin ever found its target, although Nottingham was in fact bombed during the First World War. Rather more destruction was created by the Luftwaffe in the Second but, as with so many other British cities, the damage done to Nottingham in the 20th century was largely self-inflicted. In the post-war decades, when Richard Greene was hamming it up as Robin Hood on our early television screens, the ineffably named Maid Marion Way was driven through the urban fabric to create a gulf between the city centre and the Castle. Soon after, more old streets were sacrificed to create the introverted and vile Broad Marsh shopping centre. And another horrible shopping centre was created on the site of Victoria Station on the old Great Central Railway – a trunk line which burrowed under the city and which – if post-war British governments had not been so car-obsessed and *stupid* – could now be handling Continental trains from the Channel Tunnel.

Nevertheless, Nottingham remains a city of great interest. St Mary's, the parish church, is one of the wonders of England and the subject of one of the finest etchings by the great F.L. Griggs. A masterpiece of Perpendicular Gothic, its many windows seem to form a grid of stone and glass, filling the richly furnished interior with light. And then there is the Castle which, standing on its mound, heralds the city to the visitor arriving on the surviving Midland Railway line by train. It is, in fact, a Baroque palace and, as such, unique in England, for it was rebuilt by the Duke of Newcastle in the 1670s and the walls are encrusted with heavy rustication and Mannerist aedicules. Unfortunately, the interior was burned out in 1831 by Nottingham's citizens unhappy with the then Duke's opposition to the Reform Bill. After standing as a ruin for some years, the shell was converted into the city's art gallery and museum in the 1870s and today has a collection that deserves to be better known.

What else? There is the County Hall in High Pavement by James Gandon, who went on to embellish Dublin with magnificent Classical buildings; there is a Roman Catholic cathedral by Pugin; entertaining rumbustious Gothic-cum-Tudor Late Victorian buildings by the local architect Watson Fothergill; and a grand Classical 1920s Council House by another bright local boy, Cecil Howitt. Then there are the architectural treats in the vicinity, such as Wollaton Hall, the glorious Elizabethan house by Robert Smythson which the city council had the wit to acquire in the 1920s. Rather different is the Boots Factory at Beeston, but it is rightly famous because of the pioneering and powerful factory buildings of the 1930s, all concrete and glass, by that brilliant and bloody-minded engineer, Sir Owen Williams.

And then there is the University, paid for by Jesse Boot, which is remarkable for its post-war colleges: intelligent examples of semi-traditional modern-Classical architecture by McMorran & Whitby, amongst others, placed in a pastoral landscape.

So there is much for Nottingham to be proud of. And clearly the city wishes to undo some of its worst mistakes. The Broad Marsh Centre is to be rebuilt, and 'the new development must not repeat the mistakes of the 1970s shopping centre in being designed as a mega-structure which completely disregarded the long-established street pattern...' The Old Market Square in front of the Council House – from which the market, along with the famous Goose Fair, was foolishly ejected in the 1920s – is to be improved, as are the surroundings of the railway station, a jolly piece of Late Victorian terracotta arcading. And there is talk of trying to minimise the destructive impact of Maid Marion Way and to reconnect the Castle and its grounds with the centre.

Even so, given Nottingham's recent history, one might have thought that the city council would cherish the historic buildings that survive, but this does not seem to be the case. Indeed, what is depressing is that the one central area that largely escaped post-war redevelopments and road building is now again under some threat. This is the Lace Market, an area of streets north of the parish church which is filled with many substantial 19th century lace warehouses as well as Georgian houses. Once depressed and derelict, it has seen imaginative regeneration in recent decades and is now the most interesting and enjoyable part of the city – and a conservation area. Yet, despite all the positive actions, a number of buildings in the Lace Market remain derelict and one in Pilcher Gate, a (listed) town house of c.1700 is actually proposed for demolition (a tenth of Nottingham's 971 listed buildings are regarded as 'At Risk'.)

Then there are damaging proposals for new buildings. A particular worry is the plan for building The Pod, a large hotel with restaurant and shops which is to replace a number of buildings in Fletcher Gate which, although derelict and unlisted, nevertheless make a positive contribution to the character and appearance of the conservation area (as the jargon goes). The design for the new building is by Benson & Forsyth, architects of the new National Museum of Scotland in Edinburgh, and, although interesting, is uncompromisingly aggressive. More to the point, the hotel is to be twice the height of most buildings in the Lace Market and will thus challenge the dominance of the Wrennian dome of the Council House on the skyline. Yet this project is supported by the city council, although it has provoked local opposition and, along with other proposals, greatly concerns English Heritage. Unfortunately, EH, as it is acutely conscious of being unloved by the present government, is anxious not to seem to oppose any and every new development supported by the local authority. It does, however, sensibly reiterate the government's own planning guideline (PPG 15) which advises that 'The destruction of historic buildings is in fact very seldom necessary for reasons of good planning; more often it is the result of neglect, or of failure to make imaginative efforts to find new uses for them or to incorporate them into new development.'

Now this column is intended neither to be exclusively a platform for conservation campaigns nor a travelogue. I am writing about Nottingham this month because I like the place and think its architectural delights deserve to be better known, but also because what is happening there – in the very centre of England – is representative of worrying tendencies in Britain as a whole. Nottingham is one of eight 'Core Cities' in England whose councils came together in 1995 to work to make them 'drivers of regional and national competitiveness and pros- perity with the aim of creating internationally competitive regions.' The stated objectives for Core Cities are largely con- cerned with economic growth, and I cannot find any reference to the importance of maintaining local character or to the value of historic buildings in generating real prosperity. And I fear that, despite fine words, by its actions at present Nottingham City Council is demonstrating little interest in looking after what many visitors come to see: its historic urban fabric.

None of this is surprising in the current political climate. We are living under a Labour government that is taking less interest in what we must now call 'heritage' than any of its predecessors. The influential opinion held by William Morris that history belongs to all of us and that the preservation of old buildings matters because they contribute to the general public good – a belief translated by the Attlee and Wilson governments into our planning and historic buildings legislation – seems to be of little consequence to present ministers. English Heritage is being deliberately starved of funds and thus impeded in its work while government spending on sport goes up and up and up. I do not know if the Deputy Prime Minister has ever heard of Morris: unlikely, I fear, given his evident enthusiasm for dismantling the Green Belt and covering the south-east of England with houses – let alone his Neo-Sixties utopian vision of regenerating Northern cities by bulldozing ordinary terraced houses in their tens of thousands (the so-called Pathfinder schemes).

In the circumstances, Nottingham City Council is probably being sensible by exploiting regeneration initiatives backed by the government. It seems a pity, however, that it assumes that bringing in fashionable architects to design new buildings is the best way to improve the damaged urban fabric as such designers are seldom sensitive to historic character (planning permission has just been granted for a Centre for Contemporary Arts at Weekday Cross designed by Caruso St John which seems very disappointing when compared with that firm's brilliant and thoughtful Walsall Art Gallery). But what is really depressing are the attitudes that can be detected behind the Council's recent decisions. That uncritical enthusiasm for building the new, which gravely damaged so many cities in the 1960s and was all too often blinkered self-hatred in disguise, seems to be alive and well in Nottingham today. But the city deserves better.

September 2005

[I was wrong about the design for Nottingham Contemporary, and I atoned by praising Caruso St John's new building, which heals the gash created by the Great Central Railway, in Apollo *for October 2010. As for the Labour government starving English Heritage of funds, the situation is much worse under the current Conservative-dominated Coalition government.]*

Looking After Liverpool

Behind the great 16-column Corinthian portico of St George's Hall in Liverpool, which Sir Nikolaus Pevsner described as 'the freest Neo-Grecian building in England and one of the finest in the world', are four empty plinths. It has long been my fear that someone will propose that they should be occupied by modern statues of John, Paul, George and Ringo. It could happen: The Beatles now seem to be central to Liverpool's image of itself, and it is all too easy to imagine the dire vulgarity of the result: more of the bronze-waxwork type of sculpture (by Paul Day?) that now constitutes public art all over Britain. And it would accord with the fatuous desire to be forward looking, demotic and not to be too reverential about the past, that is characteristic of those who govern Liverpool and many other cities.

Needless to say, Ringo Starr was prominent in the noisy public ceremony that inaugurated Liverpool's long-heralded year as European City of Culture in January this year. Now it would be wrong to be too cynical about this, for the city deserves credit for having pulled itself up from being Britain's principal urban basket case a quarter of a century ago, when it was known mostly for economic collapse, urban race riots and self-destructive Militant Socialism. But there is something so very exasperating about Liverpool's smug self-satisfaction, its impregnable belief in its own superiority and peculiar proletarian charm, for the simple fact is that most of what is genuinely cultured about the city – at least visually – dates from the 19th and the early decades of the 20th century. Without that legacy, the Year of Culture would be vacuous hype.

It was the city's mercantile economy, primed by the slave trade (not for nothing did Liverpool support and supply ships to the Confederacy during the American Civil War) that paid for the stupendous and imaginative buildings that expressed its overweening civic pride: St George's Hall, the two huge cathedrals (alas, Lutyens's for the Roman Catholics was hardly begun, but the Anglicans finished theirs), the three grand Edwardian piles by Pierhead now known as the Three Graces. And it was the wealth and discrimination of the merchants and ship-owners that filled Liverpool's museums and galleries with the art treasures the city now boasts. Compared with this, the recent record is not impressive. The European cultural accolade has been used as an excuse to encourage crass commercial developments at the expense of yet more of the city's historic buildings, and the one prestigious cultural project, the gratuitous new Museum of Liverpool which will disfigure Pierhead, has been marred by delays and disputes – its original Danish architects have been dismissed and there are now rows about its stone cladding.

Liverpool has often been its own worst enemy and there would be rather less to boast about today if it were not for outside interference in recent decades. Of course, the moral effect of its inexorable economic decline as a great port – the end of the TransAtlantic liners in particular – should not be under-estimated, but there is little excuse for the destructive policies pursued by its authorities. Things began badly immediately after the Second World War when the gutted but substantial ruin of the Custom House, a magnificent Neo-Classical pile by a talented local architect, John Foster, was demolished in order to 'lessen unemployment'. Presumably it did not occur to them that to *restore* the building would also have relieved unemployment – and encouraged skills and trades. Further relentless destruction of Liverpool's Georgian and Victorian fabric continued for the next few decades – not even the original Cavern Club, the celebrated basement where the Beatles first performed, was spared, thus denying the city a major tourist attraction.

Strange but true, it was the hated Conservative government of Margaret Thatcher that saved Liverpool from itself. After the 1981 Toxteth riots, Michael Heseltine, as Secretary of State for the Environment, took a close interest in the struggling city, set up a 'Task Force' to deal with urban deprivation and created the Merseyside Development Corporation. He also prevented the demolition of the former Lyceum Club designed by Thomas Harrison, the architect of Chester Castle. Sited at the bottom of Bold Street, once the city's smartest commercial street, this most handsome Neo-Classical building was to have been demolished to make way for a new shopping centre. And it was Heseltine who rescued Liverpool's museums and galleries from municipal control and mismanagement by establishing the independent National Museums & Galleries on Merseyside (now National Museums Liverpool), since when the Walker Art Gallery, the Lady Lever Art Gallery at Port Sunlight and the several other establishments have flourished.

Heseltine was also involved with the saving and restoration of two monumental structures which are today two of its principal cultural assets. One is St George's Hall, the vast Classical building of the 1840s designed by the young Harvey

Lonsdale Elmes (who won the competition at the age of 25 and was dead at 34) which stands in the heart of the city and makes the area between the Walker Art Gallery and Lime Street Station seem like a Roman forum ('SPQL' those proud Liverpudlian oligarchs had cast on its great metal doors: *The Senate and People of Liverpool*). However magnificent, the building had long been neglected; after the Second World War the sculpture in the great south pediment was taken down and apparently ended up as hard-core for road building.

Inside, in addition to Elmes's vast vaulted Great Hall and C.R. Cockerell's exquisite Concert Hall, there were two hand-some courts that remained in use. In 1984, however, following the completion of the Queen Elizabeth II Law Courts – a pecu-liarly nasty brown concrete structure which blocks the vista from the Town Hall that once ended with the dome of the Custom House – these became redundant. The vast building was then unceremoniously handed back to the City Council, which had no use for it and could not afford to run it. Fortunately, public interest in the building grew, while the Prince of Wales took an interest in it and appealed for something to be done. And something was done. Thanks to the intervention of the World Monuments Fund and English Heritage, a £23 million restoration, mostly funded by the Heritage Lottery Fund and the European Regional Development Fund, was completed last year. Largely carried out by Purcell Miller Tritton archi-tects, this has opened up the previously unused South Portico entrance and allowed the public to have access to the whole building – including the basement with its cells and elaborate heating system.

The other building is the Albert Dock, whose conversion was the real catalyst for the regeneration of Liverpool. Although it rapidly became redundant for its intended purpose as ships got bigger, this magnificent 1840s structure, designed by an engineer with a taste for the sublime, Jesse Hartley, with fire-proof brick warehouses raised above cast-iron unfluted Doric columns, was perhaps the finest surviving example of what J.M. Richards called the 'Functional Tradition' in Britain. Yet in 1966 it was threatened with demolition, although a contemporary report demonstrated it was eminently suitable for conversion to other uses. 'To pull down Albert Dock would be a black disgrace' wrote Pevsner in his *Buildings of England* volume at about this time. He was then chairman of the Victorian Society and over the following two decades the society had to fight hard against demolition, filling in the dock as a car park and other crass proposals supported by the City Council. And to assist these, in 1979, out of sheer malice, the Mersey Docks & Harbour Board opened the sluices to fill the dock with river mud.

Soon afterwards, Michael Heseltine came to the rescue. The buildings were restored, bomb-damaged parts rebuilt, and today the Albert Dock is one of Liverpool's glories, the home of the Tate Gallery and the Merseyside Maritime Museum. If anyone deserves a statue in Liverpool, it is the former Secretary of State for the Environment. But as for the Victorian Society – which, as I also pointed out in January, celebrates its 50th anniversary this year – its memorial is the fact that the Albert Dock and many other fine buildings are still standing to be enjoyed during the city's reign as European City of Culture.

March 2008

[The completed Museum of Liverpool turned out to be as offensively gratuitous as predicted while Liverpool continues to sustain its reputation for prodigal self-harm, what with the Council encouraging the monstrous overdevelopment of the Liverpool Waters docklands site north of Pierhead despite warnings from UNESCO.]

Dreamland

The painter J.M.W. Turner began to make regular visits to Margate in the 1820s. He was drawn there not so much by the amenities offered by the then fashionable watering place but by the sea and the light at the furthest eastern extremity of the county of Kent – on the remote Isle of Thanet bounded by the Thames Estuary and the English Channel; 'the skies over Thanet are the loveliest in all Europe', Ruskin recorded him once saying. Ever secretive, he was known in Margate as Mr Booth, the surname of his landlady and later mistress, Sophia, who had a house close to the stone mole with its lighthouse at the end – a Doric column – lately rebuilt by the great Scots engineer John Rennie.

Like a later artist currently enjoying celebrity, Tracy Emin, Turner had been to school in Margate. By then, the transformation of the old fishing village into a bathing resort was over half-a-century old. This was partly owing to the invention of the bathing machine, those mobile changing rooms which could be wheeled into the sea and which probably first appeared on the sands at Scarborough. However, as the seaside historian Kathryn Ferry explains, 'It was at Margate that the term "machine" was first used, specifically describing a more sophisticated bathing vehicle pioneered by local Quaker Benjamin Beale' – the sophistication consisting of the addition of a concertinaed canvas modesty hood for female bathers.

But Margate is much older than the intricate pattern of winding streets and charming small Georgian squares that lie just inland from its wide bay and chalk cliff. A little further out, now overwhelmed by Victorian suburban expansion, is the extraordinary and mysterious Shell Grotto. Apparently discovered in 1835 during the digging of a duck-pond, it consists of a winding underground passage ending in a rectangular chamber, every inch of the walls of which are lined with swirling patterns made of shells – over four million of them in all. Theories abound as to who constructed it, and when. Some guide books insist it was used by smugglers; others suggest it may have been a Roman Temple of Mithras or was dug by Phoenician traders while more recently comparisons have been made with ancient structures in Egypt and Mexico. However, to my eye, and to those of other detached commentators, it looks as if it was created not long before ... 1835. No matter: it is now a Grade I listed building and a wonder.

I first visited Margate with my father in 1957 at the age of nine. Like many thousands before us, we had come from London by boat down the Thames. That visit I remember vividly, mainly because our destination was Dreamland and, being small, I was terrified of being flung off the Scenic Railway rollercoaster. Dreamland was another of Margate's attractions. The successor to pleasure gardens, it was inspired by the fun fair at Coney Island and opened in 1920. Then, after a fire in 1931, it was given a conspicuous landmark on the seafront when the cinema was rebuilt by Leathart & Granger with a tall thin Art Deco tower. Today, alas, the cinema is closed while Dreamland itself has been devastated by the sale and removal of many of the rides – only its listing prevented the destruction of the Scenic Railway but that was damaged in an arson attack three years ago.

The decline of the British seaside resort over the last half-century owing to cheap air travel and package holidays abroad is well known, but nowhere, surely, is that more evident than in Margate. No longer, as a Regency guidebook put it, 'the constant resort of genteel people... for pleasure, as well as bathing', the town today seems poor, sad, shabby and unloved, its potentially charming townscape spoiled by tawdry new buildings or by dereliction. Hence the aim by Thanet Council and others of reversing its fortunes with the construction of an 'iconic' new public building to attract visitors. The first attempt to recreate the supposed 'Bilbao Effect' in Thanet with a striking new cultural centre – named after Turner, naturally – was a project in 2001 by the architects Snohetta & Spence to build an art gallery actually in the sea. Fortunately, common sense as well as escalating costs prevailed and the Turner Contemporary, which opened a few months ago, has been built on dry land.

The site is a prominent one, at the eastern end of Margate's wide bay where Rennie's mole meets the shore and where Sophia Booth's little house as well as the later, grander Hotel Metropole had once stood. The new building certainly does no damage to Margate as the site had long been cleared, and it makes a pleasing contrast with a happy survivor, the sweet little Doric pavilion built by the Margate Pier and Harbour Company in 1812. Towards the town, however, Turner Contemporary presents blank facades behind a concrete retaining wall: this is iconic architecture, after all, designed to draw attention to itself rather than be a polite neighbour. The architect was David Chipperfield, who has made his reputation with a series of hard-edged, minimalist structures. The exterior walls – of vertical strips of opaque and clear glass – are unarticulated and unadorned. Only a short flight of steps indicates where the entrance might be.

Inside, the entrance hall (with shop) is dominated by a glass wall overlooking the changeable sea and sky that so moved Turner. Otherwise the connection with the great 19th century landscape and topographical painter is exiguous (although a large loan Turner exhibition is promised). A staircase, arbitrarily tucked away on one side, leads to a series of plain white top-lit galleries which might be anywhere. It will be clear that I have problems with this sort of architecture, which manages to be arrogant by being insistently reticent and undemonstrative. Outside, the building is an irregular line of boxes with monopitched roofs and windows facing the sea. It is almost non-architecture, a collection of what several commentators have called mere sheds. 'If a shed is a large, multi-functional building then I think this is an elegant shed,' Chipperfield has commented. The trouble is that these boxes fail to form a coherent composition: what I understand as architecture – the balance of mass and void, light and shade, enhanced by thoughtful detailing and enriched by cultural resonance – is just not there. Early modernist buildings, by contrast, were successful as powerfully composed arrangements of plain walls and horizontal planes, and – significantly – were often the work of architects, like Maxwell Fry, who had had the benefit of a proper Classical training.

Oddly enough, Margate can boast an early work by Fry: the fine, monumental railway station, designed in the 1920s when he worked for the Southern Railway and before he discovered modernism. Apart from the Dreamland cinema, the other 20th century architectural interventions in Margate have been less happy. The most conspicuous – indeed the highest building in the town – is the contribution of High Modernism: a single, dreadful 19-storey tower of 1964 erected half-way along the seafront. Compared with that, the Late Modernism's offering in the shape of Turner Contemporary is benign and welcome.

One can only wish it well. But the Bilbao Effect is now waning through prodigal and ubiquitous repetition, and whether this modern art gallery alone can reverse Margate's fortunes must be doubtful.

Margate's real assets are its old streets and squares on which Turner Contemporary turns its back, and here there are already signs of real rejuvenation. And a project more likely to succeed, and surely more in tune with Margate's traditions, is the plan by the Dreamland Trust to reopen the famous 20-acre seaside pleasure ground as a working museum of historic fairground rides, a project which, with the support of Heritage Lottery and Thanet Council, is now under way. And it would be good if visitors from London coming to see Turner Contemporary could be diverted to the Shell Grotto, if only to learn about the old-fashioned delights of ornament and decoration.

June 2011

[I underestimated the positive effect Turner Contemporary would have on Margate in encouraging visitors, many of whom are now also going to the (restored) Grotto. And, I hope, there will soon be the revamped Dreamland to enjoy as well. As for the 19-storey tower on the seafront, called Arlington House, I fear I am now beginning to warm to it – but perhaps that is because something worse is threatened for its site. And could it really be that the Phoenicians were responsible for the Grotto?]

Lost Lululaund

Just as some pets come to resemble their owners, so some architects have the physical characteristics of their buildings – and none more so than the great American Victorian architect Henry Hobson Richardson. As photographs taken towards the end of his comparatively short life confirm, Richardson was as massive, as heavy, as wide and as striking as such masterpieces as Trinity Church Boston or the Allegheny County Buildings in Pittsburg. There is also the evidence of the portrait by the fashionable Anglo-German painter Hubert Herkomer depicting the bearded architect squeezed into a chair, his colossal stomach threatening to burst out of a double-breasted waistcoat. And it was owing to the encounter with Herkomer that Richardson was commissioned to design his only building in Britain, indeed his only work outside the United States: the painter's own house at Bushey in Hertfordshire.

In assembling a catalogue of lost and saved Victorian buildings to celebrate the 50th anniversary of the Victorian Society
this year, it seemed to me that one of the saddest disappearances
was that of '*Lululaund*', as Herkomer named his studio-house.
Built of white tufa from Bavaria and red sandstone rather than
mere English brick, it was much more remarkable – and solid
– than the houses that successful contemporary artists like
Frederick Leighton, Luke Fildes, Marcus Stone, Edwin Long
or even Whistler built for themselves in London to the designs
of Norman Shaw, E.W. Godwin and other British architects.
Above a plinth of courses of rugged stone, a wide segmental arch straddled and wrapped around two round turreted
towers below a patterned gable – so typical of Richardson.
On one side, the front door was placed beneath an elaborately
carved tympanum framed by an arch of massive stone vous-
soirs, and over this rose a colossal, flat chimney-stack.

H.H. Richardson never saw the completed building, nor
did he supervise its construction. In fact, all he provided for
Herkomer was a front elevation design in return for his portrait, and very soon afterwards, in April 1886, he died. But
the architect did in fact know England. Two decades earlier,
when a younger and thinner Richardson was studying at the
Ecole des Beaux Arts in Paris during the American Civil War,
he would cross the Channel to visit his tailor in London and
then took the opportunity to see new buildings by the leading
High Victorian Gothic Revivalists like Street, Butterfield and
Burges. Such men, under the influence of Ruskin, were interested in the colour and texture of masonry and in the integrity
of the wall surface. Such characteristics Richardson would
develop in the United States on a grander scale, while making
the crucial substitution of the round Romanesque arch for the
pointed Gothic profile. A further link between Richardson and
the great High Victorians was that all were strongly influenced
by the architecture of Normandy. Richardson's *Lululaund*, like
his libraries, railway stations, houses and public buildings in

the United States, was not different in spirit from the work of his British contemporaries, just more rugged and massive and, in many ways, better.

All Herkomer had from the American was an elevation to go with the plan of the house which he had already prepared. The interior had to be his own creation. As the artist later recalled, 'Beyond lowering the roof, concentrating the chimney stacks, and changing the upper part of the tower, I have kept strictly to Richardson's masterly outline. But now came my turn to carry out his words to me that I should "play all over it with my imagination".' And, to judge by descriptions endorsed by the tantalisingly few photographs of the interior that survive, Herkomer's imagination was given full play. The rooms he designed were German Gothic rather than Richardsonian Romanesque, extravagantly enriched with elaborate carving executed by himself and members of his family. The principal bedroom had a copper ceiling and 'richly carved walls entirely covered with gold leaf'. The hall and staircase were lined with panels of redwood, three feet wide and thirty feet high. The dining room had a fantastic carved sideboard and was decorated with a relief frieze of female figures, illustrating 'Human Sympathy' and lit by concealed electric lights. Best of all must have been the drawing room with its carved wooden panels, music gallery and vast arched chimneypiece with interlaced mouldings. The artist's own studio, with walls covered in greenish-gold metal leaf, was somewhat simpler.

Herkomer was a much more interesting figure than his somewhat lugubrious realist canvases and established Academician status might suggest. He was of Bavarian peasant stock, the son of a builder and woodcarver who left home to cross the Atlantic when his only child was two years old. But Lorenz Herkomer was unhappy in the United States and arrived in Southampton in 1857 and his son eventually studied at the South Kensington School as well as in Munich. Herkomer soon achieved success both as a portraitist and as the painter of such popular canvases as *The Last Muster* and by 1873 was able to buy a cottage in Bushey – then still a rural area outside London. The much grander house he later built there was named after his second wife, Lulu Griffiths. Her sudden death after less than two years of marriage was a great shock. Herkomer subsequently wished to mary Lulu's sister, but to do this he had to return to Bavaria – where he had built the *Mutterturm* in memory of his mother near his birthplace at Waal – and take German citizenship as such a union was illegal in Britain before the passing of the controversial Deceased Wife's Sister's Marriage Act in 1907. He then returned to Bushey, bringing with him a 'von' to add to his name as well as the third Mrs Herkomer, and resumed British citizenship, eventually acquiring a knighthood.

Herkomer did much for Bushey. In 1883 he established an art school in the village, and although most of his pupils were not distinguished William Nicholson studied there for a time. And, despite both the subject matter and style of his paintings, he was an enthusiast for the new. He was keen on electric light and motor cars – sponsoring motor races in Bavaria – and planned the interior of *Lululaund* to be practical, with the kitchen upstairs to avoid smells. Versatile as well as prodigiously hard-working, he built a theatre in the grounds which could accommodate an audience of 150, and there he staged 'pictorial-music-plays' which he partly wrote and designed himself and which are said to have influenced Edward Gordon Craig. Later, the theatre was replaced by a cinema, for Herkomer became interested in cinematography and both directed and acted in several early British films which were released commercially. He was clearly extraordinary, and was very unlike Richardson in appearance: Lee MacCormick Edwards, his modern biographer, records that Herkomer 'ate little meat and neither drank alcohol nor smoked … Until 1890 (after which he remained clean shaven) his face was covered in a thick black beard. His piercing eyes and humourless demeanour produced a rather sinister appearance.'

The remarkable career of Sir Hubert von Herkomer exemplifies the close cultural ties that existed between Britain and Germany in the 19th century. Perhaps it was a mercy, therefore, that he died early in 1914, just before the outbreak of the world war that would release the hatreds that would poison so much of the rest of the century. As for *Lululaund*, it was used for a time by the Bushey Film Corporation before falling derelict and subject to vandalism, 'the haunt of tramps, courting couples and schoolboys'. It was finally pulled down in 1939, on the eve of another world war. But a small portion of Richardson's facade survives: the front door and its tympanum, which now acts as the entrance to a club. This precious, mighty fragment, so powerful and original in design, still testifies in England to the genius of one of the greatest of American architects.

December 2008

LIST OF ILLUSTRATIONS

1. The cover of *Wiltshire* in the *Vision of England* series published by Paul Elek in 1949.
2. An 'Anti-Ugly' recommendation card issued by the New Architecture Group in 1962.
3. The title page of Andrea Palladio's *Quattro Libri* published in 1570.
4. Heathcote at Ilkley by Edwin Lutyens: photo by the author, 2000.
5. The report on preserving Monkton by SAVE Britain's Heritage and the (then) Thirties Society issued in 1986.
6. The Guinness Brewery at Park Royal, since demolished: photo by the author, 2005.
7. The Commonwealth Institute in Kensington: photo by the author, 1990.
8. The cover of *How we celebrate the Coronation* by Robert Byron published in 1937.
9. The dust-jacket for Osbert Lancaster's *Pillar to Post*, published in 1938.
10. Sir John Betjeman looking at the proofs of *Temples of Power*: photo by the author, 1979.
11. Christ Church, Spitalfields: photo by the author, 2011.
12. Seaton Delaval by Vanbrugh: photo by the author, 2013.
13. Ashridge Park by James Wyatt: photo by the author, 2009.
14. Moggerhanger Park by Sir John Soane: photo by the author, 2006.
15. The frontispiece to Pugin's *Apology for the Revival of Christian Architecture*, 1843.
16. The interior of the former Midland Grand Hotel at St Pancras: photo by the author, 2011.
17. The Wharncliffe Viaduct at Hanwell: lithograph by J.C. Bourne from his *History & Description of the Great Western Railway*, 1846.
18. The Hall of the Watermen's Guild at Ghent: etching by Ernest George c.1878.
19. The Horniman Free Museum by Harrison Townsend as illustrated in *The Studio* in 1901.
20. The interior of Coventry Cathedral: photo by the author, 1989.
21. 'Lord of the Tournament': lithograph by J.H. Nixon from his *Series of Views representing the Tournament held at Eglinton Castle...*, 1843.
22. The Wills Tower by Sir George Oatley: photo from *University of Bristol 1925*.
23. Highfort Court at Kingsbury, Middlesex, by Ernest Trobridge: photo by the author, 2005.
24. The font designed by William Burges in St Peter's Church, Draycott, Somerset: photo by courtesy of the Victorian Society.
25. The ivy-clad Charterhouse: photo from St John Adcock, ed., *Wonderful London*, c.1926.

26. Design for the crossing tower of Bury St Edmunds Cathedral by S.E. Dykes Bower, Warwick Pether & Hugh Matthew.

27. 'Christ Asleep' from *Emblems of the Christian Life* by W. Harry Rogers, 1862.

28. The east end of King's College Chapel, Cambridge, from an early 20th century postcard.

29. The tomb of the Duke of Clarence in St George's Chapel, Windsor: photo by Hollyer from Isabel McAllister, *Alfred Gilbert*, 1929.

30. The statue of W.E. Gladstone in the Aldwych, London: photo by the author.

31. Alexander Stoddart in his former studio in Paisley: photo by the author, 1991.

32. The Artillery Memorial at Hyde Park Corner by C.S. Jagger: photo by the author, 2010.

33. The Bomber Command Memorial in Piccadilly: photo by the author, 2012.

34. The Memorial to the Missing of the Somme in Thiepval, France, by Edwin Lutyens: photo by the author, 1990.

35. The Doric propylaeum at Euston Station under construction in c.1837 drawn by J.C. Bourne: from A. & P. Smithson, *The Euston Arch...*, 1968.

36. W.H. Barlow's train shed after conversion as St Pancras International: photo by the author, 2009.

37. King's Cross Station as depicted in *The London Alphabet* of the 1850s.

38. The Rotunda at Woolwich by John Nash drawn by Barbara Jones, 1952.

39. Sandycombe Lodge at Twickenham: engraving by William Havell, c.1814.

40. A villa at the top of Sydenham Hill overlooking Crystal Palace High Level Station, since demolished: photo by the author, 1968.

41. The former Post Office in central Bath: photo by the author, 2010.

42. The New City Prison, Holloway: engraving in Tallis's *Illustrated London...*, 1851,

43. The Great Roman Bath and Bath Abbey: photo from *The Book of Bath*, c.1930.

44. The airship sheds at Cardington, Bedfordshire: photo by the author, 1969.

45. A London Transport RT bus outside the Cloth Hall at Ypres: photo by the author, 1988.

46. The railings outside the British Museum: photo by the author, 2013.

47. St Mary's, Nottingham: etching by F.L. Griggs, 1929.

48. The Albert Dock and the Anglican Cathedral in Liverpool: photo by the author, 2009.

49. Margate: a postcard of the 1960s.

50. Lululaund at Bushey by H.H. Richardson: photo in A.L. Baldry, *Hubert von Herkomer, R.A.: a Study and a Biography*, 1901.

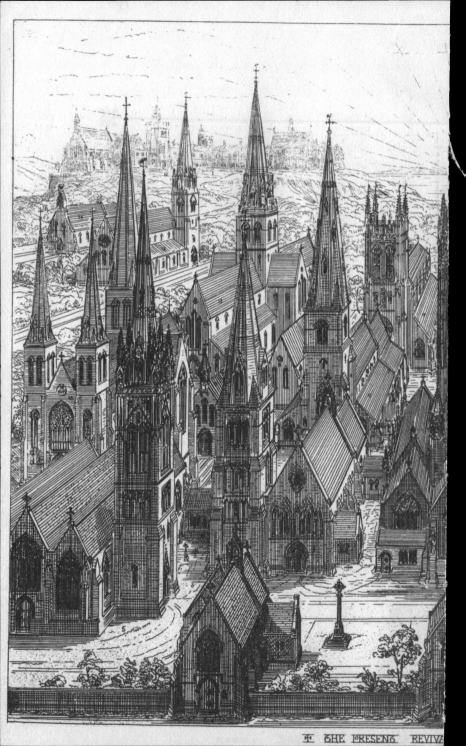

THE PRESENT REVIVAL